BOOKS BY W. S. MERWIN

Poems

Translations

PRODUCTS
OF THE
PERFECTED
CIVILIZATION

PRODUCTS
OF THE
PERFECTED
CIVILIZATION

Selected Writings of
Sébastien Roch Nicolas CHAMFORT

Translated and with an Introduction by
W. S. MERWIN

FOREWORD BY LOUIS KRONENBERGER

THE MACMILLAN COMPANY

The Macmillan Company
Collier-Macmillan Canada Ltd., Toronto, Ontario

Printed in the United States of America

for Yvonne Savage

CONTENTS

※※ ※※

FOREWORD

ALTHOUGH IT IS A PLEASURE to write this foreword, Mr. Merwin has filled his role as translator and biographer and critic so ably that for someone else to come before the curtain for even a few minutes is more to delay the proceedings than to contribute to them. Still less is there need to "introduce" so well-known and admirable a poet as Mr. Merwin. But what someone else can, perhaps, say better than he is how real the need has been for an English version of Chamfort, and how soundly and solidly—and in far greater measure than any previous translator—he has satisfied it. As it happens, only two or three years ago, lamenting that Chamfort was out of print in English, I wrote a piece to celebrate the nonpublication of his work, only to be rewarded with the news that Mr. Merwin was translating him and that help would soon be at hand.

Here indeed it is, and "help" can more happily be termed pleasure. And here, owing to Mr. Merwin's intellectual curiosity about everything concerning Chamfort, and to his editorial conscience about fully enlightening the reader, we come to know, not just an often dazzling master of a particularly French form of writing, but a fiery citizen of an age; not just the aphorist but the man. What heretofore nonscholars, which is to say most of us, had known of Chamfort resembles—to amend Coleridge—seeing him in flashes of stage lightning: the illegitimate child, the salon Figaro, the witty darling of grandees who saw him as not their judge but their jester, the champion of the French Revolution and at length its victim, dying of his attempts to commit suicide. There has perhaps been a kind of poetic justice in all this, in the fact that one of literature's most zealous collectors of anecdotes has himself survived anecdotally. In any case Mr. Merwin has put an end to the situation, has exchanged Chamfortiana for Chamfort; has, by dint of much research, chronicled Chamfort's life and then gone on, with thought and care, to appraise it. All this has real interest and value for itself, but beyond that it endows Chamfort's aphorisms with touches of inner, autobiographical illumination as well as with their outward sting and glitter; it sheds light on the man while he is shedding light on the world. No other French aphorist has worked in so impersonal a medium to leave so individual, at times outraged, an impress. Yet, along with raising his voice, cracking his whip, seizing his prey, Chamfort can offer the most polished of aphorisms.

If he has failed in English of the renown and the readership he deserves, from the fact that for years there has been no book in print to read him in, conceivably something anterior to this is most to blame: the fact that the aphorism as an established form, a traditional artistic medium, has insufficiently made its way in English, while it has for centuries occupied a prominent place in French. In one sense this is odd, for in practice the aphorism has appeared as continuously and successfully in the one language as in the other. But in English, rather than exist as a self-contained art, it has been imbedded in men's general writings, or now and then, as with a Dr. Johnson or an Oscar Wilde, run gleaming through their talk. Lord Halifax, to be sure—and he too is inexcusably out of print—was a distinguished writer of isolated maxims; and Swift, Pope, Shenstone, Blake, Shaw, and others have in various degrees turned outright aphorist. But Halifax's grandson Lord Chesterfield, along with Johnson, Hazlitt, Emerson, Wilde, Santayana, Chesterton, and many more, rather than being outright aphorists are masters of aphoristic prose—just as English is a natural language for it. Unlike French, English can dispense with both the definite and indefinite article, can let the genitive ride on the nominative's back, and prepositions dance at sentences' ends; and can thus be more pointed, more concise, more splendidly lapidary.

Nevertheless there is no sustained tradition of aphorism in English—for one reason, I would think: because there has never been, as in French, a special, indeed predominant, basis for creating it, which is to yoke the aphorist with the psychologist, to make him an observer of behavior, a student of manners, a surgeon of self-interest, a holder of the mirror up to human nature, and a manipulator of the X-ray into human motives—a registrar, in other words, of the tangled relations between man and man, man and woman, man and himself. Though its form had been perfected before his day, it was La Rochefoucauld who in the seventeenth century gave the maxim its principal subject-matter and its prevailing tone. The same period produced a more benevolent Vauvenargues and humane La Bruyère; a century later came Rivarol almost side by side with Chamfort, and thereafter, from Joubert to Valéry and beyond, the aphorism has continued to flourish. Accordingly an educated Frenchman is as naturally at home with his country's aphorists as with its essayists and poets, and an educated French worldling even more so.

La Rochefoucauld, who comes first in the great French line of psychologizing maxim writers, stands easily first in importance as well, having both perfected and systematized a union of form and substance. But Chamfort for me ranks second, both for often being exceptionally brilliant and for often seeming somewhat out of line—the most nonconformist, if one at all, of La Rochefoucauld's decendants. By birth of course the Duc de la Rochefoucauld was a great aristocrat, while Chamfort was a nobody; the duke, again, was almost clinically detached and impersonal, his urbanity worn as armor, where the pouncing Chamfort wore his wit and audacity like lace. And though the disappointments and disillusionments that made of La Rochefoucauld a kind of Olympian cynic derived from his own experience of the great world, his observations much more suggest the laboratory, where Chamfort's seem uttered in the very midst of life. He opposes a rapier wit to La Rochefoucauld's scalpel wisdom, and it must be confessed that we sometimes get from Chamfort, as from Wilde, a witticism rather than an aphorism, an impromptu rather than an *aperçu*.

Furthermore, as we discover in Mr. Merwin's text, Chamfort rifled French society as far back as Louis XIV for anecdotes. We must allow, though not always disapprovingly, that Chamfort, intruding something personal, topical, even gossipy, could produce something neither aphoristic nor equal to the aphorism in importance. His was too concrete a mind—note his talent for metaphor—for consistent generalization, too protesting a temperament for judicial impersonality. Indeed, the one English-speaking appreciator of Chamfort I know whom Mr. Merwin does not mention, George Saintsbury, has lightly bracketed Chamfort with Swift. Certainly both men took refuge—or revenge—in irony, as both had a love of puns and of plays on words. Indeed, Chamfort's final judgment on life is a play on words, as well as kindred in feeling to Swift's tombstone inscription with its "lacerated heart." "I am at last departing the world," says Chamfort, "*ou il faut que le coeur se brise ou se bronze.*" Both Chamfort and Swift were steeped in pessimism, something that Mr. Merwin, speculating about a contemporary audience for Chamfort, designates as evoking a contemporary response. And both Chamfort and Swift shared a trait evoking a response perhaps today even greater: their burning sense of protest. Although they both delighted in living among distinguished men of affairs, the one man raged over oppression in Ireland as the other in France; the one inhabited a symbolic prison, as the other an actual one. Even the blistering irony of Swift's *Modest Proposal* is pretty well matched by one short comment of Chamfort's concerning the claims of the French nobility to be intermediaries between the King and the people: "Indeed, yes; as the hounds are the intermediaries between the hunter and the hare."

Chamfort thus occupies an impressive but rather unorthodox place in a great French tradition, displaying at times an angrier manner than any other member of his tribe, constituting indeed its Angry Man, and just a little bit as Marx, as La Rochefoucauld is very much its Freud. Such matters, together with Mr. Merwin's skillful presentation both of Chamfort's life and of much of his work, bring him, I would think, into the orbit of any cultivated American reader today. Mr. Merwin is right in translating as much as he has done, uneven though it may be in bulk, or quite poor in single examples. For only so do we get the whole brunt and impact of the man, the rather ill-fitting halves of his nature, the petty contretemps and large causes, the stale gossip and stunning repartees, the world of privilege and of the dispossessed—all that troubled and tarnished a life of genuine stature, and was inescapably part of it.

LOUIS KRONENBERGER

PREFACE

⁕ ⁕

THE GENERAL READER'S acquaintance with Chamfort, I imagine, probably consists of the recollection, just out of quoting memory, of a handful of bitter and (with luck, even in translation) glittering aphorisms, many of which are to be found in W. H. Auden and Louis Kronenberger's anthology (*The Viking Book of Aphorisms*, 1962, an interesting collection with a brief but valuable introductory note on aphorisms in general) plus what he recalls of a few pages by Cyril Connolly and perhaps a remark or two by Camus. Even in French it is evident that Chamfort is often not read at all consecutively—the remnants of his work, that is, that are still assumed to be a part of literate common knowledge, the *Maxims and Thoughts* in particular. La Rochefoucauld, of course, and sometimes Vauvenargues, are assigned in schools and read through in that way. Otherwise they too would doubtless be browsed through, as are most other writers in this form. It is not one which lends itself to uninterrupted reading. It is more usual to open a collection of aphorisms somewhat at random and read in the same way until the repeated finalities of the form or some striking confirmation or contradiction of the reader's own prejudices make a natural stop. Chamfort, besides, has been particularly ill-served: despite the familiarity of his name, and the vague notoriety of his extreme pessimism and the chill cast of his mind and language, he has been given little steady and official attention by literary historians. He is not immediately engaging, nor intellectually especially original; as a revolutionary he had no influence either as a man or as a writer, and his most ardent modern admirer, Julien Teppe, gives an imposing partial list (*Chamfort, Sa Vie, Son Oeuvre, Sa Pensée,* p. 17) of the classic nineteenth- and twentieth-century works on French literature as a whole that either completely ignore Chamfort or mention him only in passing, and often disparagingly. His few partisans, on the other hand, from Mirabeau to Nietzsche and Camus, have praised him with fervor as both a moral touchstone and a master of language.

His life and his writings are full of contradictions, as well. An apostle of pessimism who declared in a variety of ways that the human species was beyond hope of redemption, and yet insisted (in the prevailing tradition of the age of enlightenment) that society must be dismantled and rebuilt piece by piece, and who flung himself, with little evidence of personal ambition, into the Revolution, until its chief protagonists and the populace behaved in a manner consistent with his own pessimism, whereupon he (who had said that he believed in the necessity of illusions but lived without any) withdrew, watched, and pronounced himself pleased to die. His life itself, as he realized, was a mass of "apparent contradictions" with his principles. And having compromised himself to some degree in the eyes of his contemporaries and of posterity, and almost certainly in his own, in order to make a career as a literary figure and man of the world in a society that he despised, his whole posthumous reputation rests on writings that were never published, and (part of the time, at any rate) were never meant to be published, at least during his lifetime.

For all his contradictions he is an oddly clear representative of his age; one would scarcely call him typical, but he is probably more so than if he had been a greater and more original figure. One should not have to labor the parallels between our age and his to make him seem relevant. Even without the most perfunctory soul-searching, a glance at our own historical moment, at any day's papers, at our sovereigns (in anyone's political theory), make pessimism, even the most extreme and desolate statement of it, hardly surprising. It, rather than its opposite which is so readily confected by the beamish jugglers in office, seems creditable and probably an usher to truth, though neither its impulse nor its final result, of course, is necessarily either of these things. But in the end Chamfort's particular statement of his pessimism is its own advocate, or it has none; and here the question is simply whether its representation in English does it any kind of justice.

W. S. MERWIN

Lot, France
April 1968

INTRODUCTION

❧ I ❧

AFTER CHAMFORT'S DEATH in 1794 his friend Guingené edited
what papers of Chamfort's he could find, and prepared a *Works*
in four volumes, which he prefaced with the memoir that has
been the chief source for subsequent biographers. More complete
editions followed in the next hundred years, but Guingené's first
brought to more than a circle of acquaintances the *Maxims,
Thoughts and Anecdotes*. In introducing them, he said:

. . . Chamfort had been for a long time in the habit of writing down
on little squares of paper the results of his reflections, drawn up as
maxims, anecdotes that he had heard, facts useful for a history of
manners, which he had observed in society, and finally the witty and
clever replies that he had heard or had uttered himself.

He tossed all these papers pell-mell into boxes. He told no one
what he meant to do with them. When he was dead, there was a
considerable number of these boxes, almost all filled; but most of
them were emptied and taken away, probably before the effects were
sealed. The justice of the peace collected what he found of the remains in two large portfolios. From the very careful choice made
from these remnants I have drawn the contents of this volume.

He found Chamfort's title, *Products of the Perfected Civilization*
and notes for organizing the material into "Maxims and
Thoughts," "Characters," and "Anecdotes," and he assumed that
they were all parts of a great unfinished work.

The title exactly suited him: he subscribed to a philosophy which saw as products of the perfecting of civilization that is boasted of, the excessive corruption of conduct, the hideous or ridiculous vices, and the faults of all kinds that he took a sly pleasure in characterizing and portraying.

It was this part of the *Works* that survived the age and is the basis for Chamfort's subsequent reputation. It perpetuated the aspects of Chamfort's character that were most apparent to his contemporaries: the observation, the glittering phrase, the multiplicity of motives, the genuine admiration of fastidiousness. He has, in the main, been treated as a marginal but discomfitting figure; the attacks on him have centered on the cruelty of his wit, his coldness, his notorious pessimism, and the ability to accept favors from institutions that he despised, while audibly attaching great importance to his contempt for them.

And he has had, as he did in his lifetime, a few fervent admirers. In our time Jean Rostand; and Camus, who wrote of him that "unlike La Rochefoucauld, he is a moralist as profound as Mme. de Lafayette or Benjamin Constant, and he takes his place, in spite of or because of his impassioned blindnesses, among the great creators of a certain art in which the truth of life is at no point sacrificed to the artifices of language." And Julien Teppe, for whom pessimism is a kind of salvation in itself, and Chamfort its prophet. One of the most interesting modern tributes to Chamfort is Nietzsche's: "Suppose Chamfort had remained one degree more a philosopher, and stayed in his ivory tower: the Revolution would have been deprived of its most tragic spirit and its sharpest sting; it would be considered a far more stupid event, and would not exert its present seductive fascination."

The Revolution has surely seduced and fascinated some who never heard Chamfort, or paid little attention to him. But as one would expect with Nietzsche, the remark is revealing: Chamfort's bitter sentences and the facts of his life epitomize an aspect of his age; they throw a cold beam on the sordors of the bored, stultified, encrusted old regime, and on those of the upheaval that replaced it. This role as a crystal reflecting certain aspects of the time is more obvious if Chamfort is considered in conjunction with his exact contemporaries, de Sade and Laclos. Taken together, despite the immense differences of character and talent, it does not seem strange that they speak from the same generation.

It would be misleading to try to draw comparisons too closely, but a few similarities that suggest themselves may be more than the result of chance.

The importance of confinement in de Sade's life and imagination is one of the salient features in both. In de Sade, violent, exploratory, and paradoxically free fantasies are a manifestation of the pressures of this heavenless circumstance. Whereas in Chamfort the fantasy, if one can put it that way, is one of stasis. In the name of freedom he progressively refuses to exist in his prison.

Of the three men, Laclos was probably the most "normal," and the Revolution did operate a genuine liberation in his circumstances and his view of them. But *Les Liaisons Dangereuses* dates from his many years of waiting, before that, in the provinces, a bored officer of artillery (not a "noble" arm) without advancement, fortune, or birth. The book's hero, Valmont, has a different kind of reality from that of de Sade's creations, but he too is part fantasy, an ambiguous fulfillment. "In portraying Valmont in the blackest of strokes, Laclos meant to avenge himself, certainly, upon the insolent individual whom he had not been able to imitate. But at the same time he depicted the insolent individual whom he would deeply have loved to be." (Roger Vailland, *Laclos par lui-même.*) So the hero is a powerful nobleman possessed of a limitless fortune, whose absorbing activity consists in conducting an act with profound moral implications, seduction, by principles as remote from moral considerations, as willed and as abstract, as possible. But Valmont becomes imprisoned in his own design. The method becomes a passion in itself, uncontrollable, a *fate*, and therefore, George Poulet argues in his essay on "Chamfort and Laclos" ("The Interior Distance," Ann Arbor, 1964) "intolerable," because it is "an existence that has escaped the control of the will, a duration no longer calculated but continually incalculable." In Poulet's word, the end of this fantasy hero was "frenzy."

What Chamfort came to, in his interpretation, was an opposite extreme, a deliberate paralysis. Whether or not this is the most appropriate term for it, Poulet's description of the process by which Chamfort arrived at it is not altogether clear. He posits a complete break between a later Chamfort "and other, previous, versions: an ambitious hack, a dandy, a passionate lover." And, he says, "nothing could be more mistaken than to want to link them up again to the true, the only Chamfort, in order to give him a background and a historical continuity." The break itself, in Poulet's thesis, was a starting point, and an essential element in Chamfort's philosophy and his confrontation of existence: he cut himself off from successive pasts and from the future as well, and lived detached from time, in a remote continuous present. One trouble with this idea (if it is to be taken as anything more than a recurrent image, in whose perspectives Chamfort tried to orient his existence, a continuous process in which a "present" Chamfort continuously adjured his other selves as though they existed in other times) is that it is hard to see how it could be possible chronologically. The real, the "only" Chamfort—remote, counseling a rationally controlled minimum of feeling, of hope, and of illusion—is there, as we shall see, in his mid-twenties, in the letter of "advice for the good of your happiness," when all three of the other versions of him cited by Poulet were certainly still present, and at least one of them would be for years. The fact that the part of his writings that comprises the most important heritage of the "only" Chamfort cannot be dated in whole or in part, but certainly represents a number of years, also makes such an argument as M. Poulet's hard to take literally. There is no reason to suppose that *all* these writings were set down after a given date, ideal or real, when all of Chamfort's "other versions" had been wholly exorcised. It is the very fixity and abstraction of his "moralist" position, over a long period, that has made critic after critic, from his time to the present, tax him with inconsistency, as they might not have done if it were clear how his relation to his eternally reiterated principles had developed from one point to another.

On the other hand, there were certainly instances of Chamfort behaving with violence toward past selves. His early life as a libertine can scarcely have been totally obliterated from his mind twenty-five or thirty years later when he took the occasion of the publication of the *Memoires* and the *Vie Privée* of Richelieu to denounce, among other abuses of power and caste, Richelieu's rakish conduct and his cruel treatment of the opposite sex, especially those members of it who were of inferior social orders, and whose illusions, in consequence, were more considerable. Temporarily, at least, Richelieu became Chamfort's Valmont; Chamfort was whipping up sexual indignation to castigate the old order and its arrogance, and he was doing so when the villains were already beyond hitting back, whereas Laclos' hero was portrayed while he was still in a position to be Laclos' jailer. It is no accident that Chamfort's villain and Laclos' hero resemble each other, and that each represents something that the author had in some sense attended, applied to, courted, and envied—before which he had been divided. The "rules" of correct libertine behavior which Roger Vailland, in the essay already quoted, deduces from *Les Liaisons Dangereuses* correspond closely with Chamfort's evocation of libertine practice in the person of Richelieu and the "school" of Grammont and Hamilton. The two authors' heroine-victims are as worthy of comparison as the hero-villains. Mme. Michelin, as Chamfort describes her, has much in common with La Presidente de Tourvel in Laclos' novel; the latter is higher in the social scale, but still a bourgeoise, and not what Richelieu would have called one of "*nous autres*." La Presidente would doubtless have proved more intelligent and more interesting than poor Mme. Michelin, but both, as their portrayers saw them, were descendants of Rousseau's "natural woman": earnest bourgeoises, sincere, loving, and simple.

There is another ideal comparison. In speaking of Valmont, and the "bitterness of the libertine," Vailland declares that "a strict virtue" (meaning adherence to a self-imposed code) "a rigorous training, the requirements of incessantly renewed acts of prowess, make of the libertine a being of extreme lucidity. He measures precisely the vanity of his victories and the illusions of the game to which he devotes his life." It is a description that comes very close to what one can imagine the young libertine Chamfort to have been like, or at least to what he may have wanted to be like. If one imagines such lucidity and such bitterness as befitted his libertine years (both of them exaggerated, perhaps, or at least kept awake by a continual comparison with the same qualities in the persons of noblemen) removed from libertine activity after they had become set as an attitude, and turned into a way of facing society itself, one is close to the "only Chamfort" of the maxims. Considering that Chamfort had learned at the Collège des Grassins, that his wits were his only weapon, it is not surprising that his wits were the weapon he chose, instead of libertine prowess, especially after his first attacks of disease, in his early thirties. As for his former libertinism, with some steady help from Rousseau, and age, he managed in the end to treat it as a symptom of a system that focused his bitterness and pessimism. The process made him one among many instances of Baudelaire's observation (which Vailland quotes) that "The Revolution was made by voluptuaries."

This particular development would seem to confirm M. Poulet's theory of a later "only Chamfort" and earlier "versions," but in fact, though it represents a clear evolution, it is an exception. In other aspects of his life he returned more than once to court what he knew he despised, knew he had to despise in order to retain his self-esteem, and (still more important) believed unquestioningly that he had to be free of if he was to respect himself. The effect on him, and on his fund of bitterness, can only be guessed. But his oppositions were no simpler than his acquiescences. And his real lucidity is more evident when he is referring to things around him than when he is talking about what he takes to be—and what bears some undeterminable relation to—himself.

But Chamfort was not a highly original philosopher: he was a dandy among moralists. "To be a philosopher," he said, "one must begin by experiencing the happiness of the dead." And so his prison, to compare him again with de Sade, was society, not simply because he hated it, but because, while genuinely despising it, he could not do without it; and the society to which he stood in this anguished relationship was above all that of his youth and ambitions and frustration: the old regime. His relation to society grew more complicated as he grew older; but until the Revolution, at least, it can hardly have changed deeply except once—when he and Mme. Buffon "retired" to her manor in the country, in 1781, "almost the only time of my life that seems to me to have been worth something." Within society the maneuvers were endless and repetitive, as with any caged creature: academic competitions, scorn of them (and the importance he attached to both); applications and efforts for literary honors, scorn of them; frequenting and use of the aristocracy, scorn of it; indignant justification of "retirement," and very limited indulgence in it except in the form of a retreat into a relative privacy; many of the maxims themselves, his refusal to publish them, are all steps traced and retraced within what can be seen as a consciousness of confinement. What one doubts, finally, is whether Chamfort wanted to be free. But one can believe that he wanted to stop.

Even so, there is no just cause for doubting that the dissidence which came to represent a more and more important part of him had called forth genuine sympathies in him as the Revolution approached. And the activity of the last years of the old order and the first of the Revolution must have seemed to be a release, and at least an illusion which he could allow himself for the time being. But with the deaths of admirations and friends, and of his hopes for the Revolution, he was left in a void. The society that had been the most complete and familiar representation of his prison was gone like the Bastille; from the viewpoint of his habits and attitudes the society around him was formless. He was left with his worn principles of retreat into the self: his "freedom." But these too had been, for years, part of a social gesture, and the theater had dissolved. And the "self" he spoke of sounds like a bounded, and almost a material place. His career, his history, his triumphs, his opinions, his prejudices, his equipment, were almost wholly secular. And he was left alone, less, it would seem, as a man is left alone with the infinite, than as he may be left alone with an empty room when his gift is not for prayer but for argument.

Poulet, speaking of what he calls Chamfort's "self-mutilation," and describing it chronologically, says that his lucidity is "sometimes . . . made up of a negative knowledge . . . the consciousness of being situated in a place in the mind from which certain inner truths are forever excluded." There is another image of self-limitation in a scene from the old order which Chamfort invokes in his essay on the *Mémoires of Richelieu:* "thirty consecutive silent sessions of Parliament, convened and adjourned without a mouth being opened, by a president who pretended to have the right to prevent the discussion of affairs." But in the end it is his limitations, as much as his "philosophy," that concern us and our society. They lead, with a peculiar bright restlessness, to one of the insistent questions of decadent and revolutionary ages: "What do you really want?"

❧ II ❧

The first facts that would ordinarily be set down about Sébastien-Roch-Nicolas, who wrote and is remembered under the name of Chamfort, turn out in his case not to be facts at all, fixed, limited, limiting, and contributing to what we can say we know. They are a collection of suppositions leading to other questions, and in this they are consistent with much that remains to us of this curious man. The recurrent enigma in the facts of his life is sometimes exasperating, but occasionally it grants us a sense of his circumstances and character which solid facts might have kept to themselves. He is remembered, after all, not for the profound resolutions of a great and wise nature, nor for the consistent penetration of an original intellect, but for the manner with which he articulated his bitterness as a witness of human behavior. And perhaps more than the obviously admirable things about him, his bewilderment, disappointment, and even the dubious and self-justifying nature of some of his conclusions help to make him still one of us, though the mystification that clouds his image is partly a deliberate legacy.

It is not certain when he was born, or where. The parish register of Saint-Genès, in Clermont-Ferrand, in the Auvergne, contains one baptismal entry reading:

Baptised, the twenty-second of June, seventeen hundred forty, Sébastien-Roch, born the same day in the parish, of unknown parents. The godfather was Sébastien-Roch Terreyre, master locksmith, and the godmother Magdelaine Marnat, the wife of Jacques-Julien, master baker, both of this parish. Signed: Terreyre, Marnet, Planeix, vicar.

At least two students of Chamfort, Dr. Goyon (*Discours sur les prix de vertue*—Académie de Clermont, 1939) and Émile Dousset (*Chamfort et Son Temps*, Fasquelle, Paris, 1943) are satisfied that this entry gives the true details of Chamfort's birth. Another, Maurice Pellisson (Chamfort, *Étude sur sa vie, son caractère, et ses écrits*, 1895), regards it with suspicion as the testimony of Thérèse Croiset, who brought up Nicolas, given by her in 1782, when she was over eighty years old. Even if the entry is, in fact, based on her late testimony, it is hard to imagine what in her character, at that age and distance from the event, could have suggested that the shifting of a few months in an entry in the baptismal register was worth the flutter. And to reduce still further the value of such speculation, another entry in the same register, in which she is named, places the birth and baptism (assuming that they refer to the same child) two and a half months earlier, rather than later. This one reads:

> Baptised, the sixth of April, seventeen hundred forty, Sébastien-Roch-Nicolas, born the same day at noon, legitimate son of François Nicolas, merchant-grocer, and Thérèse Croiset, his wife, of this parish. The godfather was Sébastien-Roch-Terreyre, master locksmith of this parish, and the godmother Catherine Chanoine, wife of Bonnet-Gautier, of the parish of St. Pierre. Signed: Terreyre, Chanoine, Planeix, vicar.

Had those involved reached some new agreement between April and June (another supposition, with other disadvantages), and who in fact were they, all of them? It is Pellisson's theory that Chamfort's father was a canon named Nicolas, a relation of the François named in the entry, and that he had persuaded the grocer and his wife to bring up the boy. But this leads us too quickly into speculations about Chamfort's parentage. To keep to the date and place, for the moment, a copy of the April 6 baptismal entry was found among Chamfort's papers after his death. It had been copied out on June 26, 1778. But in 1782, four years later, Chamfort declared to Maitre Morgantin, King's Counsel, notary at the Chatelet de Paris, that he had been born and baptised on December 20, 1742, at Duport, a village in the Auvergne. Evidently he could not, at the time, find the copy of the baptismal entry, or said he could not find it. But it is hard to imagine that he had forgotten the date and place of his birth in four years. Whether he was trying for some reason to reduce his legal age (and so changed the place, as well as the date, to prevent checking) or was convinced, as Julien Teppe believes (*ibid.*) that the April 6 entry did not refer to him, the declaration settled nothing. In the hearing that followed his suicide attempt, in 1793, the commissariat of police noted that "he says his name is Sébastien Roch Chamfort, fifty-one years old, native of Clermont in the

Auvergne." The age would put his birth in the year 1742—a date, by the way, which would mean that he had traveled across France and started school in Paris at the age of three. But the place has changed again. It was said by contemporaries that Chamfort made a secret of the facts of his birth, confiding them only to a few intimate friends, but even these friends did not leave a thoroughly consistent story. Guingené, who was close to him during his last years, said that he was born in 1740 in "a village near Clermont," combining in his account the contradictions of Chamfort's own statements. Finally, there is an entry in the mayoral archives of Clermont which places Chamfort's birth in that city in 1741.

It is possible that Chamfort did not know who his parents were. Although the April 6 baptismal entry states that he was legitimate, his friends and biographers are generally agreed that he was born out of wedlock. Sélis, who was with him when he died and wrote an article about him in the *Décade philosophique*, and Roederer, a close friend, were definite on this matter, and Guingené devotedly argued the cruelty and injustice of such circumstances. Chamfort, he says, "was permitted to know and love only his mother, but he made up for this, in a sense, by loving her very tenderly." Evidently Guingené believed that Thérèse Croiset was Chamfort's mother, rather than his foster mother, as later biographers for the most part have thought, and certainly Chamfort, in later life, referred to her as his mother.

The biographers have not managed to settle the problem and occasionally appear to have complicated it. Lescure, in his edition of Chamfort in 1879 (he was the last editor of Chamfort to see any of the original manuscripts, which shortly afterward disappeared) seems to confuse Thérèse Croiset and one of the other figures who have been suggested for the role. "Chamfort's mother," in his version, "was a companion or governess in the house where she knew her seducer. Dead in September, 1784, at the age of eighty-five, she should have been protected by her age, in 1740, against the trap into which she fell. But there are errors at forty, as there are at twenty . . ." But who is he excusing? He seems quite certain of the identity of the person in question, since he gives the date of her death. The year he names is that in which Thérèse Croiset died: the registry of her burial, again in the parish of Saint-Genès, in Clermont, says that it took place on

June 26, 1784, that she had died the day before, and that she was "about" eighty-four years old. The discrepancy of three months between the burial entry and the date given by Lescure—roughly the same length of time as that between the two baptismal entries forty-four years earlier—is reaffirmed by a letter of Chamfort's to the Abbé Roman, dated October 5 (apparently 1784) in which he says he had lost his mother two and a half months before, therefore in July. If it was Thérèse Croiset whom Lescure had in mind despite his statement that she died in September, her burial record declares that she was the widow of François Nicolas, to whom she was already married by April 6, 1740, according to the baptismal entry of that date. Can it have been she, then, who had been seduced while serving as a companion or governess? And even if it was she, since she was married to the good François Nicolas by the time Sébastien's birth was first recorded, why the problem, and why were the questions of parentage and legitimacy given such abiding importance?

There are several suggestions. According to one, his mother was a Mademoiselle de Montrodeix, and Roederer says that his father was a canon, also named Nicolas, at the Saint-Chapelle, (or at the Cathedral of Clermont in other accounts, and a Pierre Nicolas was in fact listed among the canons of the cathedral chapter from 1741, the year after the first baptismal entry, until 1783, the year before Thérèse Croiset's death entry). Canon Nicolas, in this theory, was either a relative of the grocer François Nicolas, Thérèse Croiset's husband, or took advantage of the homonym in arranging for someone to bring up the child. The imputation of Chamfort's birth to Mlle. de Montrodeix was based on a local tradition reported by Aigueperse in his *Biographie d'Auvergne*, but Pellisson distrusts the whole of his testimony. In yet another account Chamfort is said to have been born at the Château de Theix, between Clermont and Randan, and the suggestion of noble blood and indiscretions in high places would give a different sense to the "unknown parents" of the June 22 entry, instead of the imputation that he was a foundling.

The conclusion is that Chamfort, while referring on occasion to Thérèse Croiset with deep affection, as his mother, was either unwilling or unable to give a clear and full account of the details of his birth, even to close friends. It seems unlikely, from what we know of him and of the age, that mere illegitimacy could have been the cause of his reticence. Too many of his distinguished contemporaries shared that irregularity. The usual examples cited are Mlle. de Lespinasse, d'Alembert, and Jacques Delille, but the analogies might not have satisfied Chamfort, since at least two of them enjoyed compensating public advantages: d'Alembert was the acknowledged offspring of Mme. de Tencin and the Chevalier Destouches, and Jacques Delille had been recognized at the baptismal font by his father, M. Montanier, a parliamentary lawyer, who settled a small income on the child. And if such comparisons brought Chamfort any consolation, they can have done so only when he was a man; while he was growing up, he must have suffered whatever humiliation the situation afforded.

But if Chamfort was illegitimate, that was not what he kept secret. On the contrary, it is the one fact of his birth that most of his contemporaries seem to have accepted as a known fact. And if the status itself was something that he did not want referred to, he would scarcely have invited such reference, as revenge for the epigram he aimed at La Harpe:

> Ah, from your height, my friend, look down on me.
> True, I'm of recent stock, but what can I do?
> God did not grant me, as He granted you,
> Some thirty years to choose who'd fathered me.

This, of course, proves little about his real feelings in the matter, but one is left wondering whether allusions to his own illegitimacy and its harsh and frustrating consequences may not have contained some element of dramatization or mystification, there to cover his own ignorance, some other shame or disappointment of his youth, his own self-doubts, or a combination of these. It has even been suggested that what he was really ashamed of was his plebeian background, a circumstance that he may have hoped, until well into his youth, might be changed by the recognition or belevolence of an unknown or unapproachable parent. It seems improbable, from what we know of him, that he would have invented or implied a Gothic fiction to connect himself with the aristocracy, whatever contradictions there may have been in his later attitude and behavior toward titles and privileges.

Whether or not unfulfilled hopes contributed to the involved bitterness of his later years, two things that are known about his beginnings do suggest that someone besides François Nicolas the grocer, and Thérèse his wife, must have figured in the boy's origin. There is the order in which the details change from one baptismal entry to the other. It is in the earlier record that he is described as the legitimate son of the married couple. Three months later, as though a real parent or real parents had changed their minds and wanted the boy's legal situation altered, the name "Nicolas" has been dropped, and the child is said to be "of unknown parents." Such a hypothesis might also explain why the date of birth, as well as of baptism, was changed. But much more important as an indication of auspices better informed and more powerful than anyone named in the registry is the fact that Nicolas was not left with his parents or foster parents in the parish of Saint-Genès beyond the age when the schooling of a child born to advantages might have been expected to begin. He was only five when the recommendation of a Docteur Morabin, of Navarre, whom Pellisson supposes to have been a friend of the shadowy Canon Nicolas, obtained for him a scholarship to the Collège des Grassins, and he was sent to Paris.

His birth and beginnings may not be worth this much attention. His allusions to them in later years, in conversation, and in his own writings convey in the end a mixture of feeling and reticence, defensiveness and blankness that is peculiar to him, but may bespeak nothing except the completeness with which Chamfort was cut off from the first years of Nicolas. Yet it is hard not to think that the early circumstances, as he remembered them, had some bearing, however devious, on the ambiguities of his maturity, on his insistent invocation of independence, for instance, and the excited, glassy, slightly cracked resonance that the term came to have in his writing. But there is no way of envisaging Chamfort's existence during those first years. The place where he spent his early childhood left no obvious mark, and he never returned there for more than a brief visit. As a man he professed, and no doubt felt, a form of pre-Romantic love of Nature, attuned to Rousseau and the bucolics, but it was not the windy summits, high pastures, and rich valley fields of the Auvergne that moved him or called him back. In the letter to the Abbé Roman in which he speaks of his mother's death, he refers to "fifteen years of absence." Pascal too had come from Clermont and had seldom returned there, yet both men were said by contemporaries to display the stamp of the Auvergnat: concrete,

austere, practical, self-reliant, tireless. The two men would certainly have had little in common, though how like Chamfort is
Pascal's impassioned and typical assertion "I have discovered that
all of men's unhappiness arises from a single thing: They do not
know how to sit still in one room."

❦ III ❦

The Auvergne is a country of extinct volcanoes, with one level
plain, the Limagne, which follows the Allier. The whole region,
and Clermont especially, had known great wealth, and the
Auvergne was sometimes referred to as the granary of France,
but in 1738 the peasants were reduced to making bread of hemp,
beans, and bran, and in 1740, the year of Chamfort's birth, the
famous Bishop Massillon of Clermont wrote to Cardinal Fleury,
"The people of our countryside live in appalling poverty, without beds or furniture; most of them, half of the year, do not have
enough of the oat and barley bread that is their sole sustenance,
and they must snatch it from their mouths and from their children's mouths to pay their taxes." That year, in many parts of
France, the harvests had been disastrous—not as bad as in the
great famine years of the preceding century, but the differences
would not have consoled the hungry even if they had known
them. The peasants were emigrating to Spain, or leaving the land
for the cities; there were waves of rural and urban unemployed
wandering through the region after each bad harvest.

Such matters must have been discussed over the head of the
child Nicolas. And he was surely exposed to the religious climate
of the region, a compound of asceticism, cold fervor, and rather
stiff individualism that had colored the religious life of the
Auvergne through the Middle Ages, the bloody religious wars
that followed, and the Jansenism of the seventeenth century—it
is worth noting that the family of the Arnauds, as well as the
Pascals, came from the Auvergne.

But when he was five, at most, Nicolas was already in Paris.
The Collège des Grassins had been established almost two hundred years earlier, in 1569, as a school for poor children. (Its
founder, the Vicomte de Buzancy, was descended from a noble-

man of that name who had built a mosque in the Ardennes to commemorate his captivity in Palestine.) Docteur Morabin, who had recommended Nicolas for admission to the college, was on the staff there when Nicolas was enrolled and his education began.

He was not a brilliant student at first. When he began his studies at the age of five, the crisis in French education that would be brought about by the suppression in France of the Society of Jesus was still nineteen years in the future, but the controversy and the changes on emphasis in instruction that were leading toward that event were well under way. The "philosophers" represented the trend of the period—skeptical, rationalist, anticlerical—qualities that were crowned at last (literally, at the Comédie-Française, in 1778, by a crowd of enthusiasts) in the person of Voltaire. The term included almost all of the major and influential writers of the generation that dominated the middle part of the century, though it did so somewhat uneasily: the differences between Rousseau and the Encyclopedists, for instance, seemed greater to both parties than their affinities. They were unanimously opposed to leaving education in the hands of priests, and to the heavy accent on religious instruction, which most of them had experienced, in a curriculum that had been evolved largely with a view to rearing novices for the church. Humanism was becoming the order of the day, and ecclesiastical history was being demoted in favor of the history of Greece and Rome. In the schools one of the incentives to learning was a system of competitions within each college and then among the colleges, for prizes. Great importance was attached to these contests. After a time Chamfort proved to be an apt competitor: in a single year, of the five first prizes offered in rhetoric, he won four, losing only the prize for Latin verse. Guingené says:

His masters wanted him to win them all; his position as the holder of a scholarship made him dependent upon them; he was forced to repeat his studies in rhetoric and was made to understand that he must give up the scholarship that was all he had, or win, this time, all five first prizes. He won them, and . . . said to his friends, "I failed to win the prize last year because I imitated Virgil: I carried it off this year because I imitated Buchanan, Sarbiewius, and the other moderns."

The story, and its place in the system, have an interest beyond that of mere anecdote. It is reasonable to suppose that Guingené, and perhaps other friends of Chamfort's, had it from Chamfort himself, wherever else they may have heard it, and it must have been recounted long after the event, and have been colored by Chamfort's intervening years. And so certain details, as they were remembered, are suggestive; for instance, the explanation of the determination to win the prizes. The way that this is presented may of course owe something to Guingené's sympathy, but there is no reason to think that it was his invention, and it sounds a bit oversimplified. Undoubtedly the masters would have urged Nicolas to win as many prizes as possible; probably they would not have stopped short of threats, perhaps even threats in exactly the terms that are ascribed to them. On the other hand, is it likely that, in a school founded for poor boys, Chamfort was the only student whose sole asset was his scholarship? If there were any other boys there who were roughly in Nicolas's position, was it likely that the masters would deprive of his scholarship the one boy who had won four out of five first prizes in his first year of rhetoric? Of course other things must have made the winning of prizes important too, especially for a boy who felt himself to be more than usually alone, profoundly uncertain of what would become of him, utterly without prestige or protection—if he lost that which had recommended him for his scholarship in the first place. His place among his fellow students must have figured in his zeal. But it is interesting that the reason that is given for his efforts is one that comes from outside him and has nothing to do with his own wishes: the circumstances are presented as though the boy had had no choice, and the fact is equally relevant whether Chamfort believed that this was so at the time, or came to believe it afterward. For the practice of contending for prizes, and winning them, in competitions that were sometimes scarcely more than extensions of what he had known at the Collège des Grassins, claimed some of Chamfort's most assiduous efforts during the next twenty years of his life, and his attitude toward the institution and its assumptions figures among the ambiguities in his work, his view of society, and of himself. Otherwise the anecdote would be of little importance. But it seems to appear as an early instance of a contradiction that Chamfort recognized, but never, perhaps, resolved. Its hint of self-justification is reinforced by the end of the story: Chamfort's wry remark on the judgment, and by implication on the judges, the competition, and the tastes and values they embodied. Again, it makes no difference whether the remark was actually made at the time when the prizes were given, as Guingené recounts it, or later. In the former case it merely displays a precocity that is remarkable but credible, and a ready acerbity that was to become famous.

The other surviving stories of his school years are more light-hearted. His wit was habitual very early, and was obstreperous enough to earn him temporary explusions from at least one of his courses, for provoking irreverent hilarity. And before he finished his studies in philosophy, perhaps as a result of some such disciplinary action, Nicolas ran away from school altogether. He and a friend four years his elder, named Le Tourneur, who was to become known as a translator of English poetry (Young, Ossian, and Shakespeare), slipped out of the college one evening and set out on the road to Normandy. There is no record of their plans. They got as far as Cherbourg and then changed their minds and made their way to Paris again, where the Collège des Grassins indulgently took them back in.

≈ IV ≈

Chamfort's sponsors and teachers had intended him for a career in the church, and he was made an abbé. Holy orders, in eighteenth-century France, allowed for considerable scope both in ambition and mores, but Nicolas refused to take a further and irrevocable step. The abbé's gown, he said, was "a costume, and not an office." But Guingené says that he told the principal of the college, "I will never be a priest; I am too fond of repose, philosophy, women, honor, and true glory, and not fond enough of bickering, hypocrisy, honors, and money." It was quoted, again, long after the event. And it suggests that Nicolas, before the end of his days at the college, had acquired a certain worldly experience and assurance; if there was wishful thinking at any point in the suggestion, he was soon able to explore his preferences. By the time he left the college in his abbé's "costume," he appears to have won the friendship of several rich and titled personages who

welcomed his society and made available to him all the fashionable dissipations. He was known at once for his wit—a gift that
has probably never, and nowhere else, been so highly valued. All
the accounts agree that he was extremely good looking, and he
soon had a reputation for his conduct in bed. Madame de Craon,
who Guingené says was "the first beautiful lady from whom he
obtained more, or if you will, something other than friendship,
said of him, 'You think he is simply an Adonis, and he is a
Hercules.'" The pronouncement no doubt helped his opportunities, and the age itself gave them its blessing. Casanova was in
his thirties as Chamfort was being launched into a society in
which Mme. d'Epinay, Rousseau's patroness for several years,
wrote to a young bride, "You must have your diversions, your
dissipations, see the world, have affairs; in short, live like all the
women of your age"; and marital fidelity had been out of fashion
among the upper classes for years. Fifty years earlier Dancourt
had said, "Jealousy is a bourgeois passion which by now is almost
unknown among persons of quality," and in the interim the
bourgeoisie itself had conquered the passion more frequently.

The age was more democratic in a number of respects than the
current image of it, and within certain conventional limits the
beau monde could appreciate Nicolas's intellectual gifts, and welcome them. Practical help, at first, was another matter. He had
decided that he would be a writer; a man of letters, journalist,
playwright. And he took a pen name by which he was soon well
known: Sébastien-Roch-Nicolas Chamfort. (There is a village in
the Auvergne called Chamfort, but it is not known whether this
influenced his choice or whether he had ever heard of it.) His
livelihood had to be taken care of, and he resorted to his pen for
that too. He is said to have written sermons for priests who had
trouble composing their own—a source of revenue that had
served, and delighted, Diderot, some years earlier. He worked for
an old attorney in some clerkly capacity, and was promoted to
tutoring the man's children. The first tutoring position led to
others, but the sisters and wives of his employers, on occasion,
were too impressed by him for the peace of the household, and
he did not stay anywhere long.

He was hired by the Count Van Eyck to tutor the count's
nephew. The count had been in Paris since 1744 representing his
brother the Archbishop of Liége, who was himself famous for his

worldly appetites. Van Eyck was leaving for Cologne, and his young tutor went with his entourage. Dousset believes that Chamfort would have preferred to act as a secretary rather than a tutor, since he remarked later that he had no real bent for pedagogy, and that women needed "some special ordering to enable them to support, care for, and cherish children." Besides, Van Eyck is known to have been ridiculously stingy, and Chamfort despised an undue regard for money. He and his employer had a falling out, and in 1761—aged, presumably, twenty-one —he left Van Eyck's establishment, took a cure, and a trip in the late spring along the Rhine, from whose banks he sent a letter in drooping verse to a friend back in France, in which he went so far as to exclaim, of the Rhineland:

> Touching abode! Why are you not my homeland?
> Ah well, no matter . . .
> > I think of my friend.
> All one needs, to be happy, is a heart . . .

But he was soon back in Paris, announcing, more typically, that he knew of "nothing I would have been less suited to be than a German." Earning a living was a problem again, the more so as he was helping to support Thérèse Croiset, back in Clermont. His next source of income was also linked with Liége, and it may have been while he was with Van Eyck that Chamfort had met Pierre Rousseau from Toulouse, who had founded a fortnightly review of books and events, "*Le Journal Encyclopédique*," with the patronage of the Prince Palatine and the Prince d'Horion; he employed Chamfort to write for the periodical under a pseudonym, and the arrangement lasted for two years. There is no way of telling how much influence Pierre Rousseau may have had on Chamfort; he was fifteen years older than Chamfort, and had written unsuccessfully for the theater. His work as a journalist bore the skeptical, satiric stamp associated with the encyclopedists, and the first number of his journal had had to be printed on presses that had been moved twice, to Brussels, and then to Bouillon, to escape the ban of the Cardinal of Bavaria.

His labors as a journalist did not keep Chamfort in luxury, but he was engaged in things closer to his ambitions, and he said one day to his friend Sélis,

I'm a very poor devil indeed, as you see me now, but do you know what's going to become of me? I'll win a prize at the Academy; my comedy will be a success; I will find myself launched in the world and welcomed by the great whom I despise; they will make my fortune without my having to concern myself about it and I will live the life of a philosopher.

It is probably more usual to remember prophecies that come true. At the end of April, 1764, his one-act comedy, *"La Jeune Indienne,"* was performed at the Comédie-Française. The play is a pasteboard thing, and hard to take seriously except as a period piece. It is full of the cloying romantic attitudes Rousseau (Jean-Jacques) had helped to make fashionable, and it belongs in a tradition of French "noble savage" literature that included works by Bernardin de Saint Pierre and Chateaubriand, written half a century later. The hero is a young Englishman named Belton, shipwrecked and cast ashore on an island, where he is saved by an old man and his daughter, who nurse him back to health. The old man dies. Belton finds the solitude trying, pines for his home in Charlestown (South Carolina—the play was written, it will be noted, before the American Revolution), and after four years, all told, on the island, he manages to make his way home from the Ganges side, taking with him the savage maid, who loves him. At home the social conventions rear their tiresome heads, and circumstances prove so awkward for Belton what with his companion's poverty and his own compromised situation, that he is brought to the point of abandoning the friendless Betti—for this is the Indian girl's name—and marrying a rich young lady who had been chosen for him before he sailed away in the first place. His perfidy reaches Betti's ears, and she confronts him and discourses with heated eloquence on the falseness and hypocrisy that prevail in civilized society. In the end it is the father of the rich young lady who had been Belton's intended in other days—a man who is a virtuous Quaker and sees through society though he lives in it—who establishes peace once again between Belton and Betti and marries them.

Voltaire, with characteristic generosity, wrote to the young author:

La Jeune Indienne should delight all well-intentioned hearts. Besides, many of the verses are excellent. I love to be moved by comedy, as long as it is good-natured. It seems to me that you have succeeded extremely well in this mixed form, which is so difficult; I am convinced that you will go far. It is a great comfort to me to think that there are young persons of your merit in Paris.

And this although Chamfort had written some rather rude verses about *Candide* and its author in 1760, which had come to Voltaire's notice and had prompted him to write, congratulating the young man on his "touching" verses and declaring that he envied Chamfort's gift.

And the play was a success with the public. The applause was long and loud, the author was called for and pressed by the actors to take his bow. There were nine performances; Chamfort made 524 francs; Louis XV commanded a performance at Versailles; other companies performed the play; and the Comèdie-Française kept it in the repertory until 1789. But the critics, Grimm, Fréron, Collé, were unfavorable to the point of sarcasm. It was a judgment Chamfort and his friends ascribed to plain jealousy, and which would eventually figure on Chamfort's private list of justifications for avoiding society. His own mordant wit may have contributed already to the animosity with which he insisted from the start that he was surrounded (and to a tendency to expect it). He thought of it as a defense, but maxims other than Chamfort's, behavior older than man's, and the vicious postures of our own time have made clear to us the ambivalence of defense, and he was feared too early not to be disliked.

Besides, any inclination to be jealous of Chamfort was encouraged a few months after the opening of *La Jeune Indienne*, when Chamfort won a prize from the Académie for a long poem entitled, *Epistle from a Father to His Son, on the Birth of His Grandson*. The subject is education, and the views are heavily marked by those that had been widely discussed since the publication and public burning, two years earlier, of Rousseau's treatise on education, *Émile*. Chamfort had a copy sent to Rousseau, who received it with some coolness, chiding Chamfort for playing the grandfather at twenty, but declaring that he would be interested in seeing any future writings. The poem was warmly received, in general, and was read aloud at the Académie by its general secretary, d'Alembert himself, who spoke in praise of the work and its author.

The academic success had a pleasant sequel. In a gesture that was typical of the age, and surely innocent of irony, Chamfort sent his verses on education, with their recommendation of Nature in preference to lessons and masters (Mme. de Genlis had said, "since Nature gives no lessons in spelling and still less in Latin, we shall see young persons of a quite extraordinary ignorance in the world") to his old Greek teacher at the Collège des Grassins, M. Lebeau the elder, who was himself to win distinction as a member of the Academy of Inscriptions and Belles-Lettres. Chamfort inscribed the copy, "Chamfort sends his work, which won the wreath, to his former and respected master, and begs his pardon, after nine years, for Nicolas." Lebeau wrote back, "I always loved Nicolas; I admire Chamfort," and the exchange led to a reunion at which they were both moved to tears.

Of all the academicians—and at that moment the Académie included Voltaire, Marmontel, Marivaux and Buffon—Duclos was the one who showed Chamfort most favor and friendship. There were affinities between the older writer (Duclos was sixty) and the younger, and Duclos can scarcely have failed to influence Chamfort. He was a man of the world, who had enjoyed a richly varied success with the opposite sex. His integrity of character and his generosity were well known, and as a historian of the follies of the Regency he had a reputation for being a caustic satirist. Another who became Chamfort's friend at the time was Claude Crébillon, known as Crébillon the younger, a fashionable novelist then in his fifties; and at this period he formed an acquaintance with the Abbé Delille, his contemporary, another Auvergnat.

V

The literary cafés, the salons, the theater, were the main meeting places of the literati. The writer occupied a position in France at that moment which is hard for us to imagine. In 1750, says Pierre Gaxotte (*La Revolution Française*), "In all the towns there were swarms of associations of wits and thinkers, literary salons, academies, lecture halls. . . . Everyone reads; above all everyone discusses. . . . If one recalls that Rousseau's first discourse was submitted to a competition of the Academy of Dijon, one will have some idea of the tone. . . ." And de Tocqueville, in a remarkable chapter devoted to the topic in *L'ancien Régime et la Révolution* says, "France had been for a long time the most literary nation in Europe; however, men of letters had never shown the spirit that they displayed toward the middle of the eighteenth century, nor occupied the position which they then acquired." He was referring in particular to their influence on the political ideas of the time, rather than their social position, but the two were connected and influenced each other.

After his successes of 1764, Chamfort's literary plans were bruited about; they were said to include a tragedy called "Pharamonde," of which one hears no more. He did write another play, *Fanni*, of the same sort as *La Jeune Indienne*. It was performed only at a *theatre de salon*, and the text has been lost. But his interest in the theater continued, and one of his few liaisons of which we know anything dates from this period and involved a belle of the theater, a famous dancer, Mlle. Guimard.

Actresses and dancers were not received by the ladies of society, but they were of course welcomed in the literary world, and when their fortunes permitted, some of them held salons of their own and entertained brilliantly. Vanity may have played some part in Chamfort's pursuit of Mlle. Guimard; she was said to be the most sought-after woman in Paris. She had been a dancer in the ballet, scarcely turned fifteen, when she had been discovered, and "protected," according to Dousset, by M. d'Harnancourt and the president de Saint-Lubin, and others. Her attractions were described in 1761, when she was seventeen, by the police inspector du Marais: she "had the loveliest bosom in the world, and her face, while not pretty, had its charm." She had been well educated, too, it is said; in any case her protectors came to include the Maréchal Prince de Soubise, who gave her a thousand crowns a month, the Comte de Boutourlin, who was the ambassador to Russia, and the Comte de Rochefort, who was the director of the Louvre and the first valet of the King's bedchamber. She gave dinners three times a week, one for court personages and public dignitaries, one for writers, painters, philosophers, and wits, and the third for beautiful women. She reached dizzy heights of worldly success, becoming "conseillère de toilette" to Marie Antoinette, and vying with the King himself in the magnificence of her entertainments. Her house had its own theater, fitted with several grilled loges to permit ladies of the court to attend unseen. They came to see not only "legitimate" plays (Chamfort's *La Jeune Indienne* and his *Fanni* were both performed on her stage), but racier productions, in which the hostess herself took some of the chief roles. The duke of Chartres was particularly fond of a piece called *"Vérité dans le vin,"* which apparently offered, under the pretense of drunkenness, some rousing dialogue.

Chamfort's affair with Mlle. Guimard probably did not last long. Her own habits would have tended to keep it brief. When Fragonard said to her, "I love you, and you will love me, if only for a week," she had answered, "A week! None of my lovers could ever boast of anything of the kind. A week! It would be as bad as marriage!"

For all the glitter of his existence Chamfort was still poor. He lived quite literally in a garret, as many other men of letters did. And in his mid-twenties the first ominous signs of the bad health that would plague him for the rest of his life became manifest, though it is not known whether the ailment from which he suffered not long after his first successes was the persistent venereal disease to which he would be a victim from his thirties onward, or some other complaint or exhaustion. In any case it proved to be intractable. Each apparent cure was followed by a relapse. His nerves were affected; he fell into a profound depression, which became chronic, and his good looks and air of youth were permanently destroyed. Finally he kept to his room, seeing only a few friends.

Unable to work, and probably still, while he could, sending money to Thérèse Croiset, he was soon in financial trouble. This and his sickness revealed new friends, or the qualities of old ones. When the Duc de la Vallière learned of Chamfort's distress he offered assistance at once, but Chamfort was unwilling to accept more than enough to relieve his immediate wants. He and the Duc de la Vallière had known each other for some time, and Dousset says that Chamfort's vocation as a moralist dates from his acquaintance with this witty, cultivated son of a court beauty and favorite, who had herself suffered eclipse and died in a convent. There is no way of being sure of anything of the kind, but there is a strange letter dating from this period (20 August,

1765) in which that vocation is suddenly evident. There is no name at the head of the letter, so that it is not clear whether it was actually intended for a particular friend, or whether, as seems more likely, the form was simply a convention, and the letter was addressed, as it were, by Chamfort to himself, in a crisis of disillusionment. He proposes to give "advice for the good of your happiness," and the central precept is, "Protect yourself against any strong or deep feeling." For, he says:

I have noticed that whenever you are strongly affected by anything, you fall into a state of deep sadness, which is not that gentle melancholy so delicious for those who experience it. Besides, your work makes gaiety necessary for your health. Even if a profound sentiment were able to make you happy, it is certain that it would afford you no relaxation, which is something you need. Do not be afraid of losing, in this way, that sensibility that is essential to a man of letters: You had too large a dose to start with; nothing can exhaust it. . .

Never give anyone any right over you. . . . Keep everyone politely at a great distance; prostrate yourself in refusals. I believe in friendship, I believe in love (the idea is indispensable to my happiness) but I believe still more strongly that wisdom bids me renounce the hope of finding a mistress and a friend capable of filling my heart. I know that what I am saying makes you shiver, but human depravity and the reasons I have for despising men are such that I believe I am entirely excusable.

If anyone were naturally what I am advising you to be, I would shun him with all my heart. If a person is void of sensibility, he inspires a feeling that resembles aversion; if he is too sensitive, he is unhappy. What is one to decide? This: to reduce love to the pleasure of satisfying a spontaneous need, while allowing oneself at most a certain preference for one object or another. To reduce friendship to a feeling of benevolence proportioned to the merit of each person . . . your soul should never be inseparably attached to anyone else's; you must appreciate everyone and fulfill the duties of an honest man, even of a virtuous man, according to just and predetermined ideas rather than according to feelings which, though more delicious, always have something arbitrary about them.

It is through work alone that you will escape the activity of that soul of yours which devours everything. The time you spend at home will reduce by so much that which you waste out in the world, where you are so little amused, where you endure the endlessly unpleasant sense of the superiority of your soul and the inferiority of your fortune, where you discover reasons for hating and despising men.

Retirement will, at the same time, assure your repose, or to put it in other words, your happiness, your health, your fame, your fortune, and your reputation; you will have fewer opportunities for allowing yourself those pleasures which, though they do not ruin the health, do at least enfeeble the vigor of the body, impart a kind of unease, and destroy the equilibrium of the passions.

The reputation of the most celebrated of men depends upon his taking care not to be prodigal of himself. Always maintain that decent coquetry which demeans no one. Your fame will profit by it; your use of your time cannot fail to add to it, and for the same reason to your fortune as well, for believe what I say and never count on anyone but yourself.

There is one more thing that I cannot urge upon you too strongly, and which is harder for you to practice than for some, and that is thrift. I am not suggesting that you should regard money as a thing of value, but that you should consider thrift as a means of remaining independent of men, which condition is more necessary than is believed if one is to preserve one's honesty.

It stops there. At the date given, Chamfort was twenty-five —or twenty-three, if one is to lend credence to the birth date which he notarized at the Chatelet. Either way it was in the year following the triumphs of *La Jeune Indienne* and the Académie's prize; though there is no way of telling whether he was, at this moment, already sick, in need of money, in deliberate seclusion, or whether the Duc de la Vallière's offer, for instance, had yet been made. But later writings make the immediate events seem unimportant, and the letter appears to be an expression of the configuration of his character itself, already firmly set by this time.

The letter was found, apparently, among Chamfort's own papers, which increases the likelihood that it was written for himself: relatively few of the letters he sent to friends were recovered and published. But whatever the writing's ostensible destination may have been, the personal assumptions contained in its advice link the attitude of the writer to the image of the presumed reader in a regard whose narcissism so closely resembles the view of himself Chamfort presents in other and later writings that it is worth a brief examination.

The person addressed is inconveniently "sensitive" in the manner of most who had been touched by the wand of Rousseau, and Chamfort had been deeply marked by Jean-Jacques. It was a quality that his followers assumed automatically and accorded others as a kind of decency. It was one of the new hypocrisies, replacing others that had become old-fashioned. "There is an excess of sensibility that is close to insensitivity," Marmontel said (and de Sade, in *Aline and Valcour*, and Gorer, in *The Life and Ideas of the Marquis de Sade*, quoted him.) Reverdy, in *Le Livre de Mon Bord*, cites an instance at the source itself—or a stage nearer to it (for Rousseau was no more the inventor of the fiction than Chamfort was): "On one of Rousseau's manuscripts a correction has been discovered. . . . He had written, to start with, 'I could not find a single tear.' But sensibility was in fashion, and so he changed it, for the printer, to 'I felt myself dissolve into tears.' " (But the mockers also can flog dead horses.) The soul in question in Chamfort's epistle has suffered precisely because of his excess of sensibility; the writer has labored under a similar burden, and may well have been afflicted, as well, by the realization of the superiority of his own soul and the inferiority of his position, and have been led to the disparaging conclusions that are touched on.

With this and the distinction between the delicious and the tormenting kinds of melancholy, the writing and thinking are not only in an obviously romantic tradition but are almost an evocation of the embittered and misunderstood Romantic figure that was to play so important a part in the imagination of the following century. The image of unusual sensibility is not yet entirely at ease with the embittered attitude, though in fact the connection comes about naturally, and they had already been linked in Rousseau and others. And so there is the further distinction, almost a bit of dialogue, that contrasts, by way of justification, what the reader and writer *naturally* are, from the way they are *driven* to feel and behave. The distinction again is related to Rousseau, and was a familiar preoccupation of the time. But Rousseau had tried to define nature and reason and determine their relation to each other; Chamfort, throughout his writings, like many of his contemporaries, used the terms vaguely, with meanings that are largely composed of emotional overtones. The terms' relation to each other seems to shift without Chamfort being aware of the fact, so that sometimes the rational is the true expression of the natural, and sometimes, as in this letter, it contradicts it. Both the natural and the rational are here assumed to be good, however, and are entered to the credit of sensitive souls.

Chamfort was not always so sure of the values of reason; sometimes he referred to it as a burden, but when he spoke kindly of it, it was often with a certain proprietary tone, which again was especially common at the time. He has already decided, at the time of this writing, to refer to love and friendship as illusions, and is close to his formulation of the necessity of illusions for happiness—at least that is how his description of the "idea" of love as "indispensable to my happiness" can be understood. At the same time, having decided at twenty-five that his own heart cannot be adequately suited in either respect, he urges his reader to reduce both, without further hope, to relatively depersonalized gestures.

Because it is so consistent with what is recurrent and central in Chamfort's views as a moralist, and with the image of himself that he presented as a part of them, the epistle raises some of the questions that all his moralistic writings pose. What, in the first place, is his relation to them? Where they advocate or imply behavior, are they mainly notes of ways in which he thinks he really meant to behave, or codifications of ways in which he thinks he does and should behave, or excuses for ways in which he thinks he has behaved or might have behaved, but about which he is not quite at ease, or stage directions for a part he is composing, or some combination of all these? How much of their function, whatever it is, does he himself really understand?

One of the central themes of his major work, *Products of the Perfected Civilization* is the justification of his "taste for retirement," as a result of his disappointment with men and the falsities of their society and its professions. The justification is essentially the one given here, even to the generalization and the curious rigidity with which it is envisaged and set forth, qualities that suggest a certain reticence of the imagination as well as of humor, especially as they too changed very little during Chamfort's life. The most interesting thing about the justification is that as its argument recurs in letters, aphorisms, and essays, it seems to be addressed to a person who is essentially a figure of the society that is being shunned—and there are other occasions when the figure appears to be an aspect of Chamfort himself. (This is true even when the person addressed has actually "retired," in the literal and physical sense, far more thoroughly than Chamfort, as the Abbé Roman, in Provence, had done. Here it is the Abbé's unregenerate, unretired *views* that are assailed. The Abbé did not *need* Chamfort's justifications of retirement—he was living in the country.)

Chamfort never escaped that society and its attitudes for long, which is perhaps why his justification for withdrawing from it as a psychic or imaginative act was endless and essentially changeless, and why his preoccupation with leaving society often seems to be cast in the form of an attempt to convince, impress, or punish society itself; and he may have had difficulty believing in either event. Hence the fixity of the situation, relieved in the end only by violence in the society and in Chamfort's confrontation of it.

This may be why, despite his disappointments, he never entirely removed his ambitions from social contexts, and in particular, diplomacy, until both the society he despised, and the society he envisaged in its place had dissolved, and he was surrounded by public circumstances in which he did not wish to figure, or recognize himself, or live. The epistle—like many of the aphorisms, some of which may have been rehearsed in society before being copied down, and some of which may actually have been overheard and at most re-turned—owes some of its rigidity to being a part of an attitude, disguising, and in the end obstructing some other tension and retreat.

VI

After the Duc de la Vallière's assistance, another possibility of support presented itself. He had been watched over, in his sickness and need, by the dramatic poet Joseph Saurin and his wife. Among the circle of their friends Chamfort came to know the Abbé de Laroche, a man of letters whom everyone seems to have liked. Laroche had been a close friend of Helvetius, who had just died; he had no illusions about the life of a man of letters and worked at persuading Chamfort to abandon it. Early in their friendship Laroche was offered forty thousand francs by Lord Huntington, the sum to be deposited with a notary, and in exchange Laroche was to spend two years traveling in Italy as the tutor of two young Englishmen. Laroche thought that Chamfort would fill the post better than he would himself, and he suggested the substitution. But when the offer was made, Chamfort considered himself cured of his sickness and was anxious to be at liberty to resume his studies and his literary career. His poverty ceased to worry him as soon as his strength began to return, and (not surprisingly, considering the advice in his letter) he declined the offer.

He found literary employment when he was equal to it. Another friend, Charles Panckoucke, had recently opened "the most beautiful of bookshops" in Paris, and he engaged Chamfort to work on a dictionary. The terms were surely meager, but the payment evidently was regular and dependable, and the work and the arrangement as a whole contented Chamfort, who made no attempt at brilliance or originality in this kind of writing; he republished some of the articles that he wrote for Panckoucke's thirty-volume "Vocabulary" in the *Theatrical Dictionary*, eleven years later. When he had recuperated, he paid a visit to Thérèse Croiset in the Auvergne. And he continued to produce works with more literary pretention, at least, than his writings for Panckoucke: odes on "The Greatness of Man," on "Truth," on "Volcanoes," a "Verse Discourse on the Man of Letters." The last two were submitted in the competitions at the Académie, but without winning any prizes. "Two years," Guingené says, "without his fortune being advanced at all." He had taken to going out in public again, frequenting the salons.

The odes were not his first failures in the world of academic competition. In 1763 the Académie d'Amiens had proposed as a theme "How useful is literature?" a vague, distant echo, no doubt deliberate, of "Whether the progress of the sciences and the arts has tended to corrupt or to purify morals," which had been set by the Académie de Dijon fourteen years earlier, when Rousseau's essay had won the prize and made him famous overnight. The Académie d'Amiens offered only three hundred francs, but Chamfort needed money, he was unknown (*La Jeune Indienne* had not yet been performed), and he submitted an essay. He also took the trouble to alert his friends Delille and Sélis, who were both professors at the *collège* of Amiens, of his entry, and ask them to do what they could. They were forestalled, it seems, by the secretary of the Académie himself, a man named Baron—"of great pretentions and little talent," says Guingené—who had decided to enter the competition himself, and who was admirably placed to look after his own interests, since it was he who was to read the entries aloud to the assembled academicians. Apparently he hurried and mumbled through Chamfort's, which was unanimously rejected, and read his own "very well and oratorically, so that it seemed a marvel and was given the prize on the first vote." The essay Chamfort submitted was not found among his papers after his death, though Guingené said it had been there a few years earlier.

The incident does not seem to have left lasting scars. On the other hand after his verse entries had been unsuccessful for two years running at the Académie Française, he submitted no more verse, and confined his writing, except for plays and an occasional epigram, to prose. It is hard to muster much regret for the poems he might have written, but it is worth noting that his writing of verse had been, until then, voluminous. It included an antiwar poem on "The Deliverance of Salermo and the Founding of the Two Sicilies," which won a prize in his year of successes, 1765, at the Académie de Rouen, another poem that had won a prize at the Académie de Marseille, and there were besides, thirty-some libertine *contes* in the manner of La Fontaine, and several longer historical pieces.

After his fortune had undergone the two barren years of which Guingené speaks, he entered, in 1767, a composition at the Académie de Marseille; the theme they had set (again reminiscent of Rousseau's first triumph) was "To What Extent the Genius of Great Writers Influences the Spirit of Their Age." The Académie de Marseille was one of the more important assemblies of its kind, and boasted Voltaire among its members. The entries were orotund, as usual; Chamfort declared that he preferred the benign effect of men of genius to revolution, as a reforming influence, because it is stronger and more sure. Of the formation of genius itself he says, "No, it is not men who form great men. These belong to no family, to no age, to no country. . . . It is God who, in his mercy, sends them fully formed to the earth to renew man and his degenerate reason." The deity figures in argument again, in the description of the influence of genius:

its motion, once impressed, does not die with it . . . it subjugates man in order to ennoble him; it tames his will with his reason, with the noblest of his passions and of his faculties; like God it enjoys the astonishing privilege of ruling over them without limiting their powers and without taking from them the precious sense of liberty.

Chamfort won the prize, and the following year he submitted to the Académie Française his *Éloge de Molière.*

It is the first of his academic pieces that retains any interest after two hundred years. Until then the Académie had tended to set verses of Scripture for its themes; the eulogies had been reserved for military men and statesmen. Chamfort's friend Duclos was largely responsible for turning the plaudits toward literature. Chamfort, in his composition, points out that Molière had never belonged to the Académie. He calls attention to the portraits of former members on the walls and asks, "Where is Molière? One of those instances of justice that the multitude reveres and the sage respects robbed him of literary homage during his lifetime and left him only the applause of Europe." He discusses the function of comedy, as distinct from that of Cornellian heroic tragedy, which was still the more respected *genre* in France. Comedy is the school of manners, a portrait of human nature, the best moral history of society, and it contends successfully against prejudices—which in the language of the "enlightenment" meant, above all, organized religion. In his delineation of its proper activity in the hands of Molière, Chamfort's own style begins to assume the manner of his later attacks on the old order, and he ends his outline of Molière's subject matter with the remark: "society was not yet an arena where each sizes up the others with a distrust disguised as politeness." The *éloge*, naturally enough, has none of the fractious brilliance of the passages on Molière in Rousseau's "Letter to D'Alembert," published nearly twenty years before, though a few of the distinctions that Chamfort draws (particularly when talking of tragedy) recall that work. He strikes, in passing, at the school of Marivaux, contrasting Molière's fidelity to nature with the burlesqued noblemen, amorous beldames, and languishing ladies of the later comedy, "stock figures . . . in which the forced ridicule, portraying nothing, corrects nothing." The prize went to Chamfort, in the presence of one of Molière's nephews; once again it drew a generous letter from Voltaire, and annoyed some of Chamfort's contemporaries.

He turned from his new success to another play, a one-act prose comedy, suggested, it is said, by his work on Molière. Entitled *Le Marchand de Smyrne*, it was first presented at the Comédie-Française in January 1770. It is certainly the least pretentious of Chamfort's three extant plays: slight, episodic, built around stock Oriental characters that were current at the time. As with the earlier sentimental comedy, the public was enthusiastic; the play had thirteen performances. But again the critics Collé and La Harpe disliked it, and Grimm said of Chamfort:

. . . As for real talent, I fear he has none; at least his *Marchand* does not indicate anything of the kind. . . . I have found myself somewhat distressed, in the *Marchand*, by the flat and exaggerated eulogies of the French nation that one met with at every turn, which our minor authors give us as proofs of their patriotism. The art of arranging current ideas with a bit of order and a certain facility and purity is a merit of the age, of the culture in general, and not of the author. M. Chamfort's ideas of dramatic art are vague and indecisive, they are meaningless because they do not come from the source. It is obvious that they can be seized in handfuls and snatched from his head without depriving him of an atom of his own substance. What it comes to is that he is not a thinker. . . . I am no more satisfied by M. de Chamfort's manner of writing than by his ideas.

Grimm's own metaphors are not always either happy or clear, but his criticism, even allowing for its air of delight at pouncing on a reputation he resented, comes close to some of the weaknesses of Chamfort's theatrical writings, and it also reveals, in a few strokes, the Grimm who was a precursor of the Romantics, at a time when many of the critics' tastes and principles were still serving a tottering neoclassicism.

In the following year a far graver misfortune struck Chamfort. Bachaumont, in his *Mémoires*, gives most of the few details. Among Chamfort's friends was Claude de Rulhière, five or six years his elder, and secretary to the Baron de Breteuil. The baron (1730-1807) had distinguished himself by his handling, several years earlier, of a diplomatic mission to Czar Peter III. Rulhière himself, who had been a cavalry captain and a member of the royal guard, was a man of letters, wrote poetry, had published, and had acquired a reputation both as a poet and as an historian.

He used his influence to persuade the Baron de Breteuil to attach Chamfort to his staff as a personal secretary. A new mission was planned; Chamfort was attracted to the idea of a diplomatic career, and when the invitation came, he accepted it. As he was making his preparations to go abroad with the baron he was taken with an acute attack of a skin disease resembling leprosy, which this time was certainly of syphilitic origin. He had no choice but to give up his plans, stay at home, and undergo treatment.

Again, as six years before, he was reduced to extreme poverty. And again it was a friend of the Saurins who helped most: Chabanon, a young man of literary tastes who had been born in comfortable circumstances and had a pension from the *Mercure de France* of twelve hundred francs a year, which he did not need. With some difficulty he persuaded Chamfort to accept this bit of income, and the relative security it afforded allowed Chamfort to take a cure at Contrexéville, which restored his health so effectively, for the moment at least, that he moved to the country, full of literary projects, and set to work with fresh energy, writing regularly for Panckoucke's *Vocabulary* and for the *Journal Encyclopedique* and compiling a collection of anecdotes which was published as a *Dictionary of Society*. He was even credited with having written, during this period, a *roman à clé* aimed at Louis XV, but the book, it is now generally agreed, was not his. Guingené conveys an exemplary picture of him, closeted with Molière, Racine, and La Fontaine, "meditating incessantly" on these authors, "each in turn, or frequently all at once," and making notes of his observations. He worked in fact on a commentary on Racine, of which only a few fragments on *Esther* survive. But in 1774 he turned his studies on La Fontaine to account.

In that year the Académie de Marseille, which had given him a prize six years earlier, set as its theme a *Eulogy of La Fontaine*. Neither the choice of the theme nor the opinions of the judges were free from influence. M. Necker, financier, man of great wealth, patron of literature, whose wife held a famous salon and whose daughter would become famous as Mme. de Staël, had been favored with a reading of a composition on La Fontaine written by La Harpe, his protégé. He had subsequently offered a prize of two thousand francs, to be awarded by the Académie de Marseille for a composition on this author. Guingené, with his

unfailing tact (besides, Necker was still alive when he wrote, and
so was La Harpe) says, "It was a delicate gesture conceived with
a view to helping a man of letters who had already written such a
eulogy . . ." La Harpe and his friends were so certain of the
outcome that he was spoken of, well before the event, as the
winner, and warmly congratulated on the brilliance of his essay;
and Necker, in turn, was praised for the generosity of his patronage. The result of the competition was so unexpected by
everyone, including, evidently, the members of the Académie
themselves, that the wording of their award betrays their surprise. "Chance," it says, "has accorded to M. Chamfort, a very
estimable young author well known for his charming stories, first
place . . ." Even Grimm, this time, approved of what chance had
done, and said so in print; and Fréron, who had spoken severely
about *La Jeune Indienne*, now wrote an article praising Chamfort.

ᕯᕔᕯ VII ᕯᕔᕯ

The *Éloge* was one of Chamfort's productions of which Saint-
Beuve, who in the main did not like him, spoke most highly. He
shared Chamfort's love of Molière and La Fontaine, whom he
called "the two most original writers that France ever produced,"
and Chamfort's view that they belonged together and should be
thought of together. Chamfort's *Éloges* on these two writers are
the most considerable of his critical works. His final preference is
for La Fontaine, and from the point of view of a study of Chamfort it is particularly interesting that he takes pains to present it
on moral grounds. He speaks of "the charm of this indulgent
ethic which penetrates the heart without wounding it, amuses the
child in order to make him a man, and the man in order to make
him wise, and would lead us to virtue in restoring us to nature,"
before beginning a serious consideration of La Fontaine's un-
analyzable style and the implications of his simplicity and his
taste. And when he compares him with Molière, he says:

the comic poet seems to have been held, rather, by the absurdities,
and to have depicted the passing fashions of society; the writer of

fables seems to have fixed his attention on the vices, and to have presented the more universal picture of nature. The first makes me laugh more than my neighbor; the second brings me back to myself. The former avenges me for the idiocies of others; the latter makes me brood on my own. The one seems to have considered absurdities indecent, and shocking to society; the other to have seen vices as a lapse of reason, from which we ourselves are the sufferers. After reading the first I dread the opinion of the public; after reading the second it is my own conscience that I fear. In short, the man who has been chastised by Molière might well cease to become ridiculous and become wicked; chastised by La Fontaine he would no longer be either wicked or ridiculous. He would be reasonable and good, and we would discover that we were virtuous . . .

It is one of the points on which Chamfort differs sharply from Rousseau, his most frequent mentor on matters touching the relation of virtue to nature; Rousseau considered La Fontaine more conducive to vice than to virtue.

He had been writing verse for masques presented at court, during these years, and pondering other theatrical subjects as he worked on the *Theatrical Dictionary*. He made notes for a *Dissertation on the Imitation of Nature in Dramatic Works*, and a *Sketch of a Poetics for the Theater*. And he had been adding slowly to his tragedy, the theatrical work that was to decide his fate as a dramatic author. His circumstances in general had been improving, and his health had given him no trouble since 1771. In 1774 he found himself famous, and for the moment, possessed of a bit of money. His work on the *Éloge de La Fontaine* had exhausted him to a point where there was danger of a recurrence of his ailment, and at the suggestion of the famous Doctor Bouvard, who figures in several of his anecdotes, he left Paris to take the waters at Barèges in the Pyrenées.

The trip and the cure cost him the whole of his prize money, but he sounded lighthearted when he wrote from there, in mid-September, to Mme. Saurin. He had had feminine company to his taste: four ladies, of whom Mme. de Gramont occupied him most particularly. She was a woman of spirit and originality, the sister of the Duc de Choiseul, whom she had loved with a tenderness that had aroused comment. She had left at the beginning of the month, Chamfort says, writing on the fifteenth, and he adds confidentially, "I could not desire anything other than what I found in her, and we finished even better than we started." The weather at Barèges, at the time he was writing, was terrible, but he tells Mme. Saurin:

I have all kinds of reasons for being enchanted with my journey to Barèges. It seems it should be the end of all the contradictions that I have suffered, and that the circumstances have all joined to dissipate that basic melancholy that recurred too often. The return of my health, the kindnesses that I have received from everyone, this happiness so unconnected with any deserving of it but so welcome and so pleasant, at being able to arouse the interest of all with whom I occupied myself; certain real and positive advantages, hopes that could not be better founded and that are confirmed by the strictest use of reason, the public welfare and that of several persons to whom I am not unknown and by whom I am not unconsidered, the tender memory of old friends, the charm of a new but solid friendship with one of the most virtuous men in the kingdom, a man of wit, of talent, and of simplicity . . . another liaison, no less precious, with a charming woman whom I met here and who has conceived for me all the feelings of a sister, the fact that persons whose acquaintance I most wanted to make have declared a most obliging fear of failing to make mine, and finally the combination of the most tender and desirable feelings: there, you have the causes of my happiness these past three months. It seems that my evil genius has loosened his grip, and I have lived these past three months under the wand of the good fairy.

And this although, "Everything that I have mentioned has now left Barèges."

The tone of this letter is somewhat different from those that I wrote you, Madame, from the rue de Richelieu, and indeed from several conversations that I remember having had with you five or six months ago. But . . . "man goes in waves," Montaigne said. I was iron to resist pain, I am wax to receive good. The different philosophies have their virtues; it is a matter of using them appropriately. Zeno was not wrong; Epicurus was right. A sick man's diet is not that of a convalescent, etc. . . .

Mme. de Gramont's brother, the Duc de Choiseul, had been Minister of Foreign Affairs under Louis XV from 1758 to 1770, and had been "exiled" to his estates in December of the latter year, partly as a result of the intrigues connected with the rise of the new favorite, Mme. du Barry. But neither his influence nor his sister's had entirely ceased to exist, as Chamfort's friends appear to have realized: he explains to Mme. Saurin his plan of visiting the Duc de Choiseul's château at Chateloup, on the Loire near Amboise, on his way north to Paris:

M. de B. thought it foolish for me to neglect the chance of seeing M. de Choiseul; he imagines that my acquaintance with Mme. de Gramont might end by becoming something more than a mere watering-place acquaintance, which can never be the case. He is at Chanteloup at the moment; he can find out for himself, and between ourselves I think he can hardly fail to be rather surprised. However that may be I defer to his advice and to that of my friends, who scold me for my lack of zeal in the matter. But I will not be at Chanteloup before the end of October; I will stay as long as seems proper . . .

It was less than ten years since the letter of "advice for your happiness," and in referring again to the difference, Chamfort says, "My present manner of being suits me; I would return to the other if I had to, but I will try to fend off whatever would make it necessary. That is all I know."

When he had agreed to visit Chanteloup, Chamfort had canceled a proposed trip to the Languedoc, and several other prospective visits. He was welcomed to the château not only by Mme. de Gramont, but by the three other ladies whose company had given him such pleasure at Barèges, Mme. d'Amblemont, Mme. de Roncé, and Mme. de Choiseul-Gouffier. The château itself was a large place, greatly admired; the life there was a round of cultivated amusements: the periodical literature of the capital was read and discussed; music and plays were written and performed. Mme. de Choiseul was fond of acting, and as a surprise for Chamfort she had been preparing a production of his *La Jeune Indienne*, in which she herself played Betti. Renewed hopes of a diplomatic position appear to have figured in Chamfort's decision to accept the invitation to Chanteloup, but they did not keep him there, and by late October he was back in Paris, living in a cheap between-floors apartment on the Rue de Beaune. His high spirits evidently survived his return. Mlle. de Lespinasse wrote of him, in a letter of October 25: "He has come back from the waters in good health, much richer in glory than in money, with his credit improved by four ladies who are fond of him. . . . And further, I assure you that M. Chamfort is quite a contented young man, and is doing his best to be modest."

But by winter he was poverty-stricken again. Dousset says that he was drawn to gambling, which may have relieved him of whatever was left after his trip south. It was a cold winter, and he tried to do without a fire whenever he could, going to bed early. His fever came back, and he seems to have fallen into another profound depression, after the expansiveness of the summer at Barèges. He felt that friends and reputation both had abandoned him. It was an exaggeration: Sélis and the Saurins did not neglect him; but it was clear that the situation could not go on as it was. Another friend, Mme. Helvetius, arranged a lodging for him at Sèvres, and he retired there as though leaving the world altogether.

The friends who continued to see him worried about the fact that he seemed indifferent even to work, and they urged him to finish the verse tragedy that he had been working on at intervals for over a decade. He completely recast what he had written up until then, and completed all five acts.

In the meantime, the friends he had made at Barèges had been using their influence in his behalf at court, and when the tragedy was finished, it was due in part to their good offices that it was first performed at Fontainebleau, on November 1, 1776, as part of the Toussaint festivities. It was a glimpse of the court at the height of the period that heralded the Revolution. The entertainments given in the autumn after hunts had become, year by year, more lavish; the court removed from château to château, from entertainment to entertainment, in processions so elaborate that they seemed like pageants. Fontainebleau was as ornate as it had ever been. There were productions of plays, ballets, operas, invited out from Paris. The festivities in 1775 had been particularly brilliant, and those of 1776 were said to be no less so. Grimm describes the journey of the court, the enormous crowd of guests, the entertainments, gambling, horse races. But "literature," he says, "though warmly welcomed, contributed little to the pleasure of the court. Out of a dozen plays presented before Their Majesties, many were bad, a few were barely passable. Chamfort's tragedy, *Mustapha and Zeangir*, triumphed too easily."

La Harpe declares that it had won the royal approval before it was ever performed: Chamfort had read it to Louis XVI and Marie Antoinette at Versailles before the festivities, and they had expressed their pleasure. At the play's production the King was seen to shed tears. After the final curtain the Queen summoned Chamfort, "to add to the pleasure which the performance has given me, the pleasure of announcing to you that the King, in order to encourage your talents and reward your success, has made you a pension of 1200 francs, drawn on the Menus Plaisirs." Her words, and the announcement were published in the *Année Litteraire*; she plied him with further compliments; and Chamfort, for once, was at a loss for a reply. She said that she hoped he would show his thanks by having his plays performed at Versailles. The following morning she told the assembled ambassadors that she had been in a great agitation the evening before, until she had been certain of the play's success. Obviously the court, and the Queen in particular, had decided to shower him with favor. Two years later, when the play was published, Chamfort dedicated it to Marie Antoinette. The dedication was not kept in the 1789 edition.

Whether or not they were influenced by Chamfort's turn of fortune, many of the critics, too, were well disposed toward the tragedy. La Harpe, who had spoken well of him earlier in the year, when the *Theatrical Dictionary* was published, and Grimm, both found things to praise in the play. "M. Chamfort's tragedy," said the latter, "has revealed characters full of nobility, tender feelings, and exquisite plotting; it is without question the best written play that we have seen on the stage in twenty years." But six weeks later, when *Mustapha* was performed in Paris at the Comédie-Française, the public success did not equal that of his earlier plays, which the critics had not liked. At the first performance the theater was full of court personages who repeated the enthusiasm that had been made official at Fontainebleau. But on the following evenings the audience was less fervent, and the theater was not as full. La Harpe noted the fact with obvious satisfaction some time later:

The play, of a mortal coldness, without action, without interest, without flow, without situations, dragged on in a lonely fashion for a while and eventually collapsed from the weight of boredom, never to reappear. The author had said aloud that he would allow himself to be judged by this drama, especially as he had been working on it for fifteen years; there is a unanimous recognition of a total absence of tragic genius . . .

And Condorcet wrote to Voltaire, on December 21, that the tragedy was "well written, full of well-turned commonplaces," but as far as he could see, "without passion or ideas." But there were fifteen performances; they earned Chamfort nearly four thousand francs, which was good for the period; the sum was picked up at the theater and signed for by Chamfort's friend Beaumarchais. The play gave rise to at least one literary anecdote quoted by Dousset from a contemporary:

I went last night to the final performance of *Mustapha and Zeangir*, a tragedy which I esteem no more highly than is necessary, in spite of the clique that lauds it to the skies, but in which there are, no doubt, a few lovely things. An abbé came with Morellet and one of the chorus leaders of the encyclopedic sect, and his niece who was recently married to M. Marmontel. The young lady seems to have a tender heart; her tears, at the moving passages, were in marked contrast to the disdainful smile with which the abbé sat through the audience's exaggerated applause. He could not endure it: "Madame," he said tartly, "are you not ashamed to let yourself be moved by the work of a man who is not one of us? Have you forgotten that you are my niece and M. Marmontel's wife? It is shocking. You must realize that M. Chamfort, who wrote this tragedy, has refused to be included in the encyclopedia, and the intolerance of professional philosophers is more ferocious than that for which churchmen are so often blamed."

The theme of the tragedy is the love between royal half-brothers at the Byzantine court; the ambitious and unscrupulous mother of the younger brother is the cause of the intricately planned false accusations that lead to the arrest and death of the elder brother, and to the suicide of her own son, in consequence. In the opinion of the modern French critic most wholly predisposed in Chamfort's favor, Teppe, the play is "honorable, but nothing more."

One event connected with its production promised Chamfort financial security for as long as he liked. On the evening of the first performance at Fontainebleau, after the announcement of his royal pension, he was invited by the Prince de Condé to accept a position as the Prince's *secrétaire des commandements*, an office that provided a pension of a hundred *louis* a month and an apartment in the Palais-Bourbon. The post had recently fallen empty, and Chamfort's friend Dorat had advised him to apply for it. He had done so only upon the urging of friends, and he accepted, though not at once, after more of their persuasion.

The post with the Prince de Condé led into new complications, false positions, compromises. It entailed, in fact, a large and demanding correspondence, and assumed an attendance at numerous functions. His time was taken up; he found the public occasions, visits, ceremonies, receptions, oppressive. The "independence" invoked in his writings named a real need. Perhaps he did not trust himself to put his embarrassment with all possible tact, face to face: he wrote to the Prince suggesting his unfitness for the post and its advantages. The Prince answered:

Since you are absolutely set upon it, my dear Chamfort, let us say no more of functions, nor of appointments. I will leave you the title of *secrétaire de mes commandements*, which apparently you want, but I will not agree to your proposal not to accept the position that belongs with the title; it would distress me if it were a burden to you, and therefore you will keep it as long as it suits you to do so, and I shall not be in the least offended when you give it back to me. The same is true of your apartment in my house: I leave it to you to decide whether to keep it or return it to me, as you prefer. If you keep it, I ask only that you allow Grouvelle (whom you lodge there already) what he needs to do the work I give him until I decide upon another secretary. Be happy, my dear Chamfort; think, write, be well; I shall always take great interest in the successes of your intelligence and the happiness of your soul.

The secretarial duties were turned over to Grouvelle, a younger man of letters, and the situation was rendered, if anything, more complicated by the Prince's indulgence and Chamfort's wish to be diplomatic. He felt that, for the moment at least, residence at the Palais-Bourbon was incumbent upon him if he was not to offend the Prince, but he found the existence there galling. It seemed to him that he was never free of the Prince's "attentions and even his considerations" (Guingené). The result was a correspondence in which Chamfort was at pains to assure the Prince of his respect and his sense of obligation, and at the same time of the impossibility of remaining bound to him by any ties except those of friendship. The Prince, for his part, contended that there was nothing to which Chamfort objected in the Palais-Bourbon which he would not also be troubled by in the world at large; that one was not really free in any place; that he himself was not free, etc. Chamfort persisted, and early in 1777 left the Prince's service; the two men remained on good terms. He was replaced by Grouvelle, a young man who was destined for a diplomatic career, and who would read the death sentence to Louis XVI at the Temple.

Chamfort's withdrawal from the post was taken as a signal, by some, for attacking him. He was accused, on the one hand, of sycophancy, and, on the other, of ingratitude, at times by those who were obviously guilty of both. La Harpe, working to even old scores, in the end stung Chamfort into defending himself with one of his deadliest epigrams. "Monsieur de la Harpe," he said, "is a man who uses his faults to hide his vices." The repetition of the remark had the desired effect, but the growing avoidance of the court and the life of the Palais-Bourbon became, for Chamfort, part of a general withdrawal from the fashionable and literary world.

His disease had been aggravated by the winter and the restlessness, tensions, fatigues of the court, the theater, and public life. He was subject to fevers, physical pain, extreme nervous agitation and depression, and a number of other symptoms. His bitterness gained on him. He settled into what he referred to as seclusion at "my establishment at Auteuil." He continued to see Grouvelle and to attend entertainments at Chantilly. He saw a number of friends, most of them learned or literary: Beaumarchais, Condorcet—and by this time it is likely that his friendship with Mirabeau had begun. He dined once a week at Mme. d'Héricourt's in the company of the Duc de Choiseul, Delille, Marmontel, and Talleyrand. He indulged a passion for chess and frequented the Chess Society, which had been founded by the King's brother. He went to the theater. But in the main he avoided public gatherings. And it was several months before his friends became aware of a new element in his withdrawal: he had stopped writing.

⚜ VIII ⚜

His decision was established by the beginning of 1778, when Panckoucke offered him a position as theatrical critic on the *Mercure*, which Panckoucke had just acquired from Lacombe. If Chamfort had been moved at that point by ambition or malice, the offer would have provided an excellent opportunity. He wrote within twenty-four hours declining his friend's proposal, articulating principles that were surely his at the time, and still have a certain general interest:

. . . I owe you my thanks, in the first place, for the preference you show me in wishing to associate me with men of letters whom I esteem and honor; but after my thanks have been given, I beg you to accept my genuine regret at not being able to be their associate. The section that would have been my responsibility entails difficulties which they do not risk. I confess frankly that I do not know how to negotiate three times a month with the self-esteem of authors, actors, and actresses in the three theaters of Paris, and above all the Comédie-Française. If I were to be a just and stern critic, there I am at once, the enemy of all the bad actors. And though they are not numerous, they neglect no opportunity for being as dangerous as possible. If I made up my mind to be greatly indulgent, I would be dishonoring and discrediting my judgment; and what is more, and to your interest, the number of your subscribers would diminish, for what the public wants is malevolence. The article on current entertainments must be read; it must inspire curiosity, fear, hope; in a word it must stir the passions, like the theatrical works that it examines. Must I tell all, Monsieur? Keep my secret: a journal without malice is like a warship without masts, which even privateers refuse to salute.

One can argue, and pretend that it is possible to combine the most punctilious courtesy with the most severe criticism. Aside from the fact that I believe such an accord would be extremely difficult, does the wounded self-esteem of authors take into account one's self-control? The critic is abused, he is insulted, he is slandered, and in such a situation who can answer for himself? The sense of injustice is exasperating; the character is soured; one becomes unjust and ridiculous oneself, and ends by resorting to a debased conduct worthy of a public stigma and a real defamation. We have deplorable examples in the persons of M. F. and M. de La H., neither of whom was without talent, or something very like it. Who knows whether they may not even have been born honest. Truly, it is a destiny that makes one shudder. One must not run such risks. One must not tempt God . . .

His withdrawal from society and literature did not prevent him from presenting himself three times, between the years 1777 and 1780, for membership in the Académie Française—without counting a fourth application in the latter year, which he withdrew in favor of his friend Chabanon. He was finally welcomed to that body in 1781. At the time, the Académie, which Richelieu had founded fifty years earlier, was to a great extent a court institution: twenty-four of the forty members were court personages; only the remaining sixteen were men of letters. Montesquieu, in the first half of the eighteenth century, had been granted membership, not because he was a writer, but because of his position in the entourage of Monsieur (the title of the King's brother). However, the writers at the moment of Chamfort's election included Buffon, d'Alembert, Marmontel, Delille, Condorcet. The chair to which Chamfort was elected was refused, thirty years later, by Chateaubriand, because it had been occupied in the interim by a regicide. Chamfort's address of acceptance was the last of his academic bows, but it was also the lowest: "There are favors that leave no one ungrateful, but there are benefactors who dread effusions of gratitude. Replete with homage, they can be honored only by themselves; and it is to that term that you have come."

He was addressing the Académie itself, and evidently had not yet come to believe that that same phrase, those who "can be honored only by themselves," was applicable only to gifted and virtuous individuals. To the extent to which any society is regarded as a guardian and dispenser of honor, his statement was defensible. But he was soon to make it clear how unlikely he thought it was that the society he knew could have any honor to bestow. In what seem to be the later maxims the word *honor* is more common in its private sense of "moral integrity" than in its public sense of "conventional and established regard." But at the moment the distinction does not seem to have troubled him—if one takes his speech seriously at all.

Chamfort had probably chosen to live in Auteuil, rather than somewhere nearer the center of Paris, because Mme. Helvetius had settled there after the death of her husband in 1771. She had remained one of his closest friends, over the years; her "hermitage" was one of the gathering places in which he was most often to be found, and where he met many of his friends. She was the widow of a remarkable man. Helvetius had been a Farmer-General, and had written a famous book, *l'Esprit*, a defense of hedonism. He had been extremely handsome, and a friend of Mme. de Pompadour and Marie Leczinska. The dinners given by M. and Mme. Helvetius were celebrated assemblies, and the atmosphere of the household, from what one can tell at this distance, was a unique mixture of ease, warmth, freedom, and cultivation. Fontenelle is said to have stumbled by mistake into Mme. Helvetius's bathroom while she was in the bath, and according to Chamfort, the old man, who was never at a loss for the right thing to say, got out of the situation by blessing his luck and then sighing and saying, "Ah, if only I were eighty again." The company, both in M. Helvetius's lifetime and after his death, included a number of the most distinguished writers and philosophers in France, and also celebrated foreigners: Hume, Garrick—it was at Mme. Helvetius' that Chamfort met Benjamin Franklin. Her house at Auteuil had a terraced garden, which in turn gave onto her park. There she had a pavilion which was reserved for Chamfort. It was his favorite haunt for nearly six years and contributed gradually to a certain calm and peace of mind.

In the summer of 1781, the same year as his entry into the Académie, he met at Mme. Panckoucke's a widow of a doctor from Artois, a woman several years his elder, whom he found very attractive. Some time later, while on a visit to Mme. Agasse, in Boulogne, he met her again. This time, he said in a letter, he realized that he was in love with her. Mme. Buffon, Guingené says, "was no longer young, but she had an attractive figure, very beautiful eyes, an easy courtesy, and a witty turn of conversation which supplied the place of youth, and one noticed the fruits rather than the damages of age." Their liaison centered at first around Auteuil, where Chamfort gave her his apartment, and visited her there every day. They found it increasingly harder to do without each other's company or to share it, though Chamfort later declared that "there was no question of love, for there could be none, as she was some years older than I was. . . ." Love in some sense there obviously was; he spoke of it himself in other letters and in some feeble verses. In the spring of 1783 he and Mme. Buffon retired together to a small manor house named (with some sad presentiment) Vaudouleurs, which she owned in the country near Étampes. Brooks and woods surrounded the old building, closing it in on the west, and on the east allowing a glimpse of Fontainebleau through ancient trees. Once there, they saw almost no one else.

Mme. Buffon had grown up at the Duchesse de Maine's court at the Château de Sceaux, which had been a brilliant literary center during the first half of the century, the period that was ending when Chamfort was a child (the Duchesse died when he was thirteen years old), which added to its fascination for him. Mme. Buffon's recollections of the court of the Duchesse, and the literary figures who gathered there were still detailed and vivid, and they included a fund of anecdotes from an earlier generation, which had still been current when she was there. Her reminiscences contributed not only to the charm that Chamfort found in her conversation; some of them he set down in his own way, and they were eventually included in the *Characters and Anecdotes*.

It was their third summer. Chamfort's letters to his friends declared that he was happy. But the idyll was not allowed to last. He and Mme. Buffon had been at Vaudouleurs scarcely six months when she was taken fatally ill, and died on August 29, 1783. When she was gone, Chamfort stayed on alone in the house where they had been happy, a prey to his grief and despair. He appears to have received few friends, and it was evidently some time before he wrote (the letter is undated) to Mme. Agasse:

I am just beginning to lift up my soul again after the blow that has overwhelmed it. That is what has kept me, my dear friend, from answering your letter. Another feeling kept me from running to you. I confess that I dreaded your presence as much as I desire it; during those first days I was afraid of feeling choked at the sight of the person whom my friend loved best, and of whom we spoke most often. The heart knows what it needs and when it needs it. I have need of you now; I will come to see you on the first day, but in the morning, around ten. I cannot be answerable for the first moment, but I will not feel choked, because my heart can spill over in your presence. But when I think that on that same day, and probably at that very hour when I will be with you, she too would have seen you

. . . I stop there; I can write no more; the tears flow; and it is the unhappiest moment since she ceased to be.

He had refused at first to return to Paris, and it had remained for a friend, the Comte Louis de Vaudreuil, to tear him from his solitude and carry him off in a post-chaise to his own spacious house on the Rue de Bourbon, where an apartment had been made ready for him. There he was installed with a minimum of ceremony; he could receive friends or dine privately, waited upon by the Comte's servants.

The Comte de Vaudreuil was an impassioned lover of the arts and a generous patron. He gave a large dinner once a week to a circle of writers and artists, and after the meal the company adjourned to a salon where paints, pencils, pens, and musical instruments were laid out, and the company was encouraged to use them. M. de Vaudreuil practiced several arts himself, and sang. And he enjoyed a powerful influence in Marie Antoinette's entourage. From his house, early in 1784, Chamfort wrote the first of a revealing series of letters in reply to one from his friend the Abbé Roman. The Abbé was Chamfort's elder by fourteen years; he had been associated with the Encyclopedists, especially d'Alembert, La Condamine, and Rivarol. He, like Chamfort, was an impassioned chess player and had written a poem on the rules of the game, as well as a number of biographies. He translated Petrarch and other Italian and German writers, traveled in Russia, the Scandinavian countries, and England, and returned to his country retreat in Provence, where he died in 1787. It was there that Chamfort wrote to him.

You ask me, my friend, whether it is not some sort of eccentricity that leads me to regard literature as I do; whether it is not true that I enjoy a somewhat more considerable fortune than most men of letters; and lastly you wish me to confide in you under the seal of friendship what methods I have employed in order to arrive at this end, which you imagine has been the goal of my ambition. Those, if I understand correctly, are the separate headings of your curiosity, insofar as I can make a resumé of your long letter. My answers are simple.

But I must begin by saying that I am almost offended at your assuming in me a plan of conduct laid out with such an end in view. My cast of mind, my character, and circumstances, have done everything, without any connivance on my part. I have always been offended by the ridiculous and insulting notion, which is almost universally current, that a man of letters who has an annual income of four or five thousand francs is at the perigee of fortune. Having almost reached this term, I felt that I was well enough off to live unto myself, to which my taste naturally inclined me. But as my society happens to be sought after by several persons whose fortune is far more considerable, my own relative wealth has become a genuine distress, as the result of a series of duties that were imposed on me by my frequenting a world that I had not, myself, sought after. I found myself faced with the absolute necessity of either making literature a profession that would supply the fortune that I lacked, or else soliciting favors, or finally enriching myself at one stroke by a sudden retirement. The first two options did not suit me; I committed myself boldly to the third. There has been a considerable outcry; I have been called odd, peculiar. All nonsense. You know that I excel at guessing what my neighbor is thinking. Everything that was said on the subject meant, "What! Is it not sufficient reward for his efforts and trouble to be granted the honor of our company, the pleasure of amusing us, and the gratification of being treated as we treat no other man of letters?"

My answer to that is this: I am forty. As for those petty triumphs of vanity which literary figures are so in love with, I'm over my head in them. Since by your own admission I have nothing further to aspire to, allow me to retire with your blessing. If society is of no use to me, I must start to be of some use to myself. It is ridiculous to grow old as an actor in a troupe in which one cannot even boast of playing a minor role. Either I will live alone, occupied with myself and my own happiness, or if I live among you, I will enjoy some of the freedom and comforts that you accord to persons whom it would never occur to you to compare with me. I give the lie to your attitude toward men of my class. What is a man of letters, according to you, and indeed according to the generally established opinion? A man to whom one says: "You will live in poverty and be only too happy to see your name mentioned from time to time. You will be granted, not solid rewards, but a few considerations flattering to your vanity, which I count on having taken the place of the self-esteem of a man of sense. You will write, compose verse and prose, for which you will be praised occasionally, insulted often, and paid a few crowns while you wait to snap up a few twenty-five or fifty-*louis* pensions, which you will fight over, rolling in the mud like the populace to whom coins are thrown on public holidays."

My friend, I found that this existence did not suit me, and as I despised both the vainglory of the great and the vainglory of literature, I sacrificed both of them to the honor of my character and in the interest of my happiness. I said for all to hear, "I have given ample proof of my disinterestedness, and I will not beg for favors. I have very little, but I have as much or more than many deserving persons. And so I ask for nothing; but you will have to leave me in peace. It is not just that I should have to sustain at the same time the weight of poverty and the weight of the duties that go with fortune. My health is delicate; I am short-sighted; up until now I have acquired nothing out in the world but mud, colds, inflammations and indigestions, to say nothing of the risk of being run over twenty times a winter. It is time that all that was done with, and if it is not over by a given date, I shall leave."

That, my friend, is what I said; and if you are surprised that it could have such an effect, you should know that a first retirement of six months, in which I found happiness, proved invincibly that I was acting neither from caprice nor out of selfishness. It only remains for me to explain to you why my retirement gave such offense. This is something that I cannot divulge to you, at least not in the same detail. But I can tell you, without your suspecting me of vanity, I can tell you that my friends know that I am fitted for a number of things outside the sphere of literature. Several of them have banded together to help me; others have combined with their feeling a certain calculation and design, and as the circumstances were favorable, the result has been the little revolution that you deem so favorable.

It is worth remembering that he was writing to the provinces, and no doubt he would have been disappointed if his retirements had not been noticed. They have been exaggerated, largely because of the importance they had for Chamfort. Pellisson declares that a demission such as Chamfort's was a rare phenomenon in literature and probably unique in the eighteenth century, but many writers have lived far more retired lives than Chamfort, and for far longer, and have done so without troubling themselves about it or feeling that it required elaborate and continued justification. His "seclusion" was a movement away, a gesture, magnified by the social nature of literature at the time, and by his own character, especially his simultaneous rejections of his society's judgment and need for its reassurances. As for the withdrawal, both from society and from the writing of literature, one thinks of Racine, and Congrève, and in the eighteenth century itself, of Rousseau, who had decided more than once to give up writing, and had probably done so for at least as long as Chamfort did. For Chamfort did write again, and for publication, and he continued to have something of a social life, amidst his protestations.

⁂ IX *⁂*

On March 4, 1784, Chamfort wrote again in answer to the Abbé:

I have promised myself, my dear friend, always to answer your letters at once, and it takes no effort to keep my promise. I would need one to put it off, and I prefer not to contend against myself.

Ah, my friend, how surprised I was to learn that I differ from you in the very respect in which I resemble you! You admit that you have chosen the better part, and you do not wish me a like fate; you say that because you feel it. It is no doubt a good reason, but why, or rather how do you feel it? That is what surprises me. What? That miserable mania for celebrity that produces nothing but unhappiness still has a partisan, a protector! Have you forgotten that it demands almost as many miseries, imbecilities and degradations as fortune itself? And what is the reward? It is far less considerable, and it is certainly more ridiculous. Its surest effect is to teach you the full extent of human malevolence by making you the object of the most violent hatred and of the most dreadful intrigues on the part of those who cannot share this smoke with you, and who are jealous of a few miserable distinctions, which seldom fail to be boring and wearisome, to me in particular, who have been in a position to judge them all.

I was in love with fame, I will admit it; but that was at an age when experience had not taught me the true value of things, when I thought that it might exist pure, and accompanied by a degree of repose, when I thought that it was a source of pleasures dear to the heart and not an eternal conflict of vanity, and when I believed that, while it was not a means of acquiring prosperity, it was at least not an absolute impediment to it.

Time and reflection have enlightened me; I am not one of those who can tempt themselves with the prospect of dust and noise as the goal and fruit of their labors. "Apollo promises only a name and laurels"—that is what Boileau said with his fifteen thousand francs a year in gifts from the King, which would be worth twice that at present; that is what Racine said, bringing back from Versailles, on more than one occasion, purses of a thousand *louis* each. Which rendered the rivalry and hatred of a Pradon and a Boyer no less painful. To a point, indeed, where the whole thing became unendurable, and he abandoned, at thirty-six, that career of glory and infamy which has become a hundred times more turbulent and degrading since his day. As for me, who have attracted, ever since my first success, the hatred of a crowd of fools and backbiters, I think of this affliction as a stroke of great good fortune. It restores me to myself; it gives me the right to belong to myself exclusively; and since extremely powerful friends have more than once made efforts in my behalf without success, I have become weary of being a supernumerary, a kind of bauble in society. I have become indignant at the incessant proof that naked merit, born without gold and without titles, is not a thing that men share, and I have managed to derive more from myself than I could hope for from them. I conceived a hatred for celebrity that equaled my former love of fame; I retracted the whole of my life into myself: thought and feeling became the final goals of my existence and of my projects. My friends combined their efforts in vain, to shake my resolution: whatever I may write, as it were, unaware, and if I may put it so, in spite of myself, will be at most *titulus nomenque sepulcri.*

I was heartily amused by the passage in your letter where you tell me that you looked for me in the periodicals. You sounded to me like some foreigner who, on learning that I was in Paris, set about looking for me in the gaming houses and gambling dens. I had been there for a long time, when I met someone whose equal does not exist for perfection, so far as I was concerned, as I was given to see in the short space of two years that we spent together. I am speaking of a woman; and there was no love because there could be none, as she was several years my elder; but there was something more and better than love, for there was a complete union of all relations of ideas, feelings, and attitudes. I will stop, with that, because I see that I would not be able to finish. I lost her after a stay of six months in the country, in the deepest and most charming solitude. Those six months, or rather, those two years, seemed no more than an instant in my life; but the happiness of being remote from everything that I have seen in that theater of ignominies that is called literature, and in that theater of follies and iniquities that is called the world, would have been enough for me, and would always be enough for me, if deprived of the charm of sweet and gentle company and of an enchanting friendship. Independence, health, the free disposition of my time, the use, even to the point of eccentricity, of my books—that is what I need, if it is not all I need. And that is what I cannot fail to be deprived of by the success that you are so cruel as to wish upon me, and which unfortunately has become still more likely since my last letter. The donkey who wants neither to bite his neighbor nor to be bitten, in front of an empty hayrack, will have to run a few errands and trot in the ring to earn his oats if he is suddenly transformed into a plump horse in front of a full hayrack; and when I come to think that by making a move he will have more oats than he can eat, I am inclined to think that it is a fool's bargain.

You can see in that, my friend, how attached I am to the feelings that urge me to retirement, and you would see this still more clearly if you could know, fortune quite apart, how many agreeable aspects there are to my present position, what struggles I am obliged to engage in with the tenderest and most devoted of friends, what efforts I must make in order to fend off or prevent the sacrifices that they wish to make in order to keep me here. What then is this invincible pride and even this hardness of heart which makes me reject favors of a certain kind, when I admit that I would like to do more for them than they can do for me? This pride wounds and offends them; I even think that they find it small and mean; an attaching of too much importance to something that should indeed be accorded very little. My friend, I do not, I trust, have the petty and vulgar notions that are usual on this subject; neither am I a monster of pride; but I have been poisoned with sugared arsenic once, and will not be again— *manet alta mente repostum.* You say you have my soul in my first letter; I think a little was left for the second.

I accept, my friend, and most eagerly, your offer to travel together through Provence to look for a haven that would suit me, and I accept with even greater pleasure, in the thought that I will not lead you a long journey. Your country would have to have considerable disadvantages if the nearest retreat to you were not the one that suited me best.

I promised you literary news, but my personal disposition renders me quite cold on that topic, and to be able to send you any, I must be able to believe that it is really of interest to you. At the moment they are playing, with great success despite the hooting on stage and the outcry and indignation in Paris and at Versailles, Beaumarchais's *The Marriage of Figaro.* The play is full of wit, and even of comedy and talent, but it is nonetheless rendered monstrous by the admixture of execrable taste and trivialities. The boxes are sold out through the tenth and some say the twentieth performance. The play, without a curtain raiser, lasts only three hours and a quarter after the cuts that have been made. I say nothing of *Jaloux*, nor of La Harpe's very poor *Coriolanus*; the periodicals are full of those. A word about the *Danaïdes*, a new opera in which Gluck had a hand: it is a work worthy of the Hottentots, to be played to cannibals. Even so it is said that it will not have more than a dozen performances.

. . . My mother is in superb health; her one distress is that she no longer has the use of her legs; but I am very much afraid that this one impediment will shorten the life of someone so vigorous; she is more impatient, at eighty-four, than I have ever been. It seems to me that if I had to spend a year without moving, I could not go on living, and this thought troubles me considerably when I think of her condition, although I am told everything imaginable to reassure me. Farewell once again; I love and embrace you with all my heart. It seems to me that we have not ceased to understand each other.

The connection with Beaumarchais was closer than Chamfort indicates in the letter. Seven years earlier, when Beaumarchais had set out to organize a society of dramatic authors, the first in France, to protect their rights and assure them a larger share in the earnings of their plays than they had received up until then, Chamfort was one of the authors who had joined him, and it may have been in his capacity as the founder (and most impressive businessman) of that society that Beaumarchais had collected the takings of *Mustapha* at the box office. The reference to *The Marriage of Figaro*, however, raises a question about the dating of Chamfort's letter. The famous first night of that comedy took place on April 27, 1784, more than seven weeks after the date on this letter in all the French editions. It would seem more likely, on the basis of this, that Chamfort wrote to the Abbé on the "4 mai" rather than the "4 mars."

Chamfort must have been a very close witness, if not directly involved in the comedy's opening. *The Marriage of Figaro* had been known, and had been a center of controversy, for nearly three years. In 1781, when Beaumarchais had presented *The Marriage of Figaro* to the Comédie-Française, it had been accepted; but when permission to perform the play in public had been applied for, it had been summarily refused. On hearing it read, the King had leaped to his feet, during Figaro's long monologue in Act V, and exclaimed, "It is detestable! It will never be performed! For it to be harmless the Bastille would have to be done away with!" The comedy was condemned because it was a calculated mockery of the established order; the aristocracy is shown in a ridiculous light and the "natural" virtues, exemplified with insolent wit in the character of Figaro, are presented with greater sympathy; his triumph over the Count is part of the "happy ending." Nevertheless, for three years Beaumarchais's efforts to get the play performed were joined, assisted, applauded, by some of the most powerful of the aristocracy—all, in fact, who prided themselves on their advanced opinions, or who were curious or followed fashion, or set great store by being amused, or relished excitement or scandal. The Queen wanted to see the play performed, and a production was planned at the *Théâtre des Menus*; a royal order prevented it. It was the Comte de Vaudreuil who was responsible for its first performance, before three hundred guests in his own house, in 1783, not long before he arranged for Chamfort to live under his roof. The Comte had been one of the play's most determined partisans. "No salvation," he wrote, "outside *The Marriage of Figaro*." And yet de Vaudreuil exemplified a split that was more remarkable than the one between the King and most of the nobility (Louis XVI had always regarded the aristocracy as his rival anyway). For all his relatively liberal views, the Comte was so ignorant of the conditions that were pressing for change in France that Chamfort felt obliged to write to him, four years after the opening of *Figaro*, to explain why he thought the demands for social and political change had to be taken seriously.

The combination of powerful influences and the obvious fact that the play's suppression was having the same effect that had been feared in the play itself, led to *The Marriage of Figaro*'s finally being passed by six censors and put on in the new theater, now the Odéon. The nobility jammed the first performance: a long-prepared, ironic, uncomprehended triumph. In Lanson's description (*Histoire de la Literature Française*, G. Lanson; Hachette, 1903) the "Mad Day" of the comedy's subtitle could have been applied to the play's opening—"this day of intellectual madness on which the entire society of the old order applauded the ideas that would be the death of it."

Chamfort must have been under the Comte's roof at the time, surrounded by the excitement before, during, and after. His objection to the play's *taste* is doubly interesting in view of Beaumarchais's later attack, in the preface to the published version, on the deadly boredom and the critical uselessness of what he called "theatrical decency." The criticism and the defense point to a basic difference between the two men. Beaumarchais's play was being written at the time of the two productions of Chamfort's own supreme theatrical effort, *Mustapha and Zeangir*. The comedy is not only one of the triumphs of French drama in the period; in curious ways, many of them illustrated by the success of its first public performance, it typifies the period. The plot, the characters, the tone, the style, were all deliberately conceived as challenges to accepted canons, and it was its outrageousness that made it welcome. Chamfort, by contrast, appears to have been artistically more conservative, not only than Beaumarchais (his elder by eight years), but than a great many of his own age. He was certainly not the last example of a revolutionary, or proponent of revolution who was artistically resolutely old-fashioned, of course.

On the other hand the year, the occasion, the contact, mark a turning in both men's lives and dispositions. After 1784, as though the opening of *Figaro* had been the end of an epoch, or at least the last brilliant, concerted display of its temperament, a gravity gradually descended on the period, a foreshadowing of what was about to possess it. In the changing atmosphere Beaumarchais's fortune declined. Chamfort, on the other hand, moved toward a resolution of his nature during those same years. He finally abandoned writing for publication under his own name; but his political concerns came to occupy him more and more fully, and a great part of the *Products of the Perfected Civilization*, including much of what is best and most original in it, probably dates from the period between 1784 and his death.

On April 4, 1784 (a month before or a month after the letter to the Abbé Roman, above), he wrote to another friend:

Never was the life of a man less fertile in events, and yet so crammed, for better or for worse. I have covered a thousand leagues on paper: That is my story, for the greater part of the last four years. I have astonished you already in speaking of an eternal farewell to the city of Paris, last year. Indeed, my friend, it was done, and I lived for six months in the province, in the country, among no claims but friendship, a garden, and a library. It is almost the only time of my life that seems to me to have been worth something.

Only the death of the companion of my solitude could have fetched me back to the clamorous desert of Paris. I could never finish if I tried to tell you what I have lost. It is an eternal source of tender and painful memories. And it is only after six months that their pleasures have begun to outweigh their anguish and bitterness. It is only in the last two months that my soul has managed to raise itself up a little, and to lift up my body with it. It was last September that I suffered this cruel loss; a friend came in a post chaise and tore me away from that charming abode, which had come to seem horrible to me. After that I was plunged again into the kind of life from which I had at last managed to abstract myself, after two years of efforts and of what were called sacrifices, but for me were nothing of the kind. The friendship of M. le Comte de Vaudreuil, which had become much closer during the previous two years, has become a genuine devotion, and has helped greatly in relieving a part of my distress. He has forced me to accept an apartment in his house and has contrived to make it pleasant for me. He has occupied himself very seriously with my fortune, which between the time you left and my quitting Paris, foundered three times: twice as the result of unforeseen events, and the third time as the result of an act of mine, that is, through my refusing something that did not suit me, or in other words, to put it in the usual terms, which are neither yours nor mine, through my own fault. Fortune will do what she will, I will never accord wealth, in the scale of human benefits, a place higher than fourth or fifth. If she wants first place, she will have to go somewhere else. She will have no trouble finding someone to take her in.

There is some astonishment that a man who is still regarded, in spite of himself, as not being totally bereft of talent, should not wish to submit to the rule commonly imposed on men of letters: to behave like donkeys kicking and biting in front of an empty hayrack, to amuse the grooms and stableboys. Nothing revealed to me more clearly the wretchedness of this class of men than the surprise with which I am regarded for keeping to myself the writings that escape me involuntarily and through a need that is natural to my soul. On the other hand, I am quite aware that, if someone were to arrange matters so that I could live in Paris and enjoy the comforts of life and the pleasures of society, it would be hard for me to avoid the necessity of paying a tribute that would be regarded as a debt. It is for this reason that I hope my friends' efforts will come to nothing.

(I imagine that these "efforts" must have been the ones that led to Chamfort's eventual appointment to the post of secretary to Elizabeth of France—see p. 75—and that the sentence in Chamfort's "March 4" letter to the Abbé Roman, about "the success . . . which . . . has become still more likely since my last letter" refers to the same thing. If this interpretation is correct, the additional "likelihood" of the latter reference is a further reason for thinking that the letter was written in May rather than in March of that year.)

For unless they succeed, I am free; I belong to myself; the rest of my life is my own, without the thousand-headed hydra being able to deprive me of the smallest portion of it. Hence the indifference, the health, and the sense of well-being in a land where three franc crowns are worth six francs, and where the needs are those of nature, instead of those of vanity and opinion. Judge, my friend, whether, with such notions, I was not amused by the sentence in your letter where you ask me to send you a few pages instead of sending them for publication! Publication! If you knew one-quarter of what I know and have seen of men of letters, you would not suspect me of any such fancies. I have such an aversion to all that that I will not rest until I have thought of a sure way of escaping it, and arranging things so that what I write may exist without it being possible for anyone to make use of it, even if I were to be robbed of all my papers. The system that I have invented makes me the absolute master up to the gravestone and even beyond that, for I have only to keep silent, and what I have written will die with me. You see from this the profound feeling of hatred and contempt that I have for literature, as a profession and as a social position. Ah well, I love it more than ever as a cultivation of the soul, and it has occupied almost every minute of my time since I regained my faculties after last summer's irreparable loss. To such a degree is it true that nature and habit are equally intractable. Literature will be one of the greatest pleasures of my retirement, and lends charm to the prospect. But certainly that has nothing to do with a love of fame, or a mania concerning posterity. Agree with that if you can, but be assured that nothing is more true.

Somewhat later in the year, the Comte de Vaudreuil and two other aristocratic friends, the Vicomte de Narbonne and the Duc de Choiseul-Gouffier, arranged to take Chamfort on a trip to Holland, as tourists—apparently a further kind attempt to change his thoughts after the death of Mme. Buffon. Choiseul-Gouffier, until recently, had been the French ambassador to Constantinople; the Abbé Delille had been his secretary. The Vicomte de Narbonne was said to be the son of Louis XV. The one surviving anecdote of the trip sounds like a remote analogue of the first night of *Figaro*: The party was floating along a canal; someone, loudly enough to be overheard, told a story that redounded to the discredit of the French gentry. Chamfort, who had not seemed to be listening (it is Guingené's account), rose, took

Choiseul-Gouffier's hand in one of his, and the Vicomte de Narbonne's in the other, shook them both, and said, "Does either of you know anything duller and sillier than a French nobleman?" Thereupon they all laughed heartily. Chamfort came back from the trip with his health uncertain, his mordant temper thoroughly restored, and his observations and conclusions about the French nobility, seen at its best, more detailed and specific.

But on the twelfth of September, 1784, he was appointed secretary to Elizabeth of France, the King's sister. The post had been created for him at her own request, according to the commission signed by the King and the Baron de Breteuil. The Comte de Vaudreuil had no doubt contributed to the idea. Chamfort was to enjoy the honors, authorities, prerogatives, privileges, and other advantages pertaining to the office, and two thousand francs a year. He spoke of the new appointment among other matters in the third of the series of letters to the Abbé Roman, on October 5 of that year.

What must you think of me, my dear friend, and of such a long silence? You must imagine that every kind of disaster has befallen me at once. Alas, you would not be far wrong. Two and a half months ago I suffered the loss of my mother, and you are not one to be surprised at the effect that this disturbing event would have on me. It would not be like you to say that eighty-five was an age that should have prepared me for this blow, and that fifteen years of absence should make it less terrible for me. My second misfortune is to have had a double tertiary fever for the last two months, followed by an extremely disagreeable convalescence which is not yet over. I cannot say how it came about; my whole person seemed to have become a mass of bile, which prevented me from resorting to quinine. It was nature that cured me, as she would have done before the discovery of the drug. It took me a month longer, and a month of pains and torments, during which it was impossible for me to write. I did not want to send you news of me written by someone else's hand: I was afraid you would think I was dead; besides, when it comes to dictating I am of a rare stupidity.

I turn, my friend, to another subject, about which I have already said something to you: the plan of going to see you in Provence. Even if there had been no other obstacle than my illness, it was not possible, and still is not possible before the month of December. Even then it would not be practicable unless I had someone come with me in a post chaise, because traveling in public vehicles at that season would be as difficult for me as a pilgrimage to Sirius. But, my friend, there are other and greater obstacles, arising from my new post. You may have read in the papers that the office of private secretary to Madame Elizabeth, the King's sister, has been obtained for me. The position is worth two thousand francs, and though it does not make me any the richer for the moment—since in the royal household the first payments fall due only at a very distant term—it is true nevertheless that I am bound by gratitude and my devotion to those who have solicited and obtained this post for me while I was nailed to my bed and had been so for six weeks. I would be considered uncivilized and incorrigible, a desperate misanthrope, and I would be universally condemned. I must tell you besides that, quite apart from my new post, my association with Monsieur le Comte de Vaudreuil has become such that there can be no thought of leaving this part of the world. It is the most perfect and the tenderest friendship imaginable. I would be unable to write you the details, but I firmly believe that, outside England, where these matters are simple, almost no one in Europe is worthy of understanding what can unite, with such firm bonds, a secluded man of letters in search of still greater seclusion, and a courtier who enjoys the greatest possible wealth, and indeed the greatest possible favor. When I say such firm bonds, I should also say so affectionate and so disinterested, for one often sees interest mingled to produce, between men of letters and courtiers, very faithful and durable associations. But here it is a matter of friendship, and that word says everything, in your language and in mine.

There, my friend, are the reasons that keep me from coming to seek you out, and very possibly will continue to deprive me of the pleasure of seeing you in your retreat in Provence. It took nothing less, I assure you; for although in your last letter you were so barbarous as to wish to keep me in the capital, still in the interests of your mania for seeing me better off, it is nevertheless certain that in May I would have sworn that I would not spend the winter in Paris. The obstacles were of a sort that could have been overcome, and the state of my fortune was not one of them. You told me that I would need three thousand francs a year to live comfortably in Provence, and at the time when you wrote I had four thousand. That was the term I had set myself, and I was quite content. It was you who wanted me to go further. Now your wishes are granted, and it is safe to wager that six months from now they will be infinitely more so. Then one will have only to satisfy your other mania, for my celebrity. I cannot promise you that I will succeed there equally well, but whether the fancy takes me, or I retain my repugnance for that celebrity with which you seem too concerned, it is certain that once I am calm about my future I will get more work done and do it better, at that, and that I will have more titles to that celebrity if I disclose them—which I am not sure of doing, for I am hardened in sin. I think you would be on my side if you were to come and see, as I do, our Parisian public, continuously and over a long period. Besides, everything in its time; and I am not all of one piece; I am unalterable when things do not change, but I am adaptable when they do change, and especially when they change to my advantage. . . .

Send me news of yourself, talk to me of nothing but yourself. I have given you a superb example, in that respect. I warn you that I know myself by heart, and in the end one tires of oneself. . . .

There is some of the light-heartedness of the letter to Mme. Saurin, written at Barèges, ten years before, and from a similar complex of circumstances: affectionate friendships in high places contributing to his security and to the ambition that he deprecated and in the main despised, but had not entirely abandoned. And again he followed the same round of elation, precarious health with a winter coming on, and savage observations of society, the aristocracy, the world of literature, as in the year before his triumph at Fontainebleau. The generosity and thoughtfulness of his friends did not conceal the waste and the indifference to poverty that were general in their class. He is quoted as having said to Vaudreuil, one day when the Comte was taxing him with not using his patronage more freely, "I promise to borrow a hundred *louis* from you when you have paid your debts." Just as typically, it was probably while traveling, between his reception into the Académie (where he would serve the first of two terms as chancellor, the following year, and of which he would become the director in 1792) and his sinecure in the palace, that he wrote or conceived some of his most caustic passages on the ingratitude of his nation, including the long list of neglected men of letters, which he introduces by recalling the tomb of a printer which he had seen in a church in Anvers (Antwerp).

❧ X ❧

Chamfort's critical faculties can only have been encouraged by some of his new friendships. His acquaintance with Guingené dates from this time. He appears to have seen more of Talleyrand than he had before. And there was one new and close association that figured more actively than any others in the next few years: that with the Comte de Mirabeau, whom he may have met in 1780, at the house of Mme. Helvetius. Up until this time Chamfort, for one reason or another, seems to have had to do primarily with his elders. Mirabeau was nine years younger than he, and in thirty-five years had amassed a variety and violence of experience that would contribute to undermining his vigorous constitution and help to bring about his premature death in 1791—which alone prevented him, in some opinions, from leading the Revolution. It was from exile in London, in late June 1784 (thus probably after the Dutch trip, and before the long painful fever which Chamfort described to the Abbé Roman) that he wrote to Chamfort: "I await with an impatience proportionate to the object, the situation, and the opinion I have of the man and of that subject treated by such a man, the translation in question. Do not neglect it, I beg you. Your future harvests are involved. . . ."

The translation in question was almost certainly a pamphlet written by a South Carolina magistrate, Aedanus Burke, attacking the order of Cincinnatus, a nascent military organization. Chamfort's English was adequate, whereas Mirabeau's was sketchy. Burke's polemic had been given to Mirabeau in the first place by Franklin; Chamfort evidently translated it, Mirabeau wrote an imitation incorporating his own views and turning an ostensible argument against the Cincinnati into an attack on hereditary nobility, and Chamfort then went over the work adding touches of his own, including "the most eloquent passages." It was not the first time that Mirabeau had enlisted Chamfort's help in his writings. In December 1783 (four months after the death of Mme. Buffon) he had written, in the somewhat exaggerated terms that were current, asking Chamfort to give him a severe appraisal, "both regarding the substance and the form," of his work on *Lettres de cachet and State Prisons*:

... Rich as you are in moral convictions, in profound views, in fresh observations, and with a palette that is yours alone, you can infinitely enrich me. ... You who have the soul and genius of a Tacitus, with the wit of a Lucian and the muse of Voltaire when he laughs and does not grimace, if you will leave my work on your desk for a few days—mediocre though it is, it is not contemptible—it will soon deserve to be numbered among the good books. ...

His regard was not confined to literary matters. In another letter he wrote:

... But if only I had had the good fortune to meet you ten years ago, how much firmer would my morals have been! How many ravines and precipices I would have avoided! How much more my slight merit would have been developed! ... I have gained a great deal from having to do with you, and I will gain more. There are few days, and certainly there are few circumstances of any seriousness in which I do not catch myself saying, "Chamfort would frown ... We must not do that; Chamfort would be displeased" ... No one need explain to you how sweet, comforting, and encouraging a friendship is that has become habitual to this point, that offers in criticism an indisputable law, and in approbation a treasure beyond price. ...

At the same time he did not hesitate to advise Chamfort on his own personal affairs. During this same year Chamfort was attracted to the beautiful Julie Careau. Mirabeau had received his confidences and found the prospect worrying:

... With all that, my friend, I am too fond of you not to dread seeing the smallest morsel of your happiness abandoned to the hazard and inconstancy of that sex. You are too full of reason to be romantic; your imagination is too ardent and your heart is essentially too good not to be a little inclined that way. ...

(Her own comment on the matter was less melting. "I don't like wits, when it comes to love," she said. "They watch themselves go by." And it was about her that Chamfort turned the phrase about the lady who lived as honestly as possible outside marriage and celibacy. In the end she married the actor Talma, then in his early twenties.)

The adulation in Mirabeau's letters of 1783 and 1784 has a striking parallel. His father, who detested him, and was the

source of more than one *lettre de cachet* that had led to his firsthand acquaintance with state prisons forty years earlier, had so
overwhelmed with praise another moralist and aphorist, Vauvenargues, (1715–1747) that the writer had begged him to stop.
Mirabeau's correspondence with Chamfort continued throughout
1784; Chamfort's letters have been lost, but seventeen of Mirabeau's have survived. The last one of the main series (there are
two others, from 1790, shortly before Mirabeau's death) is a New
Year's note of January 1, 1785. During the latter year Mirabeau
returned to France. The friendship was inevitably interrupted by
Mirabeau's secret diplomatic mission to the court of Frederick the
Great in 1786. But in May 1789, when Mirabeau was in daily
contact, more or less secret, with the court, Chamfort (with
several other writers) was with him at Versailles, helping on his
journal and probably on a series of state papers. (It was at Versailles, at that time, that Chamfort first met Robespierre, who was
then the young deputy from Arras.) But the friendship between
Mirabeau and the man whom he had called his "best, and almost
only friend" did not survive the shifts and crises of the time
unimpaired. Mirabeau favored a strong central government and
prepared to implement a new organization under the crown;
Chamfort helped to organize a faction of deputies to oppose the
attempt, and Mirabeau did not forgive him.

At the time when the convocation of the États-Generaux was
announced for 1789, Chamfort supplied another friend, the Abbé
Sieyès with the title for a pamphlet: "What is the Third Estate?"
(It was the name given to the whole of the nation that did not
belong either to the nobility or the clergy.) The full exchange
continued: "They are everything. And what have they? Nothing." The title and the whole of the observation were more
quoted than the pamphlet.

Chamfort thought it should be possible, even in so agitated a
time, to have friends with whom one differed on matters of
politics. With such associates as Rivarol, the conservative satirist,
the positions were clear; with others he felt obliged to make them
more so, especially with friends who had been kind to him,
whose kindness he had been happy to accept, and who might be
deceived about his views. In December 1788 he set out to disa-
buse his friend and patron de Vaudreuil, who had suggested that
Chamfort write a satire on the democratic fervor of the moment:

. . . I assure you that it would be impossible for me to compose an amusing piece on a subject as serious as the one in question. It is not the moment to take up the pencils of a Swift or a Rabelais, when we are very possibly within touch of disasters, and I think that a writer who cast ridicule on all parties would be stoned at their common expense. I could not, therefore, proffer anything but a serious work, and what use would that be? If there is no single work, as yet, which presents this interesting question from all points of view, there are a great many which throw sufficient light on it if they are taken together. And what does it come to, in fact? To a suit between twenty-four million men and seven hundred thousand with privileges. I hear that the upper ranks of the nobility have formed leagues, raised outcries, etc.; it is on this subject, I think, that one can accuse most of the writers who have dealt with the question of having been clumsy or neglectful. Why did they not say, to those who are most privileged, "You think that you are being attacked personally, that it is you whom one wishes to attack. Not at all. A great nation can raise above itself, and can look up to, a few distinguished families, three hundred, four hundred, more or less; it can render this homage to services performed in the past, ancient names, memories; but in conscience, can it support seven hundred thousand with titles, who have the same rights when it comes to taxes and money as the family of Montmorency and the most ancient knightly families of France? Lament, by all means, the fatality that sends this appalling mob to tread in your footsteps, but do not burn down the house that cannot lodge them all. Are we not crushed, annihilated, under this same fatality which has finally imperiled what you call your rights and your privileges? Do you not see the necessity of changing so monstrous an arrangement, or that otherwise we will all perish equally, the clergy, the nobility, and the third estate?" I am genuinely afflicted that this observation has not been made aloud and repeated everywhere. It would have restored the prejudiced, it would have disarmed self-interest, it would have recruited pride in the service of reason, and perhaps, without any other help, it would have been enough to save those in high places from the opprobrium with which they have recently covered themselves, wholly to their own cost. Another advantage of this reflection is that it would have led at once to an appreciation of the compromise that some have ridiculously proposed: the suggestion that the third estate should be addressed in proportion to its numbers only where consent to taxes is at issue, and should be treated as a mere third of the power in debates on general legislation. Who do I hear make such a proposition? Is it a member of the ancient knighthood? Is it a secretary to the King, of the upper or lower college, since they all have the right to speak in such a way?

I will reply to this last.—No, I will do nothing of the kind: You can see that I would have an unfair advantage. To permit a people to defend its money and then deprive it of the right to influence the laws that will decide upon its honor and its life is an insult, a mockery. No, that will not happen; it cannot happen. The nation will not tolerate it, and if it does, it deserves all the misfortunes that threaten it.

But there is talk of the dangers if the third estate acquires too much influence. They go so far as to pronounce the word democracy. Democracy! In a country where the people does not possess the smallest fraction of the executive power! In a country where the slightest tool of authority finds only obedience everywhere, and indeed, too often, abjection; where the royal power has encountered resistance only from the different orders, most of whose members are hereditary noblemen, or have acquired titles in their lifetimes; where the most unbridled luxury and the most monstrous inequality of wealth will always leave too great an interval between man and man. In what country is there more liberty than in England? And is there one in which superiority of rank is more clearly defined, more respected, although the inferior is not crushed with impunity? What a multitude of false pretexts, what ignorance, or rather, what bad faith! Why not say plainly, as some have done, "I do not want to pay." I beg you not to judge others by yourself. I know that if you had five or six hundred thousand francs annual income from holdings in land, you would be the first to tax yourself scrupulously and strictly; but you remember the generous offer made by the clergy during the first assembly of notables, and the shameful protestation that it made in defense of its immunities. You see how the parliament pretends to give up its own, and the next minute keeps back the means of preserving them and even of extending their validity. And then you are acquainted with the recent events that have exposed the formal project for maintaining pecuniary privileges. M. de Chabot and M. de Castries, having set forth in a memorandum their abdication of these privileges and their intention of keeping only those rights that were purely honorific, were unable to find any of the hereditary nobility, or of those with more recent titles, who would sign after them. Did not the gentry of Brittany declare that it is not in their power to give up their effective privileges, that they are the heritage of their children, who will claim these rights sooner or later? And in this way they enlist their conscience in making the oppression of the weak the patrimony of the strong, the most revolting injustice a sacred prerogative, and tyranny itself a duty. I have heard this—and you want me to write! Ah, I would write only to set down my contempt and my horror at such principles—I am afraid that a feeling of humanity would well up from too deep in my heart, and inspire me with an eloquence that would inflame spirits already overheated; I am afraid of doing harm out of an excessive wish to do good. The future fills me with dread. I have begun to ascribe to the smallest details an importance and an interest that surprise even me. Lists are being made of those who have been for and those who have been against the people. They alternate in ascribing such and such a phrase to such and such a man, and withdrawing it again. I myself resolutely denied a statement that was attributed to M. le Comte d'Artois. It was an automatic gesture on my part, the consequence of my gratitude for the kindnesses that you have persuaded him to confer on me. This prince is said to have asked someone of note, who favored the people, 'Do you want to make commoners of us?' I do not believe he asked it, but if he did, the other might have answered, 'No, Monseigneur; I wish to ennoble the French by giving them a country.' One cannot ennoble the Bourbons, but one can render them still more illustrious by giving them, for subjects, citizens, which is something they never had. It is certainly M. le Comte d'Artois who has most to gain: it is he above all who can say to his children, *Posteri, posteri, vestra res agitur*. It is on these times that everything will depend. I make bold to declare that if the privileged classes were to win their case, the nation, crushed from within, would be as worthy of scorn from abroad, as she is now scorned. She would be, in relation to her united neighbors, what Portugal is to England; a great farm, where they would harvest, according to laws made by themselves, her wines, her grains, her produce, etc. If on the other hand what should happen does happen, as it almost certainly will, I see only prosperity for the whole nation, and for those privileged classes who are so blind and so inimical to their own interests that they do not see that the comfort of the poor contributes to the opulence of the rich. And also for the heads of state, who do not see that there is neither private liberty nor dignity except under the protection of public liberty and national honor. Oh great God, what are they afraid will happen to their dignities? Is the third estate going to take them away? Is the third estate going to fill places at court, and high offices? Do they fear for their fortunes? Is it not an established fact that in England the great landed fortunes of illustrious families all date only from the Revolution of 1688? This is the result of the increase in the value of land, an effect of public liberty and of a substantial growth of national industry, both of which, in the last analysis, profit landowners. I am so convinced of this double influence that, if I were to be asked to say in all sincerity which class of men I think would have most to gain from the revolution that is in preparation, I would say that the revolution will profit everyone, and that it will do so in proportion to the superiority of rank and of fortune which they enjoy in the present social scale. I except the clergy, whose fate troubles neither you nor me, and the present ministers (for the time, in some cases very short, during which they continue in office). But neither of these will lose the taste for the trade; and after all, one cannot prepare for everything.

That is how I regard this unique and inconceivable crisis. I wanted to make a profession of faith to you so that if, by chance, our opinions turned out to be too different, we might not return to this subject. Our opinions have been opposed more than once without keeping our hearts from understanding and loving each other; that is the main thing, or rather that is everything. I remember, among others, one very lively discussion that we had just two years ago, concerning the policy of M. de Calonne, and his project for a land subsidy, which you said would prove infallible if it was supported, as it was, with all the power of the King. I told you that the King would fail. I told you, to be exact, that the King could cut down the most enormous forest, but that no one could travel four hundred leagues on foot, over creepers, brambles, and thorn bushes. What is being undertaken today is difficult in quite another way. Suppose the nation is beaten at the forthcoming assembly of the États-Generaux (impossible though that seems), what will happen, I ask you, in 1791, when the third twentieth [a form of tax; translator's note] ceases to be due, and taxes—since the incompetence of our form of parliament has been recognized—require the national consent? Do you think that the new fifty-five millions will be collected? Do you think that the rest will be, for that matter, in any manner that is at all dependable? By no means. No, be convinced that one does not repress twenty-three or twenty-four million men without their discontent taking the form of revolt rather than of mere ill will. What then will become of those who have supported such unfortunate measures? I beg you, in the name of my tender friendship, not to take too obvious a position on this matter. I know the depths of your soul, but I know too how some will set about persuading you to antipopular leanings. Allow me to appeal to the noble part of that soul which I love, to your sensibility, your generous humanity. Is it more noble to belong to an association of men, however respectable it may be, than to a whole nation, so long debased, which as it rises to liberty will consecrate the names of those who have desired its success, but may well prove severe toward those who have been unfavorable to it? I speak to you from the depths of my cell as I would from my tomb, as the most tenderly devoted of friends, who have never loved in you anything but yourself, a stranger to fear and to hope, indifferent to all the distinctions that separate men, because their gaze is nothing to him.

It seemed to me that in writing to you with this candor I was fulfilling the noblest duty of friendship; I hope that you may be able to take it for what it is: the expression and the proof of the feeling that binds me to everything that is amiable and estimable in your nature, and to the virtues that I hope to see appreciated by others as they are by me.

The argument that the classes that would really benefit most by "this inconceivable crisis" were those that were already highest in the social scale is one of the strangest possible defenses of a coming revolution. (It would seem more cynical if Chamfort had had a chance to realize how many "revolutions" were to turn out that way.) Particular circumstances aside, he was influenced by happy views of the results of the English revolution, and by the English Whig philosophy fashionable in French pre-Revolutionary mythology. The letter to the Comte de Vaudreuil marked a separation. The Comte had bought a house still more magnificent than the one in which he had arranged the apartment for Chamfort, and Chamfort "who was genuinely fond of him, feeling that they would both be surer of the friendship lasting if they were not united by the same roof," Guingené says, took the opportunity of Vaudreuil's moving into it, to move, himself, to an apartment at Number 18, Arcades du Palais-Royal, where his comings and goings connected with activities that were soon to be a part of the Revolution were more convenient and no doubt less embarrassed. The gap between the two men widened. The Comte's "philosophical" sympathies did not embrace any of the actual changes that were bruited, and he made up his mind quickly about what he thought of the temper of the time. In July 1789, seven months after Chamfort's letter, and within a few weeks of the assembly of the États-Generaux, he and the Comte d'Artois left for England, among the first of the *émigrés*.

Chamfort made no attempt to enter into active politics at the time of the convention, when he could doubtless have been a representative if he had wished it. Nor did he enter into the debates at the Jacobin Club or the other clubs. He confined his public activity for the most part to journalism, contributing anonymously to the *Journal of 1789*, the *Feuille Villageoise*, the *Courrier de Provence*, and later to the *Gazette Nationale* and the *Gazette de France*. With Marmontel and La Harpe he worked at editing the literary section of the *Mercure de France*. He prepared, or helped to prepare, speeches for friends, among them Talleyrand: he is known to have collaborated on the speech that contributed largely to Talleyrand's becoming president of the National Assembly, in 1790. He himself was one of the founders of the "Club of 1789," with thirty-six members, many of them liberal aristocrats or intellectuals, some of whom later figured in the conservative wing of the Jacobin Club. He himself used the weekly assembly of the Club of 1789 as a chess club, and fired his remarks from the middle of games. He left the club when it ceased, in his opinion, to be an arena for ideas and became a mere center for intrigue. During 1789 and 1790, despite his poor health, he was anxious, his friend Sélis says, to be everywhere. And he did not shrink from the early manifestations of violence. He was certainly close to the principal developments that culminated in the storming of the Bastille, on July 14, 1789, and more than one account states that he was present, and among the first to enter the prison, and that his essay on the event (pp. 265–270) in his series of *Scenes From the Revolution* was largely a firsthand report. The essay was for public consumption and is touched with the rhetoric of the moment, but it was prompted by a genuine elation; and that feeling, and the conviction that a great step forward had been taken, stayed with him for some time. He is said to have announced to some aristocrats, some time later when the subject arose, that the Bastille was now doing nothing but "subsiding and becoming beautiful," and a day or so after the taking of the prison he wrote to Mme. Panckoucke:

. . . You do not seem to me very grieved over the fate of our friend the late Despotism, and you know that this death surprised me very little. I am delighted to receive my prophet's license from your hands. It is better than a witch's license, which is what several of my friends have sent me, but women are always more polite and more pleasant than men. Besides, as prophets are no longer cut up with saws, and witches are no longer burnt, I can enjoy the honors of my foresight with perfect safety. But really, it did not take much. One had only to approach the colossus to realize that it was hollow and rotten, varnished on the outside and worm-eaten within. Its fall was rather too sudden and will be inconvenient for a while, but we will manage.

I wished, these last few days, to come and talk with you, and recapitulate the thirty years that we have just lived through in three weeks, but the unbearable heat yesterday and today kept me indoors.

I will come and make it up to myself when the thermometer drops a few degrees. . . . *P.S.* Will you please relay all my compliments to M and beg him to make the *Mercure* a shade more republican? It's the only thing that will succeed now. *Item*, may the *Gazette de France* be hitched up a few notches, too, in the respectful proportion that it ought to maintain in relation to the *Mercure*. Add, I beg you as a favor, that at that price I will forgive him for the fear of bayonets that he wanted to give me—tools in which he showed too great faith for a philosopher.

In something of the same spirit he worked on a number of longer essays for the *Mercure de France,* on the recently published memoirs of Richelieu, and on the writings of his late friend Duclos, subjects which served him as occasions for attacks on the old order. He supplied journalism on a wide spectrum of subjects which had been current for years in discussion circles and now were being rushed forward all at once: penal reform, hospital reform, poverty, dueling. His friend Condorcet was preparing at that time his *Reflections on Negro Slavery*; Chamfort, in a review of a travel book, took up the question of colonialism and its degradations:

. . . If these people have come to hate the whites, it is the result of a justified horror of their cruelties; and the result of that is the atrocious slanders with which the whites attempt to vilify simple and innocent men whose vengeance they have provoked. This distressing truth, which M. le Vaillant proves with examples and facts, seems to have inspired in him a kind of passion for the savages, and a profound aversion for the whites, and in general, for civilization: a sentiment which always appears slightly peculiar, which the vulgar term misanthropic, and which on the contrary is simply a too ardent love of humanity and a violent indignation against the crimes that render men miserable in society.

The country he was referring to is now South Africa.

❧ XI ❧

Chamfort's faith in the Revolution was unabated a year after the taking of the Bastille, when a vast celebration was held on the Champ de Mars to commemorate that event. Talleyrand, as the Bishop of Autun, said mass, and the King swore allegiance to the Constitution. The next day Chamfort wrote to Mme. Panckoucke:

Good God! How I admire your courage and love your goodness! How I wished you had been where I was, facing the altar, and with a shelter close by, where one could get in out of the showers. I know where you were, and it was not well placed at all. I would almost have scolded you at that moment, but I would have loved you still more, if that is possible. . . .

I especially like your new profession of faith; we are unshakeable in our religion. As I write, I hear, shouted in my ears: "Abolition of all pensions in France!" and I say: "Abolish away, I will not change either my principles or my feelings." Men used to walk on their heads, now they walk on their feet; I am content; they will always have faults and even vices, but they will have only those of their own natures and not the monstrous deformities composed by a monstrous government.

Farewell, my dear friend, preserve yourself for your friends. Let us keep alive what is good of the good old days, which were so bad!

In the next days, when the existing pensions were, in fact, abolished, Chamfort, on a visit to his friend Marmontel, found the latter and his wife lamenting what the reform would mean to them and their children. Guingené says that Chamfort took one of the children onto his knee and said, "Come, my little friend, you are our better. One day you will weep for your father, when you hear that he had the weakness to weep for you because he had been told that you would not be as rich as he is."

Chamfort's attack on academies was written at the request of Mirabeau, who died in April, 1791, before he had had a chance to deliver it as a speech. Some of the criticisms of such institutions are perennial (as he had said of other bodies "they will not lose their taste for the trade,"); some were peculiar to the old order, and would have had few defenders at that time, when the dams were breaking. The discourse is if anything even less original than Chamfort's speech of acceptance at the Académie ten years earlier, and the studied vehemence of its rhetoric was an inflated currency of the moment.

Dousset declares that Chamfort had pressed Mirabeau to create a club that would be more popular than the one to which they both belonged, and that the result was the founding of the Jacobins. It is, to say the least, a somewhat simplified version of the origin of that club, which evolved from the original Club Breton, founded in June 1789, at Versailles, even before the representatives of the three Estates had formally convened. In November of that year, when the Assembly had moved to Paris, the club too, with some changes, had moved, and had rented for its sessions the refectory of the Jacobin convent in the Rue St. Honoré. It is true that Chamfort was a member. He had taken the oath ("I swear to live free or to die; to remain loyal to the principles of the Constitution; to obey the laws and help to enforce them; to do everything I can to perfect them, and to conform to the customs and rules of the society"), and he wore the Club's insignia on his coat buttons. But he was not active until July 1791, when, as he wrote, "after the massacre of the Champ de Mars, drawn, in spite of my sickness and suffering, by an irresistible force, I ran to the Jacobins, I the twentieth or thirtieth . . ." where he was offered and accepted the post of secretary, and continued to discharge its duties while the Jacobins were in danger, and Desmoulins and Danton had fled Paris. For a time it seemed possible that the Club might be dissolved altogether; Robespierre took advantage of the crisis to reorganize it. When the Jacobins were once again a dominant force of the Revolution, Chamfort resigned his office and ceased to attend regularly.

Despite his journalistic output—the more remarkable in view of his steadily poor and declining health—his reduced income, after the cessation of pensions, forced him to give up his apartment in the Palais-Royal and move to a cheaper one in the Rue Neuve-des-Petits-Champs. His physical condition and his work made a manservant seem indispensable, but he could not afford one and employed a housekeeper whom he had known for years. He became warmly attached to some of the neighbors in the new building, who were especially kind to him, "and he repaid them," says Guingené, "with that unrestrained intimacy in which few men, perhaps, have known so well how to give pleasure."

On January 17, 1792, he wrote to a friend, who is presumed to have been Condorcet, about the rumors of invasion and the preparations for war that preceded the fall of the monarchy:

My friend, I have not answered your last letter, first because I had not read it, and second because I knew that within three days the newspapers would answer one of the principal things that concerned us at that moment—the organizing of the émigrés in Brabant at Lille, Douai, etc. Centuries have passed since then, and everything has changed a great deal. I am living among persons (not the ones you know) who, as the result of oddly favorable circumstances, are extremely well informed about matters in the Low Countries. For over a month now they have been able to say four days in advance what was about to happen. In their opinion Leopold is more frightened of a war than the Parisian riff-raff was two years ago. They predict that his answer, on February 10, will be all that we could wish for in the most peaceable of systems; and I imagine that certain movements that are already noticeable in several of his States, in particular in Styria [province of Austria; translator's note] give him cause for concern. But let us suppose that he should wish to take hostile action in two months' time, what shall we do if, in the meantime, he addresses us as an ally and a good neighbor? Declare war on him? Invade the province of Brabant [Belgium; translator's note] as a certain faction now urges? It seems quite impossible, and even if he were to form an alliance with the German princes in order to proceed against us next spring in a war in which he would certainly involve the whole Empire, how could we force our executive power, which is in control of military plans, to march into Brabant, rather than against Liège, Trèves, etc? One laughs at the pity of it, to see that after two and a half years of revolution, the patriots cannot boast of having removed an agent in charge of war, such as M. Bessière, nor agents in charge of foreign affairs, such as Hennin and Rayneval. Will the patriots now force the King to proceed seriously against his brother-in-law, with whom he has agreements that have been thwarted by chance rather than by political design? Such action could come about only after a crisis that would still further compromise our position, and might render it still more awkward. In my view all this remains an insoluble problem, a muddled and confused drama, whose issue will fall from on high as it does in the plays of Euripides. All that I am sure of is that the general momentum will impede any partial and contradictory movements with which one seeks to delay it. . . .

That spring, in April, for the last time in his life, Chamfort was mentioned for a diplomatic post: as ambassador to the Diet of Ratisbonne. But nothing came of it. In August the monarchy fell. Chamfort is said to have witnessed the sack of the palace and the butchery that accompanied it. Two days later he wrote, possibly to the same friend:

My health continues to be good, my friend, but I keep to my regimen. This morning I went the rounds of the overturned statues of Louis XV and Louis XVI, on the Place Vendôme, the Places des Victoires. It was my day for visiting the deposed kings, and the philosophic doctors say that it is a very salubrious exercise. I am sure you would agree with them. In any case I took that much upon myself.

From Louis XV, I went on to the Château des Tuileries. No one could conceive of the spectacle there. The garden was filled with the populace as at Prato or Vienna or Potsdam. The crowd flowed through the apartments dyed with the blood of brothers and friends and pierced by the shot of the cannons that had answered those that had massacred them two nights before. The conversations corresponded with these sad objects. It is true that I did not hear the King or the Queen named; but instead there was much talk of Charles IX and of Catherine de Medicis. An old woman recounted several incidents from the history of France. A man in rags cited the anecdote of the Duchess of Marlborough's bowl and gloves as having been the cause of a war. He was mistaken: It led to one campaign less, but I was prudent enough not to revise the text. I would have been taken for an aristocrat. Besides, the mistake was so slight, and the narrator's intention was so good!

Would you like to know how many centuries opinion has traveled in two months? Think of the symptom of the French passion for royalty that I cited to you, the ease with which the Jacobin dancers, under my windows, turned from singing *Ça ira* [the song of the Revolution; translator's note] to *Vive Henri IV!* Well, the latter tune is now forbidden, and as I write the statue of that King is lying on the ground. Nothing in my life has surprised me more. I will never again say to you that those who wanted the republic would find their paths blocked by the *Henriade* and the *Lodoïx* of the university. No, that is something no longer to be feared, and I am even convinced that the *Versalicas arces* of our modern Latin poems will not protect Versailles. It took nothing less than the present court to bring about this miracle, but in the end it succeeded, glory be to it! I no longer have the slightest doubt on this subject since hearing the discussions—and not those of the street idlers, by any means—of Parisians around the royal statues that received my visit this morning. As for me, what little idle curiosity I have kept, prompted me to read a few words written under the hoof of Louis XIV's horse. What do you think I found? The name of Girardon, who hid his immortality there. Does that not strike you as the emblem itself of the egotistical protection accorded to the arts by an arrogant despot, and at the same time of the modest stupidity of an artist, a man of genius, who considers himself honored to work for the glory of a tyrant? The more I study man, the more I see nothing. But then, it would be amusing if Girardon had said to himself, "The glory of this king will not last. His statue will be overturned by a posterity outraged at his despotism, and his horse, raising its foot, will discourse of my glory to the onlookers." That artist would have had a philosophy that one might wish had been shared by Racine and Boileau.

Speaking of the King, I have been told that you had been suggested for the education of the prince royal. I can see one difficulty: how will you know what trade to teach your pupil in case the French turn out to be like the Parisians? Be careful: *it is a difficulty that is worth mentioning.*

You are happy, I am sure, that Grouvelle is the secretary of the council, and that consequently an evil genius did not settle him seven or eight days ago, as one rumor had it. He will find it an undemanding trade, after that of section president, which he held during that terrible night before last. At that moment a section president had to be neighborhood commissioner, arbitrator, justice of the peace, criminal magistrate, and something of a grave digger, since the bodies were there awaiting his orders, as happens when the executive power forces the sovereignty to have recourse to revolutionary power. I am happy, too, that Lebrun is in foreign affairs, though I have not been able to get from him, for two months, a proof of the *Gazette de France*, while he was bringing it out under my name. I hold no grudge.

Good-bye, my dear friend; I love and embrace you most tenderly. You see that, without being merry, I am not exactly sad. . . . The populace, again . . . have failed to clear the aristocrats, journalists among them, from their shores. But one must know how to take mishaps of this kind. It is what must be expected in a new people, which for three years has talked incessantly of the sublime Constitution, but is about to destroy it, and to tell the truth has not known how to organize anything but insurrection. That is not much, it is true, but it is better than nothing.

Good-bye again. I expect you within the week, and our beloved patient with you. I have not said anything to you about him, because I will write to him.

In the reorganization after the fall of the monarchy, in August, Chamfort was offered the post of director of the Bibliothèque Nationale, then housed in the Palais Mazarin, and an apartment in the building. He accepted the position, Guingené says, on the advice of friends, and after some well-founded hesitations. He shared it at first with a journalist, Carra, who was executed in the purge of the Girondins, the following year.

Neither at the time of his appointment, nor later, did Chamfort make much effort to be prudent in his comments, public or private, on the course of the Revolution, and on the principles and practices of the extreme Jacobins, Marat and Robespierre, the Committees of Public Safety, or any of the apparatus of the Terror. On the other hand, the original Club of 1789 had taken a reactionary turn, and some of its members formed a new club of "Émigrés from the Club of 1789," Chamfort among them. He clung to the ideals of the Revolution, while refusing to be numbered in any of its factions. When Hérault de Sechelles, a leader of the Dantonists, asked him to write against freedom of the press, he refused. It was an important mark against him. And there were others. Marat, accompanied by two aides, had paid a menacing surprise visit to the salon in the house of Talma one evening, hoping to frighten General Dumouriez, whom he knew he would find there. Marat himself had been worsted, humiliated, and put bodily out of the house. Everyone who had been present was included in his resentment, of course, and Chamfort had been there. At that time, in conjunction with purges of the Jacobin party and decimation of aristocrats and others so unfortunate as to displease the Committees, executions were offered as public entertainments at celebrations of revolutionary anniversaries, such as that of the death of Louis XVI. "It is the gratuity of the Convention," Chamfort said. He was arrested on May 31, 1793, with a group of Girondins who were being rounded up, and was kept for several hours in an anteroom. Robespierre passed, pretending not to know him. He was released without being questioned and without any disposition to temper his witticisms, which characterized Robespierre, Marat, and the "Sanhedrin," as he called them, as not only criminal but ridiculous.

His scorn was quoted against him by a subordinate at the Bibliothèque, named Tobiesen-Duby. This individual (who later achieved another reputation as an expert on old coins) had been an employee at the library under the two previous directors, whom he had kept informed of his dissatisfaction with his circumstances. He wanted to be director himself, and it must have been exasperating to see his superiors depart and their replacements arrive without the name of Tobiesen-Duby being raised to eminence, in consideration of all his complaints. He was of the breed that would be given hope by an era of denunciations, and he aspired to the gratitude of the Committee of Public Safety. He detailed Chamfort's irreverent sallies in a letter to the Committee, but they ignored it. He wrote again on July 21, 1793, with more vehemence and more shocking quotations. He said that Chamfort spoke in opening admiration of Charlotte Corday. Chamfort's disgust with the Terror and its officers had been intensified, that winter and spring, by the deaths, on the guillotine or by suicide, of friend after friend, and Tobiesen-Duby doubtless invented nothing, including the style, which is still with us. In his words Chamfort was a "ci-devant secretary of His rotten Highness the Prince de Condé." He warned the committee, besides, that "this Chamfort dines often with the Minister of the Interior, not that I wish to inculpate the minister, but only to tell you that this is a serpent who, with his torturous [misspelled in original; translator's note] twisting endeavors to insinuate himself into the bosom of Garat. I am a witness, myself, to his uncivic remarks, his jeremiads on the present circumstances; I will bring the accusation against him." His letter went to the committee accompained by a note from Gombaud-Lachaise, editor of the *Bulletin* of the Convention. In August, a year after the overthrow of the monarchy, Chamfort was arrested and taken, along with an aristocrat and four priests, to the prison of Les Madelonettes. The building had been an Ursuline convent, in former times; judging from pictures it had never looked inviting. It was one of the more uncomfortable and unhealthy prisons of the Revolution. Chamfort's health was particularly bad at the time of his arrest, and he required constant medical attention, which of course he could not possibly receive there, and the fact added greatly to his discomfort. He was released several days later for lack of evidence, but "he conceived, from that time onward, a profound horror of prison and swore that he would die rather than allow himself to be taken back there" (Guingené).

He immediately published an attack on Tobiesen-Duby for having denounced him as an aristocrat, and a defense of himself on the grounds of his well-known revolutionary position. He also had a long reply to Tobiesen-Duby pasted up on the walls of Paris, as an announcement. And he resigned his post at the Bibliothèque. But he made no attempt to deny the accusation of having spoken ill of Marat.

He had been released upon a condition that was frequently exercised by the Committee: a police agent was billeted on him, whose duty it was to stay with him at all times. He had the expense of keeping his jailer, and the system aimed partly at ruining the prisoners who accepted freedom on such terms. There were several others in the building who were at large on the same condition, and after a number of attempts, Chamfort succeeded in obtaining permission to have them share a single guard, and his upkeep, among them. But he continued to talk as freely in front of the guard as he had done before, and the events of the moment gave him little to admire. His surveillance continued in this manner for over a month, and in Guingené's account:

. . . one day at the end of a meal the police officer said crudely and without warning that they were to pack their bags and that he was ordered to take them at once to the house of detention. Chamfort thought that they meant to take him to Les Madelonettes and he remembered his vow. Pretending that he was going to pack, he retired to his study at the end of a gallery which held his library. He shut himself in, loaded a pistol, intending to fire at his forehead, smashed the upper part of his nose and burst his right eye. Surprised to find himself alive, and determined to die, he seized a razor and tried to cut his throat, renewing the attempt several times and cutting all the flesh to tatters. The helplessness of his hand did not alter the resolution of his soul; he dealt himself several blows, trying to reach the heart, and in a final effort, on the verge of fainting, he tried to cut both his wrists and open all his veins. At last, overcome with pain, he cried out and fell into a chair, where he stayed, almost dead. The blood flowed under the door in streams. His housekeeper heard the cry, saw the blood, called, others came, she beat on the door, then it was forced in; the spectacle that met their eyes silenced all questions. Everyone rushed to staunch the blood with handkerchiefs, cloths, bandages. The dying man was carried to his bed. Doctors and civil officials were summoned: while the former prepared what was needed for so many wounds, Chamfort, in a firm voice, dictated the following declaration to the others: "I, Sébastien-Roch-Nicolas-Chamfort, declare that it was my intention to die a free man rather than be taken, as a slave, into a house of detention. I declare that if there is a further attempt to remove me, in my present state, by violence, I still have enough strength to finish what I have begun. I am a free man; I will never be made to enter a prison alive." He signed this Roman declaration, and without deigning to notice that the room next to the study in which he had his bed was filling with persons who had been sent there from the section headquarters, he continued to give an unreserved explanation of the motives that had led him to the act which he had committed.

My wife, who had been told the news, ran to his apartment, in tears. "My dear friend," he said to her when he saw her, "You see what patriots are reduced to. I am sorry for your husband; I am sorry for you; as for me, all is said. I have nothing to reproach myself with but having lived too long." I arrived shortly afterward; I will never forget that spectacle. His head and neck were wrapped in bloody cloths; his pillow, and his sheets too, were stained with blood, and what little of his face could be seen was covered with it. He spoke less violently and was beginning to feel his weakness. I stood by him, dumb with shock, admiration, and grief. "My friend," he said to me, holding out his hand to me, "you see how one escapes them. They pretend that I missed, but I can feel the ball still in my head. They won't look for it." Everything he said was marked with the same energy and simplicity. After a moment of silence he went on calmly, and even with his habitual ironic tone, "What can you expect? That's what it is to be clumsy with one's hands. One never manages to do anything successfully, even killing oneself." Then he began to tell me how he had "perforated" his eye and the lower part of his forehead, instead of breaking in the skull; and then "mangled" his throat instead of cutting it; and "gashed" his breast without succeeding in piercing the heart. "Finally," he added, "I remembered Seneca, and in honor of Seneca I wanted to open my veins, but he was rich, he had everything he could ask for: a warm bath; all the comforts, in fact. For my part, I'm a poor devil; I don't have any of that. I've messed myself up horribly and I'm still here. But the ball is in my head, that's the main thing. A little sooner or later, that's all."

At that moment the police officer who had taken away his

companions in misfortune came into the room. Chamfort recognized his voice and asked me to call him. "Well," he said to him, "where have you taken them?" "To the Luxembourg, citizen." "Ah! Ah! I thought we were to have gone back to Les Madelonettes, and I have a horror of that place. If I'd known it was to the Luxembourg . . . maybe I wouldn't have killed myself . . . but after all, I was right to do what I've done, anyway."

Meanwhile the section officers, the justice of the peace, and the commissioners had finished their operations and wanted to station four *sans-culottes* in the patient's apartment, for whom he would have to pay. Chamfort told them that they did him too much honor, that two would be enough for his needs and far too many for his fortune. At that point a strange person came into the room among all the others who were there, a man who passes for being very learned in Greek but ignorant of many other things, and for whose benefit, after the sad death of Carra and the resignation of Chamfort, the office of librarian had been placed once again in the hands of one man. He had heard of this accident and came to see for himself. "But," he said, "M. de Chamfort apparently has not read my discourse against suicide. The work has been very successful. I prove my case *primo*, I prove it *secundo*." And with that he delivered himself, at no one's bidding, of an extract from this dissertation of his. No one uttered a word in reply, and he left without informing himself of the patient's condition, and without showing the slightest interest in him.

In defiance of everyone's expectations, including Chamfort's, he did not die of his wounds, though he did suffer a great deal from them. He was soon asking for news; he had the evening papers read to him "and usually concluded, from what he heard, that he had been right to kill himself." The eye which he had shot had been the better of the two, and he had virtually lost it, but before long he was reading a little, on his own, and translating poems from the Greek Anthology. On the "15th frimaire, IInd year of the Republic" (December 1793) he wrote to Mme. Panckoucke:

My dear friend, I feel a need to write to you, and I trust that at the moment you will be inclined to excuse the irregularities of my handwriting. I never expected, when you were tearing up your cloths for my wounds and to have lint to send me, that I would so soon be able to form with my hand the thanks that I have addressed to you from the depths of my heart. They will be brief this time, but no less warm for that. . . . They hold out hopes of my soon being at liberty. Hope is something that I accept with difficulty, but I do not wish to be so cruel to myself as to reject it this time. . . .

At the end of three weeks he was able to get up and go out.

As soon as possible he arranged to leave the apartment in the Bibliothèque Nationale; he moved into a single cheap room in the Rue Chabanais. His guards had been reduced from two to one, with whom he seems to have been on good terms. Finally he was left to himself, and the few close friends whom he continued to see. He made plans for literary work, to support himself. The periodical *la Décade Philosophique*, according to Guingené, was founded largely with a view to occupying him. And his health continued to improve. The terrible shock of his attempted suicide, and his wounds, appeared to disperse some of the chronic symptoms of ailments that had plagued him for years. Color came back into his face; he even began to put on weight. "I feel livelier than ever," he said. "It is a pity that I am not more anxious to live."

It was a severe winter. One day when the worst of it had passed, Chamfort was out for a walk and was suddenly overcome with a fever, which proved to be the beginning of a total relapse. His appetite left him entirely; he was unable to sleep; he had no energy. From the start the pains in his bladder were so severe that he was unable to walk, and on the following day the inflammation and pain increased. A famous surgeon had been sent for to look after him, but apparently he mistook the nature of the trouble, and his ministrations were of no help. The swelling and pain grew steadily worse. An operation was decided on "which might have saved him if it had been performed earlier" (Guingené). It did, in fact, afford him some relief, but the fever rose again; he grew weaker, and after two crises Chamfort died, a week and a day after the execution of Danton, on April 13, 1794. Three friends, according to Auguis, were with him at the end: Van Praet, the friend from the library who had been arrested when he had, and had been taken to the Madelonettes at the same time; and the Abbé Sieyès; and Guingené.

His obituary appeared in the journals without comment. At that moment his position in the eyes of the officers of the Terror was such that it required a certain courage to display any signs of grief at his death. Under the circumstances only a very few friends were invited to Chamfort's plain burial. But most of those who were invited came.

✺ XII ✺

Guingené, in his summary of his friend's character, admitted that he was prone to "a certain affectation, though rather in the language than in the manner in general. The worthy Auger said to him one day, 'You gave me your address so wittily that I could not find the place.' Two things are to be noted about this. Auger said it in good faith, without malicious intent; and it was Chamfort who told it." There was, he says, in Chamfort's witticisms, "a certain natural acidity which is, more often than one thinks, the companion of a good heart, but which almost always renders the goodness doubtful." He makes a resumé of what he, and other admirers of Chamfort's, have called his disinterestedness,

he abjured passionately, even in his own person, all the abuses of the old order; . . . he railed against pensions until there were none; against the Académie, whose perquisites had become his sole means of livelihood; against all idolatries, servilities, ceremonious courtesies, until not a man was left who dared show himself eager to please him; against excessive opulence, until he no longer had a friend rich enough to offer him a carriage or a dinner; . . . finally he raged against frivolity, pretensions to wit, and literature itself until all his relationships were taken up with public matters, and heedless of his writings, his comedies, his conversation. . . .

And Guingené paid tribute to Chamfort's qualities as a friend, in terms that were echoed by others.

The opposite opinion has been thoroughly aired too. It is not surprising that Chamfort had enemies and detractors all his life. Among the most complicated opinions of him, by any of those who knew him personally and whose testimony was published, was Chateaubriand's; he saw Chamfort during the late eighties, and in his early *Essay on Revolutions*, written as an émigré, in a London garret, in the early nineties, he spoke with admiration, and boasted of having had one of his key ideas "from the mouth of the famous Chamfort himself." In 1826, when the work went into a new edition, he violently retracted his earlier admiration, besides having published, five years earlier, in *Mémoires d'Outre-Tombë*, a diatribe on "the most bilious man of letters whom I knew in Paris at that time"—a passage which is incorrect in certain factual matters, and is interesting chiefly for its vehemence.

A NOTE ON THE TRANSLATION

❧ ☙

THE TRANSLATING OF A FRENCH aphorist of the classical period is a daunting undertaking. The transporting of a kind of concision, grace, and ceremony that were native to the original language into another, is obviously something that can be done only very imperfectly, and the classical period, besides, marked an attempt to carry certain peculiarly French traits of language to a pure extreme. It also employed a vocabulary of its own: not so much a use of different words as a use of usual words in a special sense. The use of language was highly self-conscious, and plays on words were frequent—including plays on the words with special contemporary meanings—and were used to make social and moral, as well as verbal distinctions. In translation, a great deal of both the usage and the grace must inevitably be left behind, and it is possible that no two readers would agree about what must be abandoned. I had begun by translating a few of the *maxims* I tended to remember, and which seemed reasonably tractable about being moved into English, and I was led from this deceptive sampling into the full haggling with approximation. I became fully aware of the difficulties, of course, only as I worked, and in many instances I am not sure that I have done more than offer a desperate proof of their existence.

The original itself varies, as I have indicated, from highly turned aphorisms to hasty jottings and repetitive passages. I have tried to follow this variety, where doing so did not conflict with clarity or content.

I have translated the *Maxims and Thoughts* complete. They are uneven; and there are entries that require or would benefit by a knowledge of the country and the period which cannot be generally assumed in English, or else a clutter of references with which I am loathe (and sometimes unable) to encumber the text; others seem trivial or unfinished, but at least this part of the *Products of the Perfected Civilization* should exist entire, in some sense, in English. It forms the core of what Chamfort must be judged by in any language. From the other parts of that collection, the *Characters and Anecdotes* and the *Philosophical Dialogues* I have made a selection (indicating by ellipses [. . .] where I have left out entries). In these sections there were far more of the sort of objections I have mentioned, and they were far more important. Many of the dialogues are very slight, and some are based on word plays the point of which evades translation. There are more "anecdotes" than "characters," taking the latter as a general and typical portrait, and the former as a specific incident.

The *genre* itself is by now something of an acquired taste, I imagine, and Chamfort's anecdotes, referring to circumstances and personages of his own age or the preceding one, are sometimes meaningless now to anyone without a detailed knowledge of the time—or a French encyclopedia. With a few borderline cases I have supplied footnotes; for the rest, I imagined that anyone with so searching an interest in the more local anecdotes of the period would almost certainly be able to read French. The same principle led me to exclude most of the works published in Chamfort's lifetime: his three plays, his academic discourses, and his journalistic writings, with exceptions that I shall mention.

In ignoring these productions I have been, in the main, in accord with the practice of even the most serious of the French selected editions. Most of what Chamfort wrote to further his career was deservedly forgotten almost before he died. But I have included the essay on "The Taking of the Bastille" from the series of *Tableaus of the Revolution*, which I have translated not for its literary merit, but as typical of the moment, its rhetoric, and Chamfort's place in both. The passages from the two essays on Richelieu and his age are included as examples of Chamfort's attitude toward a hero-villain who obviously had great importance for him. The passages also contain what must be two of the most remarkable set pieces of rhetorical indignation in that rhetorically indignant period.

PRODUCTS
OF THE
PERFECTED
CIVILIZATION

QUESTION

QUESTION: Why do you no longer offer anything to the public?

ANSWERS: For one thing the public seems to me to be running over with bad taste and the mania for denigration.

For another, a reasonable man cannot act without a purpose, and whereas a success would afford me no pleasure, the shame of a failure might cause me considerable pain.

For another, there is no reason why I should spoil my leisure simply because the gentry will have it that the gentry must be entertained.

For another, I am at work for the music hall, which is the popular theater, and at the same time proceeding with a philosophical work destined for the Royal Printing Office.

For another, the public habitually treats men of letters as the recruiting officers of the Pont St.-Michel treat their recruits: drunk the first day, ten crowns and the use of the rods for the rest of their lives.

For another, those who urge me to write do so for the same reason that one sits at windows hoping to see monkeys or men leading bears past in the street.

I am reminded of M. Thomas, insulted all his life and praised after his death.

My lords the gentlemen in waiting, actors, censors, the police, Beaumarchais.

For another, I am afraid of dying without having lived.

For another, everything that is said to persuade me to put

myself into print might just as well be said to Saint Ange or Murville.

For another, I have work to do, and successes waste time.

For another, I would rather not behave like men of letters, who are like donkeys kicking and fighting in front of an empty hayrack.

For another, if I had hurried to print all the trifles that occurred to me, there would be no more rest for me on earth.

For another, I prefer the respect of the good and honorable, and my private happiness, to a handful of eulogies, another of money, and a torrent of insults and slanders.

For another, if there is one man on earth who has the right to live unto himself, it is I, after the malice that has been leveled at me each time I have obtained any success.

For another, fame, as Bacon says, has never been known to keep company with repose.

And because the public cares only for successes that it does not respect.

Because I am content that my celebrity should not succeed half that of Jeannot's.

Because I no longer have any wish to please anyone except my own kind.

And for another thing, the more faded my literary label becomes, the happier I am.

And for another, I have known nearly all the famous men of our age and I have seen them made wretched by this glorious passion for fame, and die after debauching their moral natures in its service.

MAXIMS AND THOUGHTS

Chapter One

GENERAL MAXIMS

℃ MAXIMS AND AXIOMS, like summaries, are the works of persons of intelligence who have labored, as it seems, for the convenience of mediocre and lazy minds. The lazy are happy to find a maxim that spares them the necessity of making for themselves the observations that led the maxim's author to the conclusion to which he invites his reader. The lazy and the mediocre imagine that they need go no further, and ascribe to the maxim of generality which the author, unless he was mediocre himself, as is sometimes the case, has not claimed for it. The superior man grasps at once the resemblances, the differences, which render the maxim more or less applicable in one instance or another, or not at all. It is much the same with natural history, where the urge to simplify has led to the imagination of classifications and divisions. They could not have been framed without intelligence for the necessary comparisons and the observing of relationships; but the great naturalist, the man of genius, sees that nature is prodigal in the invention of individually different creatures, and he sees the inadequacy of divisions and classifications which are so commonly used by mediocre and lazy minds. Mediocrity and laziness: one can see a connection. Often they are the same thing. Often they are cause and effect.

℃ Most collectors of verses and sayings proceed as though they were eating cherries or oysters, choosing the best first, and ending by eating them all.

℃ What a curious work it would be which pointed out all the corrupting ideas of the human mind, of society, of morality, which are to be found either as themes or premises in the most celebrated writings and the most venerated authors; the ideas that propagate religious superstition, the bad political maxims, despotism, the vanity of rank, popular prejudices of every kind. One would see that almost all books are corrupters, and that the best do almost as much harm as good.

℃ The writing about education is endless, and the works on this subject have produced a few felicitous ideas, a few useful methods; they have furnished, in a word, a certain partial benefit. But of what general use can these writings be until the reforming of legislation, religion, and public opinion has made some head? Since education has no other end than to conform the reason of children to the public reason as regards these three subjects, what instruction is germane while these three subjects are in conflict? In training the reason of children, what are you doing but preparing it to distinguish, later, the absurdity of opinions and customs sanctified by the seal of ecclesiastical, public, or legislative authority; toward what are you leading it, therefore, but contempt?

℃ It is a source of pleasure and of philosophy to analyze the ideas that contribute to the particular judgments of individual men, and of different societies. The examination of the ideas that determine this or that public opinion is no less interesting and is often more so.

℃ Civilization, in many respects, is like cooking. When one sees on the table light dishes, wholesome and well prepared, one is happy indeed that cooking has become a science. But when one sees gravies, rich bouillons, truffled *patés*, one curses the cooks and their morbid art: it is all in the application.

℃ Man in the present state of society appears to me to be more corrupted by his reason than by his passions. His passions (by which I mean those that belong to the primitive man) have preserved, in the social order, the little of nature that is still to be found there.

℃ Society is not, as is commonly believed, the development of Nature, but rather its decomposition and total reconstruction. It is a second building, constructed from the ruins of the first. One discovers the fragments with a pleasure mingled with surprise. It is the same feeling that is evoked by the naïve expression of a natural sentiment, when anything of the kind occurs in society. Sometimes indeed it is especially pleasing when the person who voices it is someone of high rank—that is, further removed from Nature. It charms, in the person of a king, because a king is at the opposite extreme. It is a fragment of the ancient Doric or Corinthian architecture in a crude and modern edifice.

℃ In general, if society were not a fabric of pretenses, every expression of simple and true feeling would not be so remarkable as it now is. It would please without astonishing, but it astonishes as well as pleasing. Our surprise is the satire of society, and our pleasure is a homage to nature.

℃ Swindlers can always use a good name; police informers are paid less as they frequent worse company.

℃ A member of the populace, a beggar, can permit himself to be the object of contempt without provoking the imputation of baseness as long as the contempt seems to refer to his appearance only; but if the same beggar allows his conscience to be insulted, though it were by the first sovereign of Europe, he becomes as base in his person as in his station.

❡ One must admit the impossibility of living in the world without acting a part from time to time. The honest man can be distinguished from the swindler in this: he assumes a role only when he must, and to avoid danger, whereas the other goes looking for opportunities.

❡ At times one's reasoning in society is odd. One says to someone, in order to impugn his recommendation of someone else: "He's your friend." "But confound it, he's my friend because the good I have been saying of him is true, because he is as I describe him. You take the case for the effect and the effect for the cause. Why do you assume that I speak well of him simply because he is my friend, and why do you not assume, instead, that he is my friend because he merits my speaking well of him?"

❡ There are two classifications of moralists and statesmen: those who have seen human nature only from its odious and ridiculous side, and they are the greater number: Lucian, Montaigne, La Bruyère, La Rochefoucauld, Swift, Mandeville, Helvetius, etc. Those who have seen it only from its admirable side: Shaftesbury and certain others. The first are ignorant of the palace, of which they have seen only latrines. The second are enthusiasts who turn away their eyes from what offends them but nonetheless exists. *Est in medio verum.*

❡ If one wanted a proof of the complete uselessness of all books of morality, sermons, etc., one would have only to glance at the superstition of hereditary nobility. Is there any fault at which the philosophers, the orators, the poets have directed more satiric flights, and have employed wit in every form, or which has given rise to more sarcasm? And has the result been the end of pretensions, or of the fancy for riding in state coaches? Has it left Cherin[1] without a place?

---

[1] The royal genealogist.

℃ In the theater one strives for effect. But what distinguishes the good dramatic poet from the bad one is that the first pursues his effect with means that are acceptable to reason, whereas for the second all means are excellent. There is the same sort of distinction between honorable men and swindlers, both of whom wish to make their fortunes: The first employ honorable means, and the others any means at all.

℃ Philosophy, like medicine, can offer a great many drugs, a very few good remedies, and almost no specifics.

℃ Europe numbers some 150 million souls, Africa contains twice that figure, in Asia it is more than tripled; even if America and Australia held no more than half as many as our own hemisphere, it is certain that on our globe more than a hundred thousand men die every day. Even if a man lives only thirty years, he will have escaped this fearful destruction some fourteen hundred times.

℃ I have known men who were gifted with a simple and direct reason, no more, without great scope or elevation of mind, whose simple reason was enough to enable them to accord human vanities and follies the respect they deserve, to give them an awareness of their own personal dignity, and teach them to appreciate the same awareness in others. I have known women of whom more or less the same thing was true, whom real feeling, early experienced, had led to the same ideas. It follows from these two observations that those who attach great importance to those same vanities and human follies are the lowest category of our species.

℃ He who does not know how to return pleasantries and lacks a ready wit often finds himself faced with the choice of being either false or pedantic—a vexing alternative, which any man one respects escapes, ordinarily, by means of grace and good humor.

℀ Often an opinion, a custom, seems absurd to begin with, when one is very young, and as one advances in life one learns the reason for it, and it seems less so. Must one conclude, then, that certain customs have become less ridiculous? At times one is drawn to the conclusion that they were established by persons who had read the book of life entire, and are judged by others who have read only a few pages.

℀ According to the ideas that are accepted by the world and social decency, it would seem that a priest, a curate, ought to believe a little in order not to be a hypocrite, though of course he should not insist to the point of intolerance. The lordly vicar can smile at a jibe against religion, the bishop can laugh outright, the cardinal can add a touch of his own.

℀ Most noblemen remind one of their ancestors about as much as an Italian *Cicerone* reminds one of Cicero.

℀ I have read in some traveler, I forget which, that certain savages of Africa believe in the immortality of the soul. While not pretending to explain what it becomes, they believe that after death it wanders through the underbrush around the settlements, and for several mornings on end they go looking for it. When they do not find it, they abandon the search and think no more of the matter. It is more or less what our philosophers have done, with their best efforts.

℀ An honest man must assume public esteem without giving it a thought, and as it were in spite of himself. The man who solicits it shows what he is.

℀ That is a beautiful allegory, in the Bible, about the tree of the knowledge of good and evil, which produces death. Is not the meaning of this emblem that when one has pierced to the heart of things, the loss of illusions brings about the death of the soul, by which I mean a complete disinterest in all that moves and occupies other men?

℄ There must be a bit of everything in the world; even in the fictitious combinations of the social system. Inevitably men are to be found who invoke nature against society, truth against opinion, reality against what is merely accepted. It is a most telling form of intelligence and character, and its influence is greater than is generally believed. There are persons to whom one has only to show what is true for them to run to it with an unaffected and fascinated surprise. They are astonished that so striking a thing (when one knows how to present it in such a way) should have escaped them until then.

℄ It is assumed that the deaf must be unhappy in society. Is not this an expression of society's own self-importance, meaning, "How very sad for that poor man not to hear what we say"?

℄ Thought provides consolation for everything and remedies for everything. If ever it hurts you, ask it to heal the injury it has done you, and it will do it.

℄ It cannot be denied that there are a few great figures in modern history, and it is incomprehensible how they came to be formed. They seem to be out of place, like caryatids in an entresol.

℄ The best of philosophies, with regard to the world, must combine the sarcasm of good humor with the indulgence of contempt.

℄ I am no more surprised to see one man grow weary of fame than I am to see another lose patience with the noise in his antechamber.

℄ I have noticed, in the world, that the esteem of the gentle and honorable is sacrificed continually for attention, and peace for applause.

℄ According to Dorilas, one compelling proof of the existence of God is the existence of man, man at his most admirable, in the least equivocal sense, in the most exact sense, and therefore man more or less restricted, in a word, to the nobility. This is the masterpiece of Providence, or rather the one immediate work of His hands. But it is rumored, indeed with some insistence, that there exist others who resemble this privileged being in every detail. To which Dorilas answers, "Can it be true? What? Same face, same external shape?" Well then, the existence of these creatures, these men, since one will call them so, an existence which until now he denied but which, to his great surprise, he sees is recognized by several of his peers and which, though only for that reason, he does not formally reject, an existence about which his views are extremely hazy, filled with pardonable doubts which he cannot help, an existence against which he merely protests with a lofty port, a neglect of politeness, or a contemptuous bounty: the existence of all these (doubtless ill-defined) creatures—what can he make of it? How can he explain it? How can he adapt this phenomenon to his theory? In what physical, metaphysical, or if need be, mythological system will he seek the solution to this problem? He ponders, he muses, he is sincere; objection is unfounded; he is shaken. He has wit, erudition. He will find the key to the enigma; he has found it, he has it; his eyes shine with joy. Silence. In the Persian Theology one is acquainted with the doctrine of the two Principles: the Principle of Good and the Principle of Evil. Well then, do you not see? Nothing could be simpler. Genius, talents, the virtues, are contrivances of the Principle of Evil, Oriman, the Devil, for bringing to the light of day certain wretches, acknowledged plebeians, absolute commoners, or some who are barely gentry.

℄ How many distinguished members of the military, how many generals have died without having passed on their names to posterity—less fortunate in that respect than Bucephalus and even the Spanish mastiff Berecillo, who devoured the Indians of Santo Domingo, and received the pay of three soldiers!

℃ One prays that a villain will be lazy, and a fool silent.

℃ The best explanation of how the knave, and sometimes even the fool, nearly always make out better in the world than do the honest man and the man of intelligence, is that the knave and the fool have less difficulty keeping the pace and the tone of the world which, for the most part, is nothing but knavery and foolishness, whereas the honest man and the man of sense, unable to enter so unhesitatingly into commerce with the world, waste moments which, in matters of fortune, are priceless. The former are merchants who, knowing the language of the country, sell and provide for themselves immediately, while the latter are obliged to learn the language from their buyers and sellers before they can display their merchandise and come to terms with them. Often, indeed, they scorn to learn the language at all, and return without having struck a single bargain.

℃ There is a prudence that is superior to what the word is ordinarily used to describe: One is the prudence of the eagle, the other that of the mole. The first consists of boldly living according to one's character, accepting with courage whatever disadvantages and inconveniences that may entail.

℃ In order to be able to forgive reason for the harm it has done most men, one must consider what man would be without his reason. It was a necessary evil.

℃ There are presentably dressed follies just as there are well dressed fools.

℃ If one had said to Adam, on the morning after the death of Abel, that in a few centuries there would be places where seven or eight hundred thousand men would find themselves bundled and heaped together in an area of some four square leagues, would he have believed that these multitudes would ever be able to live together? Would he not have imagined crimes and monstrosities in even more horrifying profusion than is the case? One must remind oneself of this to console oneself for the abuses arising from these astonishing collections of men.

℃ Pretensions are a source of distress, and the period of happiness in a life begins when they come to an end. Though a woman may still be pretty when her beauty begins to decline, her pretensions render her ridiculous or miserable; ten years later, older and uglier, she is calm and tranquil. Or consider a man at the age when one succeeds or fails with women; he lays himself open to embarrassments and even to insults; he outlives the capacity and the uncertainties at the same time, and becomes tranquil. The harm in everything arises from the ideas not being fixed and settled; it is better to be something lesser and to be it unquestionably. The position of dukes and peers, clearly established, is preferable to that of foreign princes forced to struggle incessantly for preeminence. If Chapelain had followed the advice that Boileau gave him in the well-known phrase, "Why does he not write in prose?" he would have spared himself many torments and might have made a name for himself in some other way than as a laughingstock.

℃ "Are you not ashamed to promise more than you can perform?" Seneca asked one of his sons who could not compose the introduction to a speech he had undertaken. In the same way one might say to those who adopt principles that are beyond their characters, "Are you not ashamed to try to be more of a philosopher than you are able to be?"

℃ Most men who inhabit the world do it so vacantly, think so little, that they are quite ignorant of the world that is before their eyes. "They know nothing of it," M. de B. said with wit, "for the same reason that cockchafers know nothing of natural history."

℃ When one considers Bacon, at the beginning of the sixteenth century, pointing out to human intelligence the way it should take in order to reconstruct the edifice of the sciences, one almost ceases to admire the great men who succeeded him, such as Boyle, Locke, etc. He parcels out to them in advance the terrain which they are to clear or conquer. He is Caesar, master of the world after the victory of Pharsalia, awarding kingdoms and provinces to his supporters and favorites.

℃ Our reason sometimes renders us more unhappy than our passions, and when this happens to a man, one can say of him that he is a patient poisoned by his doctor.

℃ The moment when one loses the illusions and passsions of youth often leaves regrets, but sometimes we hate the spell that deceived us. So it is that Armida burns and razes the palace where she was enchanted.

℃ Doctors can see no more clearly than laymen into ailments, and the interior of the human body. They are both blind, but the doctors are the Hospital of the Blind: They know the streets better, and manage better.

℃ You ask how one makes one's fortune. Consider what happens in the pit, at the theater, on a day when it is crowded: Some stay at the back, some at the front move to the rear, those behind are pressed forward. The image is so apt that the description of it has passed into the vulgar parlance that refers to making one's fortune as "getting ahead": "my son, or my nephew will get ahead." The quality say, "advance oneself," or "succeed"—gentler expressions, which avoid the implication of force, of violence, of grossness, but keep the main idea.

℃ The physical world seems to be the work of a powerful and good being who has been forced to abandon to a wicked being the execution of part of his plan. But the moral world seems to be the product of a devil who has lost his mind.

℃ Those who offer their bare word in support of a statement that has been thoroughly proved are like the man who said, "I have the honor of assuring you that the earth turns around the sun."

℃ In affairs of importance men show themselves at their best advantage; in small matters they are seen as they are.

℃ What is a philosopher? He is a man who opposes nature with law, custom with reason, opinion with conscience, and error with his judgment.

℃ A fool who displays a flicker of intelligence astonishes and shocks, like coach horses at a gallop.

℃ Not to be worked by anyone's hand, to be no one's man, to draw one's principles, one's feelings, from no one else, this is the rarest thing I have seen.

℃ Instead of trying to break men of certain faults that are intolerable to society, it would have been better to correct the weakness of those who endure them.

℃ Out of any four so-called follies, three are mere foolishness.

℃ Opinion is the queen of the world, because foolishness is the queen of fools.

ℂ We must know how to perform the foolishness that our characters require.

ℂ Rank without merit earns deference without respect.

ℂ Great or small, there is no avoiding it, one must say to oneself as the coachman said to the courtesans in "Javelle's Mill": "The likes of you and the likes of us, we can't manage without each other."

ℂ Someone said that Providence was the Christian name of chance; a pious soul might say that chance is a familiar name for Providence.

ℂ Few men permit themselves a vigorous and intrepid use of their reason and dare to direct it upon every object in its full force. The time has come when it must be directed toward every point of morality, of politics, of society; toward kings, ministers, the great, philosophers; toward the leaders in the sciences, in the arts, etc.: there is no other way out of mediocrity.

ℂ There are men who are driven to be first, who must get above the rest at whatever cost. Nothing matters to them as long as they have a prominent place on the charlatan's platform; on a stage, a throne, or a scaffold they will always be quite happy as long as they are the center of attention.

ℂ Men become little as they become alike. They are Milton's devils, forced to become pygmies in order to find room in Pandemonium.

ℂ One obliterates one's character for fear of being noticed and stared at, and flings oneself headlong into nullity to escape the threat of portrayal.

❡ Physical disasters and the calamities of human nature have rendered society necessary. To the miseries of nature, society has added its own. The difficulties of society have evolved the necessity for government, and government has added to the miseries of society. This is the history of human nature.

❡ Ambition seizes upon little souls more easily than upon great ones, as fire catches more easily in straw, in thatched cottages, than in palaces.

❡ Man lives with himself much of the time, and then he needs virtue. When he lives with others, he needs honor.

❡ The fable of Tantalus has been used almost exclusively as an emblem of avarice, but it is at least as applicable to ambition, the love of fame, and virtually all the passions.

❡ Nature, in giving birth at once to reason and to the passions, seems to have wished to help man to alleviate, with her second gift, the harm she did him with the first, and in allowing him only a few years of life after the loss of his passions, she seems to have taken pity on him, relieving him quickly of a life reduced to no resource but reason.

❡ All of the passions lead to exaggeration. That is why they are passions.

❡ The philosopher who wants the passions snuffed out is like the alchemist who wants to do without his fire.

❡ The first of nature's gifts is this force of reason which raises you above your own passions and your weaknesses and puts you in control of your capacities, your talents, and your virtues.

ℂ Why are men such fools, so enslaved by custom and by the dread of making a will, in a word such imbeciles, that they must leave their possessions to those who will rejoice at their deaths, instead of to those who will grieve.

ℂ Nature intended illusions for the wise as well as for fools lest the former should be rendered too miserable by their wisdom.

ℂ To see how patients are treated in hospitals, one would say that man had contrived these dismal resorts not to care for the sick, but to huddle them out of sight of the fortunate, lest these wretches disturb their pleasures.

ℂ In our day, those who love nature are accused of being romantic.

ℂ Tragic drama has the great moral disadvantage of attaching too much importance to life and death.

ℂ That of all days is the most completely wasted in which one did not once laugh.

ℂ Most follies are merely the result of foolishness.

ℂ One betrays one's intelligence, one's conscience, one's understanding, as one ruins one's stomach.

ℂ The principles of secrecy and of the strongbox are the same.

ℂ Often the mind is to the heart merely what the château library is to the lord of the manor.

℀ All that the poets, the orators, and even certain philosophers tell us about the love of fame we were told at school to urge us to win prizes. All that is said to encourage children to prefer the praise of their mentors to a piece of pie is repeated to men to make them consider their personal profit less desirable than the plaudits of their contemporaries and of posterity.

℀ If one wishes to become a philosopher one must not be revolted by the first afflicting discoveries that one makes in one's acquaintance with men. In order to know them, one must overcome the repugnance that they provoke, as the anatomist triumphs over nature, over his own organs and his taste, in order to become adept at his art.

℀ In studying the ills of nature, one acquires a contempt for death. In studying the ills of society, one acquires a contempt for life.

℀ The value of different men is like that of diamonds: given a certain size, purity, and perfection, they have their fixed and marked price. Beyond these measurements they remain priceless, and find no buyers.

Chapter Two

GENERAL MAXIMS: CONTINUED

℀ IN FRANCE everyone seems intelligent, and the reason is simple: Since everything is a series of contradictions, it requires only the slightest attention to notice and connect two contradictory things. This results in quite natural contrasts, which confer upon their discoverers an aura of great intelligence. One has only to recount in order to caricature. The ordinary journalist cannot help writing farce, just as, one day, the historian will seem to be a satirist.

⟮ The public never believes in the purity of certain virtues and certain feelings. And in general the public rises only to the level of base concepts.

⟮ It is not possible for any man, unaided, to be as contemptible as an organization. And it is not possible for an organization to be as contemptible as the public.

⟮ For centuries public opinion has been the worst opinion of all.

⟮ Hope is merely a charlatan who deceives us without end, and for my part happiness begins only when I have lost it. I would gladly inscribe over the gate of Heaven the verse which Dante set over the doors of Hell:

You who enter, leave every hope behind.

⟮ The man who is poor but independent of men is at the command of necessity alone. The man who is rich but dependent may be commanded by another, or others.

⟮ The man whose ambition has miscarried and who lives in despair makes me think of Ixion fastened to his wheel for having embraced a cloud.

⟮ The ill-disposed man of intelligence differs from the good and respectable man of intelligence as the assassin differs from the man of the world who is a practiced swordsman.

⟮ What good is it to appear to have less weaknesses than others, fewer gaps in one's defenses? One is enough, if it is known. One would have to be an Achilles without his heel, and that is what is impossible.

℃ Such is the wretched condition of men that they must turn to
society to allay the harshness of nature, and to nature to comfort
them for the evils of society. How many men have found distraction for their sufferings neither in the one nor in the other!

℃ The most one-sided and absurd suit, which would be con-
temptuously rejected as untenable in a society of self-respecting
men chosen as arbiters, is made the basis of a trial with full legal
ceremony. Every trial can be won or lost; one might just as well
bet for as against. Furthermore, any opinion, any statement, however ridiculous, if it becomes the subject of a debate between two
parties in an assembly or parliament, may well end by gaining a
majority vote.

℃ It is a recognized fact that our century has restored words to
their places; that in banishing scholastic, dialectical, and metaphysical subtleties, it has returned to the simple and the true, in
physics, in ethics, and in politics. To speak only of ethics, one is
aware of the complex and metaphysical ideas contained, for instance, in the word "honor." Our century has recognized the
inconvenience of such complexity, and in order to restore everything to simplicity and prevent the misuse of words, it has established that "honor" was the unalloyed property of every man
who had never been taken into the hands of the law. Before, this
word was a source of equivocations and arguments; now, nothing
could be clearer. Has a man been put in the pillory or has he not?
That is all there is to it. It is a simple question of fact which can
be determined by a glance at the court record. A man who has
not been in the pillory is a man of honor, who can aspire to
anything—to positions in the ministries, etc.; he can belong to
organizations and academies; he can be received at court. It is
obvious how many arguments and disputes are avoided by this
clarity and precision, and how much easier and more convenient
the traffic of life is made.

℃ The love of fame a virtue? Extraordinary virtue which makes
use of the activity of all the vices, which is spurred on by pride,

ambition, envy, vanity and sometimes even avarice! Would Titus be Titus if he had had for his ministers Sejanus, Narcissus, and Tigellinus?

℮ Fame often puts an honest man to the same proofs as wealth. Both, before acquiescing to his suit, force him to do or to endure things unworthy of his character. And so the man of unswerving virtue rejects the one as the other, and wraps himself in obscurity or poverty, and sometimes in both.

℮ He who is exactly midway between our enemy and us seems to be nearer to us than to our enemy. It is an effect of the laws of optics, like that which makes the jet of a fountain seem closer to the far side than to the side where one is standing.

℮ The opinion of the public is a judgment which the honest man should never entirely accept and which he should never reject.

℮ Vain means empty; thus vanity is so poverty-stricken that its own name is the worst thing one can say about it. It makes out to be exactly what it is.

℮ It is commonly believed that the art of pleasing is a great means of achieving wealth; knowing how to be bored is an art which succeeds still better. The talent for acquiring wealth, like the one for succeeding with women, can be reduced practically to that.

℮ There are few men of great character who do not have a strain of the romantic somewhere in the head or the heart. The man in whom there is nothing of the sort, however worthy and however intelligent he may be, is to a great character what an artist who is extremely skillful but does not aspire to the sublime is to an artist who is a man of genius and has made the sublime familiar.

℃ There are certain men in whom virtue shines brighter in private than it would do in any public function. The surroundings would detract from them. The more beautiful the diamond the lighter must be the setting. The richer the setting, the less one notices the diamond.

℃ If one wishes to avoid being a charlatan, one must shun platforms, for if one sets foot on them, a charlatan one must be, otherwise the crowd will throw stones.

℃ There are few vices that will so readily prevent a man from having many friends as will the possession of inordinate talents or virtues.

℃ There are superiorities and pretensions that have only to be ignored to be annihilated, and others that, if unnoticed, are ineffectual.

℃ One would be much advanced in the study of ethics if one could recognize all the traits that distinguish pride from vanity. The first is lofty, calm, arrogant, tranquil, unshakable. The second is base, unsure, shifty, restless, and wavering. The former magnifies a man, the latter inflates him. The former is a source of countless virtues, the latter gives rise to most of the vices and to every deceit. There is a form of pride in which all the commandments of God are comprehended, and a form of vanity which contains the seven deadly sins.

℃ Living is an ailment which is relieved every sixteen hours by sleep. A palliative. Death is the cure.

℃ Nature seems to use men for her purposes without regard to the tools she is employing, rather as tyrants who dispatch those of whom they have made use.

℃ There are two things that one must get used to or one will find life unendurable: the damages of time and the injustices of men.

℃ I can imagine no wisdom without caution. Scripture says, "the fear of the Lord is the beginning of wisdom"; I would have said, "the fear of men."

℃ There are certain faults that protect one from epidemic vices; as it has been remarked that during a plague the sufferers from quartain fever escape the contagion.

℃ The great calamity of the passions is not the torments they cause but the wrongs, the base actions that they lead one to commit, and which degrade men. Without these hindrances the advantages of the passions would far outweigh those of cold reason, which renders no one happy. The passions make a man live; wisdom merely makes him last.

℃ A man of no elevation of spirit could never be good, but merely amiable.

℃ What one needs is to be able to combine opposites: the love of virtue with an indifference to public regard, the love of work with an indifference toward fame, and a regard for one's health with an indifference toward living.

℃ The man who cures a dropsy victim of his thirst does him more good than the man who gives him a barrel of wine. Apply that to riches.

ℂ The malevolent at times commit good actions, as though they wanted to see whether in fact they afford as much pleasure as good people pretend.

℃ If Diogenes were alive now, he would need a shutter for his lantern.

℃ It must be admitted that in order to live happily in the world there are sides of one's soul that must be totally paralyzed.

℃ Fortune and the drapery with which it is surrounded present life as a spectacle in the midst of which any man, however honest, ends by play-acting in spite of himself.

℃ Things are miscellanies; men are patchworks. Ethics and physics are concerned with mixtures. Nothing is simple, nothing is pure.

℃ If the cruel truths, the painful discoveries, the secrets of society that make up the knowledge of a man of the world at the age of forty had been known to him when he was twenty, he would either have fallen into despair or would have set out to corrupt himself; and nevertheless one sees a certain number of wise men who have reached that age, versed in all these matters, thoroughly enlightened, and neither corrupted nor unhappy. Prudence pilots their virtues through the public corruption, and the strength of their characters, together with the insights of a broadly cultivated intelligence, lift them above the distressing perversity of men.

℃ If you want to see to what extent any social calling corrupts men, think of what they are like when they have undergone its influence for a great while, I mean in their old age. Look at an old courtier, an old priest, an old judge, an old solicitor, an old surgeon, etc.

❡ A man without principles is usually also a man without character, for if he had been born with character, he would have felt the need to make principles for himself.

❡ Esteem is worth more than celebrity, respect is worth more than renown, and honor is worth more than fame.

❡ Often vanity has been the motive that has incited a man to display the full energy of his soul. A bit of wood added to a steel point makes a dart; two feathers attached to the wood make an arrow.

❡ The weak are the light infantry of the army of the ill-intentioned. They do more harm than the army itself; they harry and they lay waste.

❡ Some things can more easily be rendered legal than legitimate.

❡ Celebrity: the advantage of being known by those who do not know you.

❡ One is happy to share the benevolence of one's friends toward persons who do not in themselves interest one; but hatred, even when thoroughly justified, is not easily adopted.

❡ A certain man has been dreaded because of his talents, detested because of his virtues; only his character proved reassuring. But what a time it took before justice was done.

❡ In the natural order as in the social order, one must not hope to be more than one can be.

℄ Stupidity would not be totally stupid if it did not go in terror of intelligence. Vice would not be entirely vicious if it did not hate virtue.

℄ It is not true (as Rousseau said, speaking of Plutarch) that the more one thinks the less one feels; but it is true that the more one judges the less one loves. Few men provide one with exceptions to this rule.

℄ Those who defer in everything to the general opinion are like actors who act badly in the hope of applause, when the public's taste is bad. Some of them would be able to act well, if the public's taste were good. An honest man plays his part as well as he can, without a thought for the gallery.

℄ There is a certain pleasure in courage that sets itself above fortune. To scorn money is to dethrone a king. There is a joy in it.

℄ There is a kind of indulgence toward one's enemies that seems mere stupidity rather than goodness or nobility of soul. M. de C——'s, for instance, which to my mind renders him ridiculous. To me he is like Harlequin saying, "You struck me! Well! I'm not angry." One must have the wit to hate one's enemies.

℄ Robinson on his island, deprived of everything and forced to undertake the most onerous labors in order to subsist from day to day, managed to live and even, as he tells us, to taste a few moments of happiness. Suppose his island had been enchanted and furnished with everything that renders life pleasant; idleness might have rendered his existence intolerable.

℄ The ideas of men are like cards and other games. Ideas that at one time, to my own knowledge, were considered dangerous and rash, have since become general, almost commonplace, and have descended to men who are little worthy of them. Some of those that we call daring will seem feeble and ordinary to our descendants.

℃ I have often noticed in my reading that the first gesture of those who have performed some heroic action, who have carried out some generous impulse, who have rescued the unfortunate, run some great risk and acquired some great benefit either for the public or for individuals—I have, I say, noticed that their first gesture has been to refuse the reward that was offered to them. This urge is to be found in the hearts of the most indigent of men and in the most humble of the populace. What is it, then, this moral instinct that informs a man of no education that the reward for his acts is in the heart of him who performs them? Evidently if we are paid for them, this is taken away from us.

℃ A virtuous action, a sacrifice either of one's self-interest or one's self, is necessary to a noble soul, to the self-respect of a generous heart, and in some sense to the egotism of a great character.

℃ The harmony of brothers is so rare that the fable names only two who were friends, and it supposes that they never saw each other, since they went alternately from the earth to the Elysian fields, thus avoiding all possible occasion for dispute and hostility.

℃ There are more fools than wise men, and even in the wise there is more folly than wisdom.

℃ Precepts are to conduct what practice is to the arts.

℃ Conviction is the conscience of the mind.

℀ One is happy or unhappy as the result of a multitude of unseen things which one does not refer to and could not describe.

℀ Pleasure may be based on illusion, but happiness rests on truth. Truth alone can afford us whatever happiness the nature of man is capable of receiving. The man who has been made happy by an illusion is speculating with his fortune; the man who has been made happy by the truth has his fortune in land and sound investments.

℀ There are very few things in the world upon which a self-respecting man can allow his soul or his thought to rest, with pleasure.

℀ When it is maintained that the insensitive, on the whole, are happiest, I remember the Indian proverb: "It is better to be sitting than standing; it is better to be lying down than sitting; it is better to be dead than anything."

℀ Cleverness is to trickery what manual dexterity is to picking pockets.

℀ Obstinacy displays character more or less as a temperament displays love.

℀ Love: agreeable folly. Ambition: serious imbecility.

℀ Prejudice, vanity, scheming, these are what govern the world. He whose only principles of conduct are reason, truth, and sensibility has almost nothing in common with society. It is within himself that he must seek out and find virtually all his happiness.

❡ One must be just before one can be generous, as one must have shirts before one can have lace.

❡ The Dutch have no pity for those who fall into debt. To their minds, a man in debt lives at the expense of his fellow citizens if he is poor, and of his heirs if he is rich.

❡ Fortune is often like rich but extravagant wives, who ruin households to which they have brought rich dowries.

❡ The changing of fashion is the tax that the industry of the poor levies upon the vanity of the rich.

❡ Concern for money is the great test of small natures; but is scarcely a test at all for those who rise above the ordinary; and there is a long way between the man who scorns money and the one who is genuinely honest.

❡ He who is frugal is the richest of men, and the miser is the poorest.

❡ Sometimes two men are drawn together and united for some time by deceptive resemblances of character. But the error is dissipated by degrees, and they are then surprised to discover themselves at some distance from each other, repelled, in a sense, by all their points of contact.

❡ Is it not amusing to consider that the fame of certain great men is the result of their having spent their lives combatting prejudices or stupidities that move one to pity, and should never have found places, obviously, in the human head? Bayle, for instance, is celebrated for having demonstrated the absurdity of philosophical and scholastic subtleties that would have made a peasant of the Gatinais, with his rich endowment of natural common sense, shrug his shoulders. And Locke for having proved that one should not talk about what one does not understand, nor pretend to understand what one does not. And a number of philosophers for having composed heavy volumes against superstitions that would make a Canadian savage flee in contempt. And Montesquieu and several others before him, for having intimated (while respecting a horde of miserable prejudices) that governments are made for the sake of the governed, and not the governed for the sake of governments. If the dream of the philosophers who believe in the perfectability of society is fulfilled, what will posterity say when it sees that such great efforts were necessary to arrive at results so simple and so natural?

¶ A man who is wise as well as honest owes it to himself to complement the purity that satisfies his conscience with the prudence that divines and forsees calumny.

¶ The role of the man who forsees is a sad one. He afflicts his friends with warnings of the misfortunes they court with their imprudence. He is not believed; and when the misfortunes occur, those same friends resent him for the ills he predicted, and their self-regard lowers their eyes before the friend who should be their comforter, and whom they would have chosen if his presence did not humiliate them.

¶ He who tries to make his happiness depend too much on his reason, who holds it up for examination, who quibbles, as it were, with his delights, and admits no indelicate pleasures, ends by having none at all. He is a man who cards the wool of his mattress until nothing is left, and he ends by sleeping on the boards.

¶ Time diminishes what the metaphysicans would call our *absolute* pleasures, but apparently it increases the *relative* ones, and I suspect that this is the artifice that Nature has employed to bind men to life after the loss of the objects or the pleasures that rendered it most agreeable.

⟪ When one has been racked and exhausted by one's own sensibility, one learns that one must live from day to day, forget a great deal, and in short *erase life* as it passes from us.

⟪ False modesty is the most decent of all lies.

⟪ We are told that we should make an effort to reduce our necessities day by day. It is above all to the necessities of self-love that this rule should be applied. They are the most dictatorial, and the ones that we most need to fight against.

⟪ It is not rare to see the faint-hearted, as a result of keeping company with spirits of a more vigorous temper, transcend their own natures. This produces incongruities that are as amusing as a fool's pretensions to wit.

⟪ Virtue is not the sovereign good any more than health is. It is the site of good rather than the good itself. It is more certain that vice renders unhappy than it is that virtue confers happiness. The reason virtue is supremely desirable is because it is the opposite of vice.

Chapter Three

ON SOCIETY, THE GREAT, RICHES, PERSONS OF FASHION

⟪ No ONE ever comes to know the world through books. That has often been said, but what has not been said is the reason, which is this. The knowledge of the world is the result of a thousand delicate observations which one's self-love dares not admit to anyone, even one's best friend. One is afraid of appearing to be someone who concerns himself with trifles, though these same trifles are very important to the success of the greatest affairs.

℃ Reading through the memoirs and literary monuments of the century of Louis XIV, one finds even in the bad company of that age something that is missing in the good of our own.

℃ What is society when it is not sewn together by reason, when the affections lend it no interest, when it is not an exchange of agreeable thoughts and genuine benevolence? A fair, a gambling den, a tavern, a wood, a neighborhood of ill-repute and its addresses: that is all it is, each in turn, for most of those who are its members.

℃ One can imagine the metaphysical edifice of society as a material edifice composed of different niches or compartments of various sizes. The social positions, with their prerogatives, their rights, etc., form those different compartments or niches. They remain, and men pass away. Sometimes the occupants are tall, sometimes short, and none of them, or almost none, fits his place. There you have a giant hunched or squatting in his niche; there you have a dwarf in an arcade: the niche is seldom made for the statue. Around the edifice circles a crowd of men of different sizes. They are all waiting for a niche to fall vacant so that they can occupy it, whatever it is. Each one boasts of his rights—by which he means his birth, or his protectors—to be admitted. And he who tried to obtain the preference by pointing out that a correspondence exists between the niche and the man, the instrument and the sheath, would be greeted with howls. The contestants themselves refrain from accusing an adversary of being a bad fit.

℃ One cannot live in society beyond the age of the passions. It is only tolerable during the period when one is using one's stomach to amuse oneself and one's person to kill time.

❧ The legal profession, the magistrature, know about as much of the affairs of the moment, and what goes on at court, as students who have obtained leave and have dined outside their college know of the world.

❧ Everything that is said at gatherings, in salons, at dinners and public assemblies, in books, even the ones that set out to reveal the nature of society—it is all false or insufficient. One could apply to it the Italian phrase *per la predica* (matter for sermons) or the Latin *ad populum phaleras* (throw your baubles to the crowd). What is true, what is instructive, is what the consciousness of an honest man who has seen much and observed it well relates to his friend as they sit by the fire. A number of conversations of this kind have taught me more than all the books and all the ordinary commerce of society. They set me in the right direction with more assurance, and gave me more to think about.

❧ The influence on our minds of a moral idea that conflicts with physical and material objects can be seen in many circumstances, but never so clearly as when the shift is sudden and unexpected. Go for a walk on the boulevard in the evening. You see a charming garden with a salon at the end of it, lit with taste. You catch sight of groups of pretty women, little groves, and among them a shaded walk winding out of sight, in which you hear laughter. You imagine that those must be nymphs, from the grace of their figures. "Who is that one?" you ask, and you learn, "That is Madame de B——, the lady of the house." As ill luck will have it, it turns out that you know her, and the spell is broken.

❧ When you meet the Baron de Breteuil he regales you with the account of his good fortunes, his crude love affairs, etc., and he ends by showing you a portrait of the queen, in the middle of a rose, set in diamonds.

❧ A fool, proud of some decoration or other, seems to me inferior to that absurd man who, in the course of his pleasures, had his mistress stick peacock feathers into his behind. At least he had the pleasure of . . . But the other! The Baron de Breteuil is far inferior to Peixoto.

℄ One can see from the example of Breteuil that a man can jingle in his pockets the portraits in diamonds of a dozen or more sovereigns, and still be an absolute fool.

℄ He's a fool, he's a fool, it's soon said: See how extreme you are in everything? What does it mean, after all? He mistakes his position for his person, his importance for merit, and his credit for a virtue. But doesn't everyone? Is there really anything in this to exclaim about?

℄ When fools leave office, whether they have been ministers or chief clerks, they retain a lofty manner and a ridiculous pomposity.

℄ Anyone who is intelligent can tell a thousand good stories about the stupidities and servilities which he himself has witnessed; there are a hundred examples. As the source of them is an evil as old as the monarchy, there is no better proof that it is incurable. Judging from a thousand parables that I have heard, I must conclude that if monkeys had the talent of parrots they would readily be made ministers.

℄ There is nothing so difficult to unsettle as a trivial idea or an accepted proverb. Louis XV has been bankrupt some three or four times altogether, and gentlemen swear as roundly as ever by their words as gentlemen. The word of M. de Guimenée[2] could scarcely be better.

---

[2] Nephew of Cardinal de Rohan, who was one of the organizers of the famous Necklace Affair; Guimenée saw his own vast wealth sold off to pay his debts.

℃ Persons of fashion have only to be herded together to fancy that they are in society.

℃ I have seen men betray their own conscience to please another who was wearing the hat of the president of the Assembly or the robe of the Keeper of the Seals. Why be astonished, then, at those who exchange theirs for the hat or the robe itself? All equally vile, and the former more absurd than the latter.

℃ Society is made up of two great classes: those who have more dinners than appetite, and those who have more appetite than dinners.

℃ One gives ten- or twenty-guinea meals to persons in favor, for whose good digestion of the same meals one would not give a shilling a head.

℃ In practicing the arts of raillery and banter, it would be good to make it a principle that the author of the jest, in each case, must be certain of amusing the object of it, and that if the latter is offended, the former is in the wrong.

℃ M—— told me that I had one great misfortune; I did not reckon with the omnipotence of fools. He was right, and I have noticed, on entering some fashionable gathering, that any fool was at a great advantage: that of being among his peers. Each was like Brother Deadweight in the Temple of Nonsense:

> When he arrived he liked it all so well
> He thought himself home in his cloister still!

℃ At times, seeing the petty thieveries of the petty, and the robberies of those in office, one is tempted to regard society as a wood full of thieves, of which the most dangerous are the officers set there to arrest the others.

❦ Persons of fashion and of the court ascribe to men and to things a conventional value and then are astonished at being deceived by it themselves. They are like accountants who, in adding up a column, give the figures a variable and arbitrary value, and then, when they arrive at the total, in which they give them their real and correct value again, are amazed that the sum does not balance.

❦ There are moments when the world seems to be aware of its real worth. I have often noticed its respect for those who had none for it; often a sovereign contempt for it is a recommendation in its eyes, provided the contempt is genuine, sincere, candid, unaffected, and unboastful.

❦ The world is so contemptible that the few decent persons who are to be found in it respect those who despise it and are influenced by the contempt itself.

❦ Court friendship, honesty of foxes, and society of wolves.

❦ I would advise anyone who wished to obtain a favor from a minister to approach him with a mournful air rather than a lighthearted one. No one likes to see those who are happier than himself.

❦ A cruel truth, but one that must be recognized, is that in the world, and especially in the fashionable world, all is artifice, calculation, contrivance, even what appears to be simplicity and the most delightful spontaneity. I have seen men in whom what seemed to have the grace of pure impulse was in fact rehearsed, and came out more nimbly too, however turned and schooled. I have seen the most deliberate contrivance assume the apparent naïveté of the most heedless abandon. This is the studied negligence of the coquette, from which art has banished everything that resembles art. It is troublesome but necessary. In general, woe to the man who, even in his most intimate friendship, reveals his weakness and shows how he can be taken. I have seen the closest friends inflict wounds on the self-respect of those whose secrets they had discovered by surprise. In the present state of society (I am speaking, in all this, of the fashionable world) it seems that it would be impossible for a single man to reveal the depths of his soul, the details of his character, and above all his weakness, to his best friend. One must (in this same world) carry refinement so far that it can never be so much as suspected, were it only to avoid being despised as a bad actor in a troop of excellent comedians.

ℭ Those who imagine that they love a prince at the moment when they receive some mark of his favor make me think of children who wish to be priests the day after a gorgeous procession, or soldiers the day after they have seen a parade.

ℭ Court favorites and those in power at times show a disposition to attach to themselves persons of merit, but they require a preliminary debasement which repels to a great distance all those who have any shame. I have known men whom a favorite or a minister might have had cheaply, as outraged by this propensity as though they had been men of spotless virtue. One of them said to me, "The great expect one to degrade oneself not for profit but for a hope. They expect to buy one not with a prize but with a lottery ticket. I know swindlers who look as though they were enjoying their bounty, when in fact they have done no better than if they had been the most honest folk in the world."

ℭ Useful acts, however spectacular, or the most genuine and important services that could possibly be rendered to the nation and to the court itself, if they do not find favor at court are merely what the theologians call splendid sins.

ℭ Few have any idea how much wit it takes never to be ridiculous.

℃ Any man who lives much in the world convinces me that he is insensitive, for I see almost nothing there that can interest the heart, or rather nothing that does not tend to harden it: one has only to consider the callousness, frivolity, and vanity that govern the place.

℃ When princes set aside their miserable ceremony it is never for someone of merit, but for a whore or a clown. When women are frank it is almost never to a worthy man, but rather to a *species*. In general, when someone breaks the yoke of opinion it is seldom in order to rise above it, almost always in order to fall below it.

℃ There are errors of conduct that are no longer committed in our day, or far less frequently than they used to be. We have grown so refined that even a boor, with a little reflection, can make up with wit what he lacks in soul, and avoid certain basenesses which at one time might have proven successful. I have observed disreputable men at times maintain a proud and decent bearing in the presence of a prince or a minister, refuse to be intimidated, etc. This deceives the young and inexperienced, who do not know, or else forget, that a man must be judged by the sum of his principles and his character.

℃ When one sees how the social conventions seem to have been contrived to exclude merit from all the posts in which it might have been useful to society, and examines the alliance of imbeciles against persons of intelligence, one has the impression that one is watching valets conspiring to undo their masters.

℃ What does a young man find when he enters the world? Those who wish to protect him, pretend to *honor* him, govern him, advise him. I am not speaking of those who wish to mislead him, harm him, ruin him, or cheat him. If his character is sufficiently elevated for him to want to be protected by nothing but his own manners, to be honored in nothing nor by anyone, to govern himself by his principles and advise himself according to his own lights, by his character, and in keeping with the position which he knows better than anyone, there will be no lack of insistence that he is eccentric, peculiar, and intractable. But if he has little intelligence, no elevation of character to speak of, few principles, he does not notice that he is being protected, or that anyone wishes to have control over him, and if he becomes the instrument of those who take him up he is pronounced charming, and is, as they say, the most agreeable child in the world.

℄ Society, which is called the world, is nothing but the contention of a thousand clashing petty interests, an eternal conflict of all the vanities that cross each other, strike against each other, are wounded and humiliated by each other in turn, and expiate on the morrow, in the bitterness of defeat, the triumph of the day before. To live alone, to avoid the bruises of wretched serapes in which one attracts all eyes one minute only to be trampled on the next, is to be what they call nothing, to have no existence. Poor humanity!

℄ There is a certain profound insensibility to the virtues that is more startling and far more shocking than vice itself. Those whom the public in its baseness calls the powers that be, or the great, those in office, seem for the most part to be endowed with this odious insensibility. Is not this the result of a vague and ill-developed notion that they have, that men who possess those virtues are not fitted to be instruments of intrigue? They neglect those men as being useless to themselves and to others, in a country in which, without intrigue, deception, and falsehood, one can accomplish nothing.

℄ What does one see in the world? Everywhere a naïve and sincere respect for absurd conventions, for some nonsense or other (the fools salute their queen) or else the precautions necessitated by this same nonsense (persons of intelligence go in dread of their tyrant).

ℂ The bourgeois, out of a ridiculous vanity, make of their daughters a manure for the lands of persons of quality.

ℂ Imagine twenty men, even decent and honest men, all of whom know and respect one man of recognized merit, Dorilas, for instance; praise, extol his gifts and his virtues, about which everyone is agreed. One of those present adds, "What a pity he is so little favored by fortune." "What do you mean?" another answers. "It's just that his modesty makes him live without luxury. Are you not aware that he has an income of twenty-five thousand *livres* a year?" "Really?" "Indeed; I have proof." Then let this same man appear and compare his welcome in their society with the cool albeit distinguished manner in which he had been received before. This is what he did; he made the comparison, and sighed. But among them there happened to be one man whose demeanor toward him remained the same. "One in twenty," said our philosopher. "I am content."

ℂ What a life most courtiers lead! They permit themselves to be bored, importuned, debased, made use of, and tormented, for miserable ends. In order to live and be happy, they await the deaths of their enemies, of the rivals to their ambition, even of those whom they call their friends; and while they invoke this death with their wishes, they themselves dry up, they wither and die, asking for news of the health of Monsieur So-and-so or Madame So-and-so, who insists on remaining alive.

ℂ Whatever nonsense may have been written by certain physiognomists of our day, it is certain that our habits of thought can affect particular traits of our physiognomy. Many are the courtiers whose eye is false for the same reason that most tailors are knock-kneed.

ℂ It may not be true that great fortunes always imply intelligence, as I have often heard said by people of intelligence; but it is far truer that there are concentrations of intelligence and cleverness from which fortune cannot escape, even when the possessor of them is endowed with the purest of honesty, an obstacle which, as one knows, fortune finds the most forbidding of all.

℃ When Montaigne said of nobility, "Since we cannot achieve it let us avenge ourselves by speaking ill of it," he said something amusing, something which is often true, but appalling; something which gives arms to those fools whom fortune has favored. Often the hatred of inequality is inspired by nothing but pettiness of spirit, but it would be possible for a man who was genuinely wise and honest to hate it because he saw it as the barrier that separates souls that were made to understand each other. There are few men of any distinction of character who have not had to deny themselves feelings inspired in them by someone or other of a superior rank, and have not repulsed, at the cost of their own pain, some friendship or other which should have been a source of delight and solace. Any of these, instead of repeating Montaigne's phrase, might say, "I detest that nobility which made me avoid what I loved, or could have loved."

℃ Is there anyone whose acquaintances are without exception creditable? Who is there who does not see someone for whom he must make excuses to his friends? Is there any woman who has never been in the position of having to explain to the assembled company the visit of some woman or other whom one would not have expected to find under her roof?

℃ Are you the friend of some courtier, or as they say, some man of quality, and do you wish to arouse in him the liveliest attachment of which the human heart is capable? Do not be content with lavishing on him all the solicitude of the tenderest friendship, soothing his woes, allaying his sufferings, consecrating to him all your time and vindicating his honor or saving his life; do not waste your time on such trifles. Go further; do better; draw up his genealogy.

℃ You imagine that a minister, a man in office, has some principle or other, and you imagine this because you have heard him say it. And therefore you refrain from asking of him some favor or other which would be inconsistent with his favorite maxim. You soon learn that you have been deceived, and you see him doing things that prove to you that a minister has no principles at all, but is moved by habit and the tic of saying some particular thing.

℃ A number of courtiers are hated without gaining anything by it, simply for the pleasure of being hated. They are lizards that have got nothing by climbing except the loss of their tails.

℃ Degrade themselves as they will, institutions (parliaments, academies, assemblies) sustain themselves by sheer bulk, and no one can do anything against them. Dishonor and ridicule slide off them like musket balls off the hide of a boar or a crocodile.

℃ At the sight of what goes on in the world, the most misanthropic of men must end by being amused, and Heraclitus must die laughing.

℃ It seems to me that if they were equal in intelligence and enlightenment, a man born rich would never be able to acquire as profound an understanding of the human heart and of society as would a man born poor. For where the former could afford a pleasure, the latter must console himself with a reflection.

℃ At the sight of princes performing of their own free will certain decent actions, one is tempted to blame most of their errors and weaknesses on those around them; one says to oneself, "What a pity that this prince has friends such as Damis and Aramont!" One quite forgets that if Damis or Aramont had had any genuine nobility or character, they would not have been this prince's friends.

❡ As soon as philosophy makes a bit of progress, foolishness redoubles its efforts to consolidate the empire of prejudice. Consider how the government favors every notion that has to do with birth and breeding. Until it has reached the point where there are only two classes of women: women of quality and women of pleasure; the rest are nothing. No virtue can raise a woman above her station; only vice can remove her from it.

❡ To acquire fortune and distinction in spite of the disadvantage of having no ancestors, and to do it in the midst of that crowd who received everything at birth, is like winning, or stale-mating a game of chess after giving one's adversary a rook, or castle. Often the others have too many conventional advantages over you, so that there is nothing for it but to concede the game. One can manage without a castle, but not without the queen.

❡ Those who bring up princes and pretend to give them a good education after first grounding them in their formalities and their degrading etiquettes are like teachers of arithmetic trying to produce great calculators after having persuaded their students that three and three make eight.

❡ Who is most foreign to those about him? A Frenchman in Peking or Macao? A Lapp in Senegal? Or might it not be, perhaps, a man of merit but with no money and no title, surrounded by those who have one or the other, or perhaps both of these advantages at once? Is it not remarkable how society proceeds with its tacit agreement to exclude from a share in its rights nineteen-twentieths of society itself?

❡ The world and society are like a library in which at first sight everything appears to be in order because the books are arranged according to the format and size of the volumes, but in which everything turns out to be in disorder because nothing is arranged according to its field of knowledge, its subject, or its author.

℃ The fact that one has distinguished and even illustrious friends can no longer be a recommendation for anyone in a country in which one pleases, frequently, with one's vices, and is sometimes sought out for one's silliness.

℃ There are men who are not especially likable themselves but do not prevent others from being so. They are endurable, from time to time. There are others who are not only not agreeable themselves, but their mere presence is enough to spoil the sociable inclinations of others; these, on the other hand, are insupportable, and illustrate the great nuisance of pedantry.

℃ Experience, which enlightens private individuals, corrupts princes and those in office.

℃ The public in our day is like modern tragedy: absurd, atrocious, and flat.

℃ The courtier practices a trade which he has tried to make into a science. Everyone tries to better himself.

℃ Most relations in society—camaraderies, etc.—are to friendship what cavalier-servantism is to love.

℃ The art of parenthesis is one of the great secrets of eloquence in society.

℃ At court everyone is a courtier: the prince of the blood, the week's chaplain, the local surgeon, the apothecary.

℃ Magistrates who are responsible for public order—the Criminal Prosecutor, for instance, the Civil Prosecutor, the Chief of

Police, and many others, almost invariably develop a horrible view of society. They think they know mankind and they know only the dregs. One does not judge a city by its sewers nor a house by its latrines. Most of these magistrates remind me constantly of the school where the monitors have a little hut beside the conveniences, from which they emerge only to apply the rod.

℃ It is raillery that should mete out justice to all the wrongs of men and of society. It saves us from being compromised. It allows us to put everything into place without leaving our own. It attests to our superiority over the things and the persons that are the objects of our ridicule, without their being able to take offense unless they lack humor or manners. The reputation for being able to handle this weapon skillfully earns, for the man of no distinction of birth, the same sort of consideration in the world and in the best company that the military accords to those who handle the sword particularly well. I have heard a man of wit say, "Strip raillery of its sovereignty and I will give up society tomorrow." It is a sort of duel in which no blood is shed, and which, like the other sort, renders men more circumspect and more polite.

℃ No one suspects, at a mere glance, how much harm it does to aspire to the common phrase of approval, "M. So-and-so is most agreeable." It happens, I am not sure how, that there is a sort of facility, of carelessness, of weakness, which is very winning, when these qualities are found mixed with wit; and that the man with whom one can do what one will, who belongs to the moment, is more agreeable than the one who is consistent, who has character and principles, does not forget his sick or absent friend, and is able to leave a pleasant gathering in order to do him a service, etc. It would make a dreary list if one were to set down all the faults, errors, and transgressions that please. And so it is that the worldly, who have given the art of pleasing more thought than is supposed, and more than they themselves imagine, have more of these faults than anyone, all arising from having to have it said of themselves, "M. So-and-so is most agreeable."

℄ There are things that a well-born young man would never be able to imagine. How, at the age of twenty, could he know to be suspicious of a police spy wearing the red sash of the Order of St. Louis?

℄ The most absurd conventions, the most ridiculous formalities enjoy in France and elsewhere the protection of the phrase, "It's the custom." It is the very phrase with which the Hottentots answer when the Europeans ask them why they eat grasshoppers, why they devour the vermin that crawl on them. They too say, "It's the custom."

℄ The most absurd and unjust pretension, which would be hissed down in any assembly of honest men, can become the subject of a suit at law and in due course be legitimized; for every suit can be won or lost, just as, in assemblies, the silliest and most ridiculous opinion can be admitted, and the wisest counsel rejected with scorn. To have defenders, a thing has only to be made a party principle, and nothing could be easier when most assemblies are divided into opposing parties.

℄ What is an ass without his asininity? Take the wings off a butterfly and you have a grasshopper.

℄ Courtiers are poor men who have become rich by begging.

℄ It is easy to reduce to simple terms the exact value of celebrity. Anyone who becomes known for some talent or some virtue exposes himself to the inactive benevolence of a few good persons and to the active malice of all the other sort. Count the two categories and weigh up the two forces.

℄ Few can love a philosopher. He is almost a public enemy who confronts the different pretensions of men and the mendacity of things and says to each man and each thing, "I take you only for what you are; I appreciate you only at your worth." It is not the easiest thing in the world to be loved and esteemed when one has announced that this is one's firm intention.

℃ When one is too forcibly struck by the evils of society and by the horrors that are everywhere visible in the capitals and the large cities, one must say to oneself, "Worse calamities than these could have been engendered by the series of arrangements that has made twenty-five million men the subjects of one, and has assembled seven hundred thousand men in an area of two square leagues."

℃ Qualities that are too far above the average often render a man less fitted for society. One does not go to market with gold bars but with silver coin and small change.

℃ Society, its different circles, its salons, all that is called the world, is a wretched play, a bad opera, without interest; insofar as it keeps our attention at all, it does so with its machinery and its decorations.

℃ In order to view things correctly, one must give words the opposite sense to the one the world gives them. Misanthrope, for instance, means philanthrope; bad Frenchman means good citizen, which implies certain monstrous abuses; philosopher means, "a simple man, who knows that two and two make four, etc."

℃ In our day a painter will do your portrait in seven minutes, another will teach you to paint in three days, a third will teach you English in forty lessons. They propose to teach you eight languages with pictures that represent the objects and their names under them in the eight languages. If it were finally possible to gather up the pleasures, the feelings, and the ideas of a whole life and huddle them into the space of twenty-four hours it would be done; they would get you to swallow the pill and then say, "Now, be off with you."

⟨ One must not regard Burrhus as an absolutely virtuous man. He was so only by contrast with Narcissus. Seneca and Burrhus were the honest men of a century that had none.

⟨ When one wishes to charm, in society, one must resign oneself to being taught many things that one knows by people who do not know them.

⟨ If one only half knows a man, one does not know him at all. If one knows only three quarters of a thing, one is completely ignorant of it. These two considerations are enough to allow one to assess almost all of the statements that are propounded in society.

⟨ In a country where everyone is trying to be noticed, many must believe, and indeed do believe, that it is better to be bankrupt than to be nothing.

⟨ The threat of the neglected cold is for doctors what Purgatory is for priests: a gold mine.

⟨ Conversations are like travel by sea: we move away from the land almost without noticing it, and become aware that we have left the shore only when it is already some way off.

⟨ A man of intelligence maintained in the company of several very rich men that one could be happy on an annual income of two thousand crowns. They argued the contrary with asperity and even some passion. When he left them, he tried to think of the cause of such harshness in persons who he knew were dis-

posed to be his friends. He found it at last. His contention had
proved to them that he was not dependent on them. Any man
whose needs are few seems to threaten the rich with the possibility of his escaping them. Tyrants are thereby faced with the
prospect of losing a slave. One can apply this reflection generally
to all the passions. A man who has overcome his weakness for
love evinces an indifference which women never fail to find odious. They lose interest in him at once. Perhaps it is for this same
reason that no one troubles himself about the fortune of a philosopher: a man who lacks those passions that move society. Everyone becomes aware of being able to add almost nothing to his
happiness, and he is left as he is.

ℂ It is dangerous for a philosopher who is in the service of one
of the rich and powerful (if the rich and powerful ever have
philosophers in their service) to reveal his full disinterest. He
would be taken literally. He must hide his true feelings, and he is,
as one might say, one of nature's hypocrites.

Chapter Four

ON THE TASTE FOR RETIREMENT, AND ON DIGNITY OF CHARACTER

ℂ A PHILOSOPHER LOOKS upon "a place in the world" as Tartars
look upon cities: as a prison. It is a circle in which the ideas
shrink, draw together, meanwhile robbing the soul and the mind
of breadth and development. A man whose place in the world is
large has a larger and more ornate prison. He whose place is small
has a cell. The man who has none is free, provided he has means,
or at least is not dependent on men.

ℂ The most modest of men, if he lives in the world, should have
a thoroughly assured livelihood, to prevent anyone from taking
advantage of him. Then his pride can be the ornament of his
modesty.

℃ Weakness of character or lack of ideas, in a word all the things that can prevent us from living with ourselves, are what save many from becoming misanthropic.

℃ One is happier in solitude than one is in the world. Is that not because in solitude one thinks about things, whereas in the world one has to think about men?

℃ The thoughts of a man who lives in solitude, a man of sense even if rather ordinary, would be inconsiderable indeed if they were not worth at least as much as what is said and done in the world.

℃ A man who maintains both his reason and his integrity (or at least his fastidiousness) inflexible despite the weight of all the absurd and dishonest conventions of society, who never bends on the occasions when it would be to his interest to do so, infallibly ends with no one taking his part, and no friend but an abstract being called virtue, who will let you die of hunger.

℃ One must not be limited to being able to live only with those who are able to appreciate one. That would bespeak a too diffi-cult, delicate, and critical self-regard. But one must not lay the foundations of one's daily life among any except those who can prize one according to one's true worth. Even the philosopher does not condemn this sort of self-regard.

℃ Sometimes it is said of a man who lives alone, "He does not like society." Often it is as though one were to say that a man did not like walking because he would not willingly walk at night in the forest of Bondy.

℃ Is it absolutely certain that a man whose reason was wholly undeviating, whose moral sense was absolutely fastidious, could live with anyone? By live I do not mean occupy the same place without fighting, I mean delight each other, love each other, deal pleasantly with each other.

℀ A man of intelligence is lost if his intelligence is not combined with energy of character. When one has Diogenes' lantern one also needs his stick.

℀ No one has more enemies in the world than the man who is honest, proud, and sensitive, with an inclination to leave persons and things as they are instead of taking them for what they are not.

℀ The world hardens most men's hearts. But those hearts that are less susceptible of being hardened are obliged to make for themselves a factitious insensibility, to avoid becoming the dupes of men, or of women. The feeling with which an honest man comes away after several days given up to society is usually troubled and sad. Its only advantage is the pleasure it lends to retirement.

℀ The public's ideas are seldom anything but vile and base. As it relishes nothing but scandals and acts of flagrant indecency, it splashes all the events and talk that come its way with those same colors. Show it an attachment of the noblest kind between a great lord and a person of merit, between a man in office and a private person, and what does it see? In the first case a protector and a client, and in the second calculation and informing. In an act of generosity, undertaken in noble and moving circumstances, it often sees only money lent to a clever man by a dupe. In the making public of what is often a most touching passion between a virtuous woman and a man worthy of love, it sees nothing but abandon and debauchery. These judgments have been determined in advance by the great number of cases in which there was cause for condemnation and scorn. It is plain, from these observations, that the decent and honest will be better off if they can avoid the public altogether.

❡ Nature did not say to me, "Do not be poor"; still less, "Be rich"; but she cried out to me, "Be independent."

❡ The philosopher gives himself out to be someone who prizes men only at their proper worth, when it is perfectly clear that this form of assessment pleases no one.

❡ The man of the world, the friend of fortune, even the lover of glory, mark out for themselves a straight line that leads them to an unknown end. The sage, the lover of himself, describes a circle, whose extremity brings him back to himself. It is the "rounded ball over which everything glides" of which Horace speaks.

❡ There is no reason to be surprised at J. J. Rousseau's preference for solitude; souls such as his are given to being alone, to living in isolation, like the eagle; but like him also, the scope of their view and the height of their soaring are the delights of their solitude.

❡ He who has no character is not a man but a thing.

❡ The "myself" of Medea[3] has been called sublime, but he who cannot say it in all the circumstances of life amounts to little, or rather, he is nothing.

❡ One does not know at all the man whom one does not know well; but few men are worth studying. It follows that a man of genuine merit should, as a general thing, show no great inclination for being known. He realizes that few are capable of appreciating him, and that of this small number each one has his attachments, his interests, his self-regard, which prevent him

[3] Corneille, *Medea,* Act I, sc. V, v. 320
Nerine: In so great a calamity what remains to you?
Medea: Myself.

from granting to merit the attention that would be needed to judge it correctly. As for the ordinary eulogies that are proffered when anyone suspects its existence, it would be impossible for merit to find these flattering.

℃ When a man has risen by means of his own character to the point where, in justice to him, one should be able to predict how he will behave in all circumstances in which honesty could participate, he is studiously disparaged and shunned not only by swindlers but by the semihonest as well. Furthermore, the honest sort, who have been convinced by his fidelity to his principles that they will find him in all circumstances in which they may need him, permit themselves to neglect him, and attend instead to assuring themselves of those whom they still doubt.

℃ Almost all men are slaves, for the reason that the Spartans gave for the servitude of the Persians: the inability to pronounce the syllable "no." The ability to pronounce this word, and the ability to live to oneself, are the only two ways of preserving one's liberty and one's character.

℃ When a man has made up his mind to see only those with whom he can discuss morality, virtue, reason, and truth, while regarding conventions, vanities, ceremonies, as nothing but the props of civil society—when, I say, he has made up his mind to do this (and he must, or brand himself foolish, feeble, or base) he ends by living virtually in solitude.

℃ Any man who is certain of the nobility of his feelings has the right to act in accord with his character rather than with his position, in order to obtain the treatment he deserves.

Chapter Five

THOUGHTS ON MORALITY

℃ THE PHILOSOPHERS RECOGNIZE four cardinal virtues from which according to them, all the others derive. These virtues are justice, moderation, strength, and prudence. One might say that this last reinforces the first two, justice and temperance, and that to some degree it can take the place of force, in sparing a man who is so unfortunate as to be ill-provided with that virtue many of the occasions that require it.

℃ Moralists, like those philosophers who have constructed systems of physics or metaphysics, have overgeneralized, and laid down too many maxims. What, for instance, becomes of that phrase of Tacitus, "A woman who has lost her modesty will not be able to refuse anything afterward," when confronted with the examples of so many women whom a moment of weakness has not prevented from practicing a number of virtues. I have seen Madame de L——, after a youth which differed little from that of Manon Lescaut, conceive in her riper years a passion worthy of Heloise. But it would be rash to uphold in books the morality of these examples. One must simply note them so as not to be taken in by the moralists and their mountebanks' tricks.

℃ In society, bad behavior has been purified of everything that would offend good taste; the reform is a thing of the last ten years.

℃ The soul, when sick, behaves just as the body does: It torments itself and flings itself about, but in the end it finds a bit of calm. It comes to rest at last in feelings and ideas of the kind that are necessary to its repose.

❡ There are men to whom illusions about the things that interest them are as necessary as life itself. Even so, their perceptions would make one think, at times, that they were near the truth; but they retreat at once, like children who chase a man in a mask and run away if he turns around.

❡ The feeling we have for most benefactors is like our gratitude to those who pull our teeth. We tell ourselves that they have done us good, that they have saved us from something bad, but we remember the pain they caused us, and no longer love them with any tenderness.

❡ A tactful benefactor should realize that there is, in the gift he confers, a material side, which he must prevent the object of it from noticing. Any reminder of it should be, as it were, swallowed up, enveloped in the feeling that prompted the giving, just as, between two lovers, the idea of pleasure is enveloped and ennobled in the charm that gave it birth.

❡ Every gift that is not dear to the heart is odious. It is a relic, a dead man's bone. One must find a setting for it or trample it under foot.

❡ Most benefactors who pretend to be anonymous hide, after conferring their gifts, in the manner of Virgil's Galatea, "who fled, but first made sure that she was seen."

❡ It is generally said that we become attached to our benefactors. It is a kindness of Nature. It is only just that love should be the reward for doing good.

❡ Calumny is like some annoying wasp, against which one must make no move unless one is sure of killing it, or else it will return to the charge more furiously than ever.

℃ The new friends we make after a certain age, in the hopes of replacing those whom we have lost, are to our old friends what glass eyes, false teeth, and wooden legs are to real eyes, natural teeth, and legs of flesh and blood.

℃ Sometimes in the naïvetés of a gifted child there is a pleasant philosophy.

℃ Most friendships are hedged round with "ifs" and "buts" and become in the end mere associations that subsist on unspoken assumptions.

℃ Between the ways of the Ancients and our own there is the same relation that there is between Aristides, the treasurer of Athens, and the Abbé Terray.

℃ The human species, evil by nature, has become more so through society. Each man has certain faults: first, those that are common to all men; second, those that are peculiarly his own; third, those of his class in the social order. These faults grow worse with time, and each man, as he advances in age, and suffers from the faults of others, and from his own, conceives for humanity and for society a contempt which can be turned on them alone.

℃ Happiness is like watches. The least complicated give the least trouble. The repeater is less dependable. If it shows the minutes as well, that is one more thing to go wrong. Those that show the day of the week and the month of the year are even more likely to be continually out of order.

℃ All is equally vain in men—their joys and their griefs. But it is better for the soap bubble to be golden or azure than for it to be black or grayish.

℧ He who disguises tyranny, patronage, or even generosity under the name and manner of friendship reminds me of that villainous priest who used his communion wafer to administer poison.

℧ There are few benefactors who do not say, as Satan did, "All these things will I give thee if thou wilt fall down and worship me."

℧ Poverty keeps down the price of crime.

℧ The Stoics are a race of visionaries who extend poetic exaltation and enthusiasm into morality.

℧ If it were possible for someone, without using intelligence, to feel the grace, the delicacy, the scope, and the different intellectual qualities of another, and to show that he felt them, the society of such a person, though it produced nothing else, would nevertheless be highly sought after. Same result if one makes the same supposition with regard to spiritual qualities.

℧ In observing or enduring the sufferings that are bound up with extremes of feeling, whether in love or friendship, whether through the death of a loved one, or the hazards of life, one is tempted to believe that dissipation and frivolity are not as foolish as they are made out to be, and that life is worth no more than the worldly make of it.

℧ In certain impassioned friendships one enjoys the happiness of the passions and the approbation of reason as well.

℧ Fervent and delicate friendship is often injured by the opening of a rose.

℀ Generosity is simply the pity of noble souls.

℀ Enjoy and give pleasure, without doing harm to yourself or to anyone else—that, I think, is the whole of morality.

℀ For men who are genuinely honest and have certain principles, the Commandments of God were graven in an abridged form over the gate of the Abbaye de Thelème: *Do what you please.*

℀ Education should be constructed on two bases: morality and prudence. Morality in order to assist virtue, and prudence in order to defend you against the vices of others. In tipping the scales toward morality, you merely produce dupes and martyrs. In tipping it the other way, you produce egotistical schemers. The principle of all society is to do justice to oneself and to others. If one should love one's neighbor as oneself, it is at least equally just to love oneself as one does one's neighbor.

℀ Nothing except absolute friendship develops all the qualities of soul and mind in certain persons. Ordinary society gives them scope to unfold only a few graces. They are beautiful fruits which fully ripen only in the sun, and which would have produced only a few charming but useless leaves in the greenhouse.

℀ When I was young, with the urgencies of the passions drawing me into the world, forced to seek in society and in pleasure a few distractions from real sufferings, they preached to me about the love of retirement, of work; I was belabored with pedantic sermons on the subject. Having reached the age of forty and lost the passions that render society endurable, seeing nothing in it any longer but wretchedness and futility, no longer needing company in order to escape from sufferings that no longer exist, my taste for retirement and work has become very lively and replaced all the rest. I have stopped going out into society, and now they never give up importuning me to go back to it. I have been accused of being a misanthrope, etc. What am I to conclude from this incongruous change? That men have an urge to criticize everything.

℄ I study only what I like; I occupy my mind only with the ideas that interest me. They may or may not prove useful, either to me or to others. Time either will or it will not bring about the circumstances that will lead me to a profitable employment of my acquisitions. In any case I will have had the inestimable advantage of not having been at odds with myself, and of having obeyed the promptings of my own mind and character.

℄ I have destroyed my passions rather as a violent man kills his horse, because he cannot control it.

℄ The first occasions of grief armored me against those that followed.

℄ I retain for M. de la B—— the feeling that a decent man feels when passing the tomb of a friend.

℄ To be sure I have cause to complain of things and perhaps of men, but I hold my tongue about the latter. I confine my complaints to things, and if I avoid men, it is because I prefer not to live among those who make things a burden to me.

℄ Fortune, in order to arrive at me, will have to conform to certain conditions imposed on it by my character.

℄ When my heart has need of tenderness, I recall the loss of friends who are mine no longer, the women whom death has taken from me; I live in their coffins, I send my soul to wander around theirs. Alas, I have three tombs!

℃ When I have performed some good action, and it has been discovered, I feel that I have been punished, not rewarded.

℃ In renouncing the world and fortune, I have found happiness, tranquility, health, even wealth; and whatever the proverb says, I conclude that he who leaves the game wins it.

℃ Celebrity is the scourge of merit and the punishment of talent. Mine, such as it is, seems to me no better than an informer, born to trouble my rest. In destroying it I experience the joy of overcoming an enemy. Sensibility, in me, has overcome even self-regard; and literary vanity has perished in the destruction of the interest which I took in men.

℃ Delicate and true friendship cannot bear to have any other feeling mixed with it. I consider it a great happiness that the friendship between M—— (Mirabeau) and me was already perfect when I had occasion, recently, to render him a service, which I alone could do. If everything that he has done for me could have been tainted with the suspicion of having been prompted by the hope of finding me as he did in this circumstance, if it had been possible for him to predict it, my life would have been irrevocably poisoned.

℃ My whole life is a fabric of apparent contrasts with my principles. I have no love for princes, and I am attached to a princess and a prince. I am known for my republican maxims, and several of my friends wear decorations presented by the monarchy. I love voluntary poverty, and I live with the rich. I flee from honors, and one or two have sought me out. Literature is almost my only comfort and I do not keep company with wits nor attend the Academy. Add to this that I believe that illusions are necessary for men, and I live with none; that I believe that passions are of more use than reason, and I no longer know what they are, etc.

℃ What I have learned, I no longer know. The little that I still know, I have guessed.

℃ One of the great misfortunes of man is that even his good qualities are sometimes of no use to him, and that the art of using them and controlling them properly is often a late fruit of experience.

℃ Indecision and anxiety are to the spirit and the soul what examination by torture is to the body.

℃ The honest man disabused of his illusions is man at his best. However limited his intelligence, his company is extremely pleasant. It would be inconceivable for him to be pedantic, since he attaches no importance to anything. He is indulgent, remembering that he once had illusions himself, as others still do. His coolness results in a sure hand in business; he allows himself to be neither repetitive nor fretful. If someone else, in conversing with him, is either of these, he forgets it or dismisses it. Usually he is more amusing than the next person, since he is continually coining epigrams about his neighbor. He is in the right, and he laughs at the gropings and stumblings of those who are in the wrong. He is a man who can see with an enlightened vision, in a dark room, the ridiculous gestures of those who are walking at random in there. He breaks, with a laugh, the false weights and measures that are applied to men and things.

℃ One is frightened by violent points of view, but they are suited to strong souls, and vigorous characters find rest in extremes.

℃ The contemplative life is often miserable. One must act more, think less, and not watch oneself live.

℃ Man can aspire to virtue; he cannot reasonably pretend to find truth.

℃ The Jansenism of the Christians is the stoicism of the pagans, defaced and rendered available to the Christian populace; and this sect has been defended by Pascals and Arnauds!

Chapter Six

OF WOMEN, OF LOVE, OF MARRIAGE, AND OF GALLANTRY

℃ I AM ASHAMED of your opinion of me. I have not always been such a Romeo as I now seem to you. If I were to tell you of three or four episodes from my youth, you would see that they were none too savory and were quite worthy of the best company.

℃ Love is a feeling which, to appear honest, must be made up of nothing but itself, and live and subsist by its own means entirely.

℃ Whenever I see infatuation in a woman, or indeed in a man, I begin to suspect their sensibilities. This rule has never failed me.

℃ With the feelings, what can be evaluated is of no value.

℃ Love is like epidemic diseases. The more one fears it the more likely one is to contract it.

℄ A man in love is a man who wishes to be more attractive than it is possible for him to be, which is why almost all lovers are ridiculous.

℄ One could name a woman who has made herself wretched for life and braved loss and dishonor for a lover whom she subsequently ceased to love because he removed his powder or trimmed a fingernail badly, or put on his stocking wrong side out.

℄ A proud and honest soul that has felt strong passions flees them, fears them, scorns gallantry, as that soul that has felt friendship scorns ordinary attachments and petty interests.

℄ It is sometimes asked why women make a display of men. Several explanations have been given, most of them unflattering to men. The real one is that they cannot otherwise exercise their powers over them.

℄ Women of the middle ranks of society whose hope or obsession it is to be something in the world enjoy the advantages of neither nature nor opinion. They are the most wretched creatures I have known.

℄ Society, which greatly shrinks men, reduces women to almost nothing.

℄ Women have fantasies, infatuations, sometimes tastes. They can even rise to passions; what they are less susceptible to is attachment. They are made to traffic with our weaknesses, with our folly, but not with our reason. Between them and men there are sympathies of the epidermis, and very few sympathies of intelligence, soul, and character. This is proved by the small account women take of a man of forty. I mean even those who are themselves nearly that age. Note that when they accord him a preference it is nearly always after discreditable considerations, after a weighing up of interest or vanity, so that the exception proves the rule. Let us add that the axiom "He who proves too much proves nothing" is not applicable here.

℄ Love seduces us through our self-love. Ah, how can we resist a feeling that increases our admiration for what we have, restores to us what we have lost, and gives us what we do not have?

℄ When a man and a woman have a violent passion for each other, it always seems to me that, whatever obstacles may separate them, a husband, relatives, etc., they belong to each other "by nature," "by divine right," despite human laws and conventions.

℄ Remove self-love from love, and not much would be left. Once purged of vanity, it is a frail convalescent that can scarcely drag itself about.

℄ Love as it exists in society is merely the mingling of two fantasies and the contact of two skins.

℄ One is told occasionally, to encourage one to frequent some woman or other, "She is very loveable." But what if I do not wish to love her! It would be better to say, "She is very loving," because there are more who want to be loved than who want to love.

℄ If one wants to form an idea of the self-love of women in their youth, one has only to judge by how much remains to them when they are no longer of an age to be attractive.

❡ "It seems to me," said M. de——, "that the truth about women's favors is that they are open to competition, but are never the reward of either feeling or merit."

❡ Young women share one misfortune with kings. They have no friends. But luckily this misfortune saddens them no more than it does kings. Greatness in the one, vanity in the other, relieve them of feeling it.

❡ In politics they say that the wise make no conquests; it is just as true of courtship.

❡ It is amusing that the phrase "to know a woman" means to go to bed with her, and means that in several ancient languages and in those ways of living that are simplest and closest to nature, as though one could not know a woman without that. If the patriarchs had already made that discovery, they were more advanced than is usually believed.

❡ Women wage with men a war in which the latter have an immense advantage, in that the loose women are all on their side.

❡ There are girls who manage to sell themselves, whom no one would take as gifts.

❡ The most worthy of loves exposes the soul to petty passions. Marriage exposes your soul to the petty passions of your wife, ambition, vanity, etc.

❡ You may be as charming and honorable as can be, and may love the most perfect woman imaginable; you will still find that you have to overlook your predecessor, or your successor.

℀ Perhaps one has to have felt love in order really to know friendship.

℀ The relations between men and women are like those between Europe and the Indies: at once commerce and a war.

℀ In order for a relation between a man and a woman to amount to anything, they must share pleasure, memory, or desire.

℀ A woman of wit one day told me, in one sentence, what may be the secret of her sex, which is that every woman, in taking a lover, pays more attention to how he is regarded by other women than to how she regards him herself.

℀ Madame de —— has gone to join her lover in England in order to offer proof of a great tenderness which she does not feel. In our day scandals are undertaken as a matter of decency.

℀ I remember a man who gave up the ladies of the Opera because he found them, he said, as false as honest women.

℀ The ear and the mind are aware of repetitions. For the heart they do not exist.

℀ Feeling leads to thought. Almost anyone would agree about that. But they would agree less easily that thought leads to feeling, which is just as true.

℀ What is a mistress? A woman in whose presence we forget what we know by heart: all the failings of her sex.

❧ In affairs of the heart, time has made the excitement of scandal succeed the excitement of mystery.

❧ Love apparently does not seek out real perfections; one would be tempted to say that it shuns them. It loves only the ones that it creates or imagines; it is like those kings who recognize no honors except the ones they themselves have made.

❧ The naturalists tell us that in every species degeneration begins with the females. The philosopher can apply that to morals, in civilized society.

❧ What renders the company of women so stimulating is the number of implications involved; between men implications are irritating or at best insipid; between men and women they are pleasurable.

❧ It is often said that "The most beautiful woman in the world can give no more than she has," which is quite false. She gives exactly what one imagines one receives, for in these things it is the imagination that determines the value of what is received.

❧ Indecency, lack of modesty, are absurd in any system: in the philosophy of indulgence just as in that of abstinence.

❧ I have noticed in reading Scripture that in several passages, when humanity is being reproached for its outrages or crimes, the Author speaks of "the children of men," and when it is a question of follies and foibles, "the children of women."

❧ We would be too wretched if, in the presence of women, we remembered what we know by heart.

℃ It is as though nature, in rendering men's taste for women utterly indestructible, had had some notion that without this precaution the contempt that the vices of their sex inspire, and in particular their vanity, would prove a great obstacle to the sustenance and propagation of the species.

℃ "No man who has not had a great deal to do with whores can know women," I was told gravely by a man who is a great admirer of his wife, who is deceiving him.

℃ Marriage and celibacy both have their disadvantages. One must prefer the one whose disadvantages are not irremediable.

℃ In love it is enough if one's attractions and one's charms give pleasure. But in marriage, to be happy, we must love each other, or at least be suited to each other's faults.

℃ Love is more pleasant than marriage for the same reason that novels are more amusing than history.

℃ Marriage succeeds love as smoke does a flame.

℃ The most reasonable and moderate pronouncement that has been made on the subject of celibacy and marriage is this: "Whichever you choose, you will regret it." Fontenelle, in his last years, repented never having married. He forgot ninety-five years spent without a care.

℃ In contracting marriages, only what is reasonable is openly agreed upon; only what is mad is interesting. All the rest is a low scheme.

❡ Women are married before they are anyone and before they have had a chance to become anyone. A husband is a sort of process that awakens his wife's body, drafts the outlines of her mind, and sketches in her soul.

❡ Marriage, as it is practiced among the rich and well born, is an accepted indecency.

❡ We have seen men who were supposed to be honest, from respectable milieus, laud the happiness of Mlle.——, a young woman of beauty, wit, and virtue who had the luck to become the bride of M.——, a repugnant old person in bad health, dishonest and an imbecile, but rich. If there is one thing that characterizes a despicable age, it is the regarding of such events as triumphs; it is the absurdity of such rejoicing; it is this reversal of all moral and natural ideas.

❡ The condition of husband is disagreeable in that a husband, however intelligent, may well be in the way wherever he is, even at home; he may be a bore without opening his mouth, and be ridiculous in saying the simplest thing. Being loved by one's wife is a partial safeguard against this awkwardness. That was why M.—— said to his wife, "My dear, help me not to be ridiculous."

❡ Divorce is so natural a thing that in many households it goes to bed nightly between man and wife.

❡ The passion of women forces the most honest of men to be either a husband or a gallant, either a rake or impotent.

❡ The worst of all misalliances are arranged by the heart.

℃ To be loved is not everything; we must be appreciated, and it is impossible to be appreciated except by what is like us. This is why love does not exist, or at least does not last, between persons one of whom is too far the inferior of the other. And this is not a question of vanity, but of a just self-regard, which it would be absurd and impossible to eradicate from human nature. Vanity belongs only to a weak or corrupt nature; but self-regard, properly understood, belongs to a nature that is as it was meant to be.

℃ Women give to friendship only what they borrow from love. An imperious and ugly woman trying to be attractive is a pauper asking for charity.

℃ The lover who is too much beloved by his mistress seems to love less, and vice versa. Can it be that the heart's feelings are like material benefits? When one can no longer hope to repay them, one sinks into ingratitude.

℃ The woman who esteems herself more for the qualities of her soul or her mind than for her beauty is superior to her sex. She who esteems herself more for her beauty than for her mind or the qualities of her soul is typical of her sex. But she who esteems herself more for her birth or her rank than for her beauty is alien to her sex, and beneath it.

℃ It would seem that women's brains had one compartment less and their hearts one string more than men's. They needed some special ordering to enable them to support, care for, and cherish children.

℃ Nature has confided the preservation of all creatures to mother-love; and to assure mothers of their reward, it has been woven into the pleasures and even into the sufferings of that delicious sentiment.

℄ In love everything is true, everything is false; it is the only subject about which nothing one can say is absurd.

℄ A man who is in love and looks upon a reasonable man pityingly seems to me like a man reading fairy tales and ridiculing those who read history.

℄ Love is a stormy commerce that always ends in bankruptcy, and it is the person who is bankrupted who is dishonored.

℄ One of the best possible reasons for never marrying is that one is never entirely the dupe of a woman as long as she is not one's wife.

℄ Have you ever known a woman who, on seeing one of her friends courting another woman, assumed that the latter would refuse him? From this one can deduce their opinion of each other. Draw your own conclusions.

℄ However low an opinion a man may have of women, every woman's is worse.

℄ A few men were able to rise above the wretched considerations that drag men down to below what they are capable of; but marriage, affairs with women, have brought them down to the level of those who before could not be compared with them. Marriage, gallantry, are a sort of conductor that brought the petty passions along to them.

℄ I have known men and women in the world who did not seek an exchange of feelings but an exchange of behavior, and would have given up this latter bargain if it could have led to the former.

Chapter Seven

OF THE LEARNED, AND OF MEN OF LETTERS

℄ THERE IS A CERTAIN FERVENT ENERGY, the mother or necessary companion of at least one species of talent, which commonly condemns its possessors to the misfortune, not of immorality nor a complete incapacity for admirable behavior, but to the frequent indulgence in aberrations, which would seem to indicate a total absence of morality. It is a consuming sourness, which they cannot control and which renders them quite odious. It is sad to think that Pope and Swift in England, Voltaire and Rousseau in France, judged not out of hatred or jealousy, but with equity and benevolence, on the basis of facts that have been advanced and admitted by their friends and admirers, would be charged and convicted of thoroughly reprehensible acts, and of sentiments that at times were thoroughly perverse. O Altitudo!

℄ It has been noted that writers on physics, natural history, physiology, chemistry, were usually men of a gentle, even, and for the most part, happy temperament, while on the contrary writers on politics, law, and even moral philosophy were of a sad, melancholy turn, etc. Nothing could be explained more easily. The former study nature, the latter society; the former contemplate the work of the great Being, the latter allow their regard to rest on the works of men. One would expect the results to differ.

℄ If one were to examine carefully the combination of rare qualities of mind and soul that are needed in order to judge, feel, and appreciate good verse—the delicacy of feeling, of the senses, of the ear and of the intelligence, etc.—one would conclude that, despite the pretensions of all classes of society to be able to judge works intended to please, the poets, in this respect, have fewer real judges than mathematicians have. And so the poets, taking no account of the public, and concerning themselves only with connoisseurs, would doubtless do with their works what the famous mathematician Viète did with his, at a time when the study of mathematics was less widespread than it is now. He had only a few copies printed, which he had distributed to those who were capable of understanding and enjoying his book, or to whom it would be of use. As for the others, he never gave them a thought. But Viète was rich, and poets, for the most part, are poor. And then, a mathematician is not so vain as a poet, or if he is, his calculations on the subject are probably better.

℃ There are men in whom the mind (that universal instrument) is merely a talent by which they seem to be dominated, which they cannot control, and which is not at the command of their reason.

℃ I would be happy to say of metaphysicians what Scaliger said of the Basques: "They are said to understand each other but I do not believe it."

℃ Has the philosopher, who does everything for the sake of vanity, any right to despise the courtier, who does everything for the sake of interest? It seems to me that the one carries off the louis d'or and that the other retires content with the sound of their chinking. Is D'Alembert, Voltaire's courtier, whose interest is vanity, much superior to those around Louis XIV, who wanted a pension or a place?

℃ When an agreeable man covets the minor benefits of charming more than the circle of his friends, as so many do (especially men of letters, for whom charm is almost an occupation), it is plain that he cannot have been led to it by any promptings except those of interest or vanity. He must choose between the roles of courtier or coquette, or comedian, if you will. The man who sets out to be agreeable to one circle of acquaintances because he likes their company is the only one who is playing the role of an honest man.

℃ Someone said that to steal from the classics was piracy on the high seas, but that to pillage the moderns was to pick pockets at street corners.

℃ Verses can add wit to the thought of a man who may not otherwise have much; this is what is called talent. Often they expel wit from the thought of a man who is naturally intelligent; this is the best possible proof that he has no talent for verse.

℃ Most books of the day seem to have been written in one day from books read the day before.

℃ Good taste, tact, and style have more in common than men of letters affect to believe. Tact is good taste applied to deportment and conduct. Style is good taste applied to discourse and conversation.

℃ Aristotle remarks with great point, in his *Rhetoric*, that all metaphors based on analogy should be equally true if reversed. Thus one says of old age that it is the winter of life; reverse the metaphor and you find that it is quite as true that winter is the old age of the year.

℃ In order to be a great man in the world of letters, or at least in order to bring about a revolution of any importance, one must, just as in the world of politics, find everything ready, and be born conveniently.

℃ Great lords and celebrated wits are two classes that seek each other out in the hope of uniting two species of men, of which the one makes more dust than is common, and the other more noise.

℃ Men of letters love those whom they entertain, as travelers love those whom they astonish.

℃ What is a man of letters who is not given some special help by his own character, and the goodness of his friends, and a bit of income? If this last advantage is so utterly lacking that he cannot decently occupy the place in society to which his merit calls him, what need has he of the fashionable world? Is not his only course then to choose a retreat where he can cultivate his soul, his character, and his mind, in peace? Must he go on enduring society without gleaning a single one of the advantages which it offers to its citizens in other classes? More than one man of letters, forced to adopt this course, has found in it a happiness which he would have looked for in vain anywhere else. He is one who can truthfully say that when everything was refused him everything was given him. How many occasions there are when we could cite Themistocles' saying, "Alas, we would perish if we had not perished!"

℃ One says, and repeats, after reading some work overflowing with virtue, "What a pity that authors do not portray themselves in their writings, and that one cannot conclude from such a work that the author is what he makes himself out to be." It is true that there are many examples on which to base such a thought; but I have noticed that the reflection is often made instead of honoring the virtues portrayed in the writings of an honest man.

℃ An author, a man of taste, in the midst of this surfeited public is like a young woman in a circle of old reprobates.

℃ A little philosophy leads to a contempt for learning; a great deal of philosophy leads to a respect for it.

℃ The works of a poet, and often those of a man of letters, do not earn much for their authors, who find themselves, where the public is concerned, somewhere between "thank you very much" and "be off with you." Their fortune is limited to what pleasure they can find in themselves and their time.

℄ The reprose of a writer who has written good things is more respected by the public than the active fecundity of an author who proliferates mediocre works. In the same way the silence of a man who is known for his wit is more imposing than the chatter of a dull talker.

℄ The success of a great many works is based on an affinity between the mediocrity of the author's ideas and the mediocrity of the public's.

℄ The composition of the Académie Française would lead me to think that it had taken for its motto the verse of Lucretius: "Contesting of wit, and of titles."

℄ The honor of belonging to the Académie Française is like the Cross of St. Louis, which is to be seen both at dinners at Marly and in the cheapest taverns.

℄ The Académie Française is like the Opera, which is kept going by things that have nothing to do with it—the taxes that are drawn for it from the comic-operas of the provinces, the revenue from permits to go from the orchestra into the wings, etc. In the same way the Académie keeps itself going by means of all the advantages it procures. It is like Gresset's heroine Cidalise:

> Take her; you owe her that, in any case.
> You'll have time to esteem her later, if you can.

℄ Literary reputations, and particularly those in the theater, are somewhat like the fortunes that used to be made in the Indies. It was hardly necessary to do more than go, to acquire vast wealth; but fortunes so made have damaged those of the next generation. The worked-out lands no longer yield so abundantly.

ℂ In our day theatrical and literary successes are no longer anything but laughingstocks.

ℂ It is philosophy that discovers the useful virtues in ethics and politics. It is eloquence that renders them popular. It is poetry that renders them, one might say, proverbial.

ℂ A sophist who is eloquent but without logic is to a philosophical orator what a parlor-trickster is to a mathematician, or Pinetti to Archimedes.

ℂ One is not a man of wit simply because one has a great many ideas, any more than one is a good general simply because one has a great many soldiers.

ℂ Men of letters who retire from the world are often severely criticized. They are called upon to take an interest in a society from which they receive almost no benefits; they are importuned to be everlastingly present at a lottery in which they have no ticket.

ℂ What I admire in the ancient philosophers is the desire to make their conduct conform to their writings. One notices it in Plato, Theophrastes, and a number of others. Practical ethics was so essential to their philosophy that several of them were placed at the heads of schools without having written anything: Xenocrates, for example, Polemon, Heusippus, etc. Socrates, without having offered a single work to the public, and without having studied any science except ethics, was the chief philosopher of his age.

❡ What one knows best is, (1) what one has guessed; (2) what one has learned from experience of men and things; (3) what one has learned not from books but as a result of books, through the reflections to which they have given rise; (4) what one has learned from books and from teachers.

❡ Men of letters, poets especially, are like peacocks; occasionally a few niggardly grains are tossed to them in their pen, and sometimes they are let out to spread their tails where they can be seen, whereas cocks, hens, ducks, and turkeys go free in the barnyard and stuff their crops at their ease.

❡ Success produces success as money produces money.

❡ There are books that the cleverest of men would not be able to write without a baggage train: that is, without going to consult men, things, libraries, manuscripts, etc.

❡ It is almost impossible for a philosopher or a poet not be misanthropic, (1) because his taste and his talent lead him to observe society, a study which is an endless torment to the heart; (2) because his talent is almost never rewarded by society (in fact he is lucky not to be punished for it) and this saddening fact merely redoubles his tendency to melancholy.

❡ The memoirs which men of office or of letters—even those who have seemed to be the most modest—leave to serve as histories of their lives betray their secret vanity, and remind one of that saint who left a hundred thousand crowns to contribute toward his canonization.

❡ It is a great misfortune to lose, as the result of our characters, the rights that our talents would allow us to claim in society.

℄ The great have produced their masterpieces after the age of the passions; after the eruptions of volcanoes the soil grows more fertile.

℄ The vanity of persons of fashion continually makes use of the vanity of men of letters. The latter have made more than one reputation that has risen to great heights. It is nothing but wind, in the first place, on both sides; but those who are skillful at intrigue manage to use it to swell the sails of their fortunes.

℄ An economist is a surgeon with an excellent scalpel and a rough-edged lancet, who operates beautifully on the dead and tortures the living.

℄ Men of letters are seldom jealous of the occasionally exaggerated reputations of books written by persons of the court. They regard such successes as honest women do the fortunes made by courtesans.

℄ The theater confirms customs or changes them. It must either correct what is ridiculous or propagate it. In France it has been seen to do both, alternately.

℄ More men of letters than one might suppose think they love glory when what they love is merely vanity. These two things are not only different but opposed, for the one is a petty passion, the other a great one. There is the same difference between vanity and glory that there is between a pompous ass and a lover.

℄ Posterity judges men of letters by their works alone, without considering the positions they have held. The principle seems to be "What they have done, not what they have been."

❦ Speron-Speroni gives a very lucid explanation of how an author can state clearly, as he imagines, what his reader, in fact, finds extremely obscure. "The author," he says, "proceeds from thought to expression, whereas the reader goes from expression to thought."

❦ The works that an author writes for the pleasure of it are often the best, as love-children are often the most beautiful.

❦ In the arts, and in fact in many other things, one really knows only what one has never learned.

❦ The painter gives soul to a face, and the poet lends a face to a feeling and an idea.

❦ When La Fontaine is bad, it is because he is careless. When Lamothe is, it is because he is making an effort.

❦ In a comedy of character, perfection consists in working out the plot so that its combinations would not do just as well in some other play. Perhaps the only one in the repertory that escapes this criticism is Tartuffe.

❦ There is an amusing way of proving that in France the philosophers are society's worst citizens. Thus the philosophers have printed a vast quantity of important truths about politics and economics, and have given a number of practical suggestions in their books, which have been followed by most of the sovereigns of Europe, almost everywhere except in France. As a result the prosperity of other countries has added to their power, while the prosperity and power of France have not changed, the same abuses continue here, etc., and France will end by being inferior to other nations, a fact for which the philosophers are obviously to blame. We know the Duke of Tuscany's remark on this subject, made to a Frenchman with reference to certain happy innovations which the former had made in his domains. "You praise me too highly," he said. "All of my ideas are out of French books."

ℭ At Anvers, in one of the main churches, I saw the tomb of Plantin, a famous printer, embellished with superb paintings by Rubens, dedicated to his memory. The sight made me think of the Étienne brothers, Henri and Robert, whose Greek and Latin erudition has rendered immense service, and who eked out a miserable existence in France; and Charles-Étienne, their successor, who died in the paupers' hospital after having made contributions nearly as great to the progress of literature. I remembered how André Duchêne, who may be considered the father of French history, was forced by poverty to leave Paris and take refuge on a small farm he had in Champagne. He was killed in a fall from a loaded hay wagon that had been piled to a great height. Adrien de Valois, the pioneer of the history of metals, enjoyed no better fate. Samson, the father of geography, went out on foot, at the age of seventy, to give lessons, in order to keep alive. Everyone knows how Duryer fared, and Tristan and Maynard, and countless others. There was not enough broth for Corneille in his last illness. La Fontaine was no better off. If Racine, Boileau, Molière and Quinault were more fortunate, it is because their talents were consecrated more particularly to the king. The Abbé Delonguerue, who has brought together, and recounts a number of these anecdotes concerning the sad lot of illustrious men of letters in France, adds, "This is the way it has always been in this wretched country." The famous list of men of letters to whom the king wished to give pensions, which was presented to Colbert, had been drawn up by Chapelain, Perrault, Tallemand, and the Abbé Gallois, who omitted the names of those of their colleagues whom they hated, while including those of several foreign scholars, knowing perfectly well that the king and minister would take more pleasure in being praised four hundred leagues from Paris.

Chapter Eight

ON SLAVERY AND LIBERTY;
ON FRANCE BEFORE AND SINCE
THE REVOLUTION

℃ A GREAT DEAL of ridicule has been heaped on those who spoke with enthusiasm of the state of nature, contrasting it with the order of society. But I would like to know how these three objections can be answered. There is not a single known case, among savages, of: (1) madness; (2) suicide; (3) a savage wishing to embrace society; whereas there are a great many Europeans, both on the Cape and in the Americas, who, after having once lived among savages and then been restored to their compatriots, returned to the forests. Account for that without verbiage, or sophism.

℃ The misfortune of humanity, in society, is that whereas in ethics and politics it is possible to define evil as "that which does harm," one cannot say that good is "that which is of use," because what is of use at one moment may be harmful for a long time afterward, or forever.

℃ When one considers that the outcome of the labors and intellects of thirty or forty centuries has been to deliver up three hundred million men, over the whole surface of the globe, into the hands of some thirty despots, most of them ignorant and feeble-minded, and each of them in the sway of three or four scoundrels (and frequently stupid ones) what can one think of humanity, and what hope can one have for its future?

℃ Almost the whole of history is nothing but a series of horrors. If tyrants detest it while they are alive, their successors seem willing to allow the crimes of their predecessors to be transmitted to posterity, to divert attention from the horror that they themselves inspire. In fact there is no longer any way of consoling the people except by teaching them that their forebears were as wretched as they are, or more so.

ℭ The natural character of the Frenchman is a mixture of monkey and bird dog. Comical and given to capering about, like the monkey, and at heart, like him, thoroughly malicious; like the hunting dog he is ignoble from the moment he is born: he fawns, licks the master who strikes him, allows himself to be put on a chain and then leaps for joy when he is let off it to go hunting.

ℭ At one time the royal treasury was called "the savings." They blushed at a name which seemed a contradiction, since the treasures of the realm have been squandered, and they have come to call it, simply, "the royal treasury."

ℭ The most honored title to French nobility is direct descent from one or more of those thirty thousand helmeted, breast-plated, arm-and-leg-plated men who, mounted on great iron-clad horses, ground under foot eight or nine million naked men who are the forebears of the present nation. What an incontestable right to the love and respect of the descendants! And to render this nobility unimpeachably respectable, it reinforces itself by enlisting and adding to its ranks those men who have acquired fortunes by despoiling the hovels of those too poor to pay their taxes. Wretched human institutions, made to inspire scorn and abhorrence, and then insisting on one's respect and reverence!

ℭ It makes as much sense to have to be a member of the gentry in order to be a ship's captain as it would if one had to be a king's secretary in order to be a cabin boy.

℀ The impossibility of attaining high positions unless one was born with a title is one of the gloomiest absurdities in most countries. It is as though donkeys were to try to keep horses off merry-go-rounds and out of tournaments.

℀ Nature does not go to consult Cherin when she wishes to make a virtuous man or a man of genius.

℀ What does it matter whether there is a Tiberius or a Titus on the throne if each of the ministers is a Sejanus?

℀ If a historian such as Tacitus had written the histories of our best kings, with precise accounts of their tyrannical actions, and all their abuses of authority, most of which have been buried in the deepest obscurity, there are few reigns that would not arouse in us the same horror as that of Tiberius.

℀ One might say that there was no civil government in Rome after the death of Tiberius-Gracchus; and Scipio-Nasa, by leaving the senate and using violence against the tribune, taught the Romans that only force could give laws to the forum. It was he, before Sylla, who brought this unhappy secret to light.

℀ The hidden interest that binds one so firmly to the reading of Tacitus is the continual, and continually fresh contrast between the ancient republican liberty and the base slaves whom the author depicts. It is the comparison between the Scauri, Scipios, etc., of the old days, with the cowardice of their descendants. In a word, part of the effect of Tacitus is due to Titus-Livy.

℀ Kings and priests, in forbidding the justification of suicide, have meant to make our slavery last as long as possible. They want to keep us shut up in a cell from which there is no escape, like that scoundrel in Dante who walled up the wretched Ugolino's prison door.

℃ Books have been written about the interests of princes, and there are those who talk of studying the interests of princes. Has anyone ever talked of studying the interests of the people?

℃ No history is worthy of attention except that of free peoples. The history of peoples under the yoke of despotism is a mere collection of anecdotes.

℃ The real Turkey of Europe was France. There are perhaps twenty English writers in whom one finds the phrase, "despotisms, such as France and Turkey."

℃ Ministers are only men of affairs, and they are as important as they are only because the gentleman, their master, is someone of consequence.

℃ A minister, in inducing his masters to commit errors and stupidities injurious to the public, often actually consolidates his own position. One might say that he is bound to them more firmly by complicity.

℃ How does it happen that in France a minister remains in office after a hundred reprehensible actions, and is dismissed for his only good one?

℃ Strange as it seems, despotism has its defenders who pretend that it is essential to the encouragement of the arts. It is hard to believe how many people the brilliance of the age of Louis XIV has converted to this way of thinking. According to them the goal of all human society is to have beautiful tragedies, comedies, etc. They would pardon all the evils that have been done by priests with the thought that if there had been no priests, there would be no Tartuffe.

❡ In France, merit and reputation no more help their owners to attain office than the rose garland that is the village maiden's prize for virtue gives her the right to be presented at court.

❡ France: a country in which it is often useful to display one's vices, and always dangerous to show one's virtues.

❡ Paris: an extraordinary place, where one must pay thirty sous for one's dinner, four francs to take the air, a hundred louis for a superfluity of those things that are necessary, and four hundred louis for no more than is necessary of those things that are superfluous.

❡ Paris: a ciy of amusements, pleasures, etc., in which four-fifths of the inhabitants die of want.

❡ One could apply to Paris St. Theresa's definition of Hell: "The place that stinks and where no one loves."

❡ It is remarkable how much ceremony there is in a nation as lively and gay as ours. It is surprising, too, to see the spirit of pedantry and heaviness in the institutions and assemblies; it is as though the legislator had set out to make a counterweight to hold down the natural lightness of the French.

❡ It has been established that when M. de Guibert was appointed governor of the Invalides there were found in that military hospital six hundred pretended soldiers who had never been wounded, and who, with very few exceptions, had never been present at any seige or battle, but who, to make up for it, had been coachmen or lackeys of peers or men in office. What a text and subject for meditation!

℄ In France they ignore those who set fires and punish those who give the alarm.

℄ Most of the women at Versailles, and in Paris, when the latter are anyone at all, are merely bourgeois of quality like Madame Naquart, whether they have been presented at court or not.

℄ In France there is no longer a public, nor a nation, for the same reason that lint is not linen.

℄ The public is governed according to its own ways of thinking. It has the right to talk nonsense, as the ministers have the right to enact it.

℄ Whenever some public folly is committed, I remember a handful of foreigners who are in Paris, and I am ashamed, for I still love my country.

℄ The English are the only people who have found a way of limiting the power of a man whose face is stamped on a little piece of money.

℄ How is it that under the most appalling despotism people still make up their minds to reproduce? It is because nature's laws are softer but more powerful than those of tyrants, and the child smiles at his mother under Domitian as under Titus.

℄ A philosopher said, "I do not know how a Frenchman who has once been in the king's antechamber, or in the *oeil-de-boeuf* at Versailles, can say of anyone at all, "that is a great lord.""

℄ The flatterers of princes have said that hunting was an image of warfare, and indeed the peasants whose fields are ravaged by the hunt must find it a reasonable facsimile.

℄ It is unfortunate for men, but perhaps fortunate for tyrants, that the poor, the unfortunate, lack the instinct or the pride that keeps the elephant from reproducing in captivity.

℄ In the eternal struggle that society conducts between the poor and the rich, the noble and the plebeian, the man who has a name and the unknown, there are two observations to be made: the first is that their actions and what they say are weighed on different scales, and where the one registers a pound the other will register ten or a hundred by an accepted disproportion that has been fixed from the beginning; this in itself is horrible. This evaluation of persons, authorized by law and custom, is one of the enormous vices of society, and would be enough in itself to explain all the others.

The other observation is that in starting from this irregularity another malpractice ensues: the poor man's, the commoner's pound is devalued, it is reduced to a quarter, while the rich man's or the nobleman's ten come to be worth a hundred, his hundred a thousand, etc. It is the natural and necessary consequence of their respective positions, the poor and common being envied by all their equals, and the rich man and the nobleman enjoying the support and complicity of the small number of his own kind who lend him help in order to share his advantages and gain others like them.

℄ It is an undeniable fact that there are in France seven million men who beg for alms and twelve million with none to give them.

℄ "The nobility," say the nobles, "is an intermediary between the king and the people . . ." No doubt: just as the hunting dog is an intermediary between the hunter and the hares.

❧ What is a cardinal? A priest dressed in red, who has a hundred thousand crowns from the king so that he can laugh at him in the name of the Pope.

❧ Most social institutions seem to exist in order to maintain man in a mediocrity of mind and feelings that render him more fit for governing or being governed.

❧ A citizen of Virginia, owning fifty acres of fertile soil, pays forty-two sous of our money in order to enjoy, in peace, under just and benevolent laws, the protection of the government, the safety of his person and his property, civil and religious liberty, the right to vote at elections, to be a member of Congress and consequently a legislator, etc. The French peasant who corresponds to him, in the Auvergne or the Limousin, is crushed with taxes, rates, levies, and requisitions of all kinds on his labor, so that he can be insulted by some underdelegate, imprisoned arbitrarily, etc., and transmit to a half-naked family this heritage of misfortune and degradation.

❧ North America is the part of the universe in which the rights of man are best known. The Americans are the worthy descendants of those famous republicans who went into exile to flee from tyranny. It is there that men were bred and reared who were worthy to fight with the English themselves and defeat them, at a time when the latter had recovered their liberty and had succeeded in making the most superb government that has ever existed. The American Revolution will prove useful to England herself, forcing her to reexamine her constitution and rid it of its abuses. What will happen? The English, driven from the continent of North America, will fling themselves upon the islands and the French and Spanish possessions, and will give these their English government, which is founded on men's natural love of liberty, and encourages it. In the Spanish and French islands, and above all in the Hispanic continent, when it has become Anglicized, new constitutions will be formed, with liberty as their principle and their basis. Thus the English will have the unique glory of having formed almost the only free people in the universe, the only ones, properly speaking, who are worthy of being called men, since they alone will have known and upheld the rights of men. But how many years will it take to bring about this revolution? The French and the Spaniards will have to have been driven from their enormous territories, where it will not be possible to do more than establish enclaves, into which Englishmen might be transplanted as bearers of the first seeds of liberty. These seeds will grow, and yielding new fruit, bring about the revolution that will drive the English themselves from both Americas and all the islands.

⟨ An Englishman respects the law and despises authority. A Frenchman, on the contrary, respects authority and despises the law. He must be taught to do the opposite, and that may not be possible, considering the ignorance in which the nation is kept, an ignorance that must not be disclaimed by pointing to the enlightenment that is relatively common in the capitals.

⟨ I am everything, the rest are nothing: there we have despotism, the aristocracy, and their partisans. I am my neighbor, my neighbor is me: there we have the popular doctrine and its partisans. Now choose.

⟨ Everything that emerges from the people arms itself against them to oppress them, whether it is the member of the militia, the merchant who has become the king's secretary, the preacher, risen from a village to deliver sermons advocating submission to arbitrary power, the historian of bourgeois parentage, etc. They are the soldiers of Cadmus: the first ones who are armed turn against their brothers and attack them.

⟨ The poor are the Negroes of Europe.

❦ As some animals cannot breathe the air of certain altitudes without dying, the slave dies in the atmosphere of liberty.

❦ It is the head that governs men. A kind heart is of no use in a chess game.

❦ Human society must be started over again, as Bacon said must be done with human understanding.

❦ Diminish the sufferings of the populace and you diminish its ferocity, as you cure illness with bouillon.

❦ I have observed that the most remarkable of men, who have led revolutions that appear to have been products of their unaided genius, were seconded by the most favorable of circumstances, and by the spirit of their age. It is common knowledge how many attempts were made before Vasco de Gama's great voyage to the Indies. It should not be forgotten that several navigators held the opinion that there were large islands, and probably a continent, to the west, before Columbus discovered it, and that he himself had with him the papers of a famous pilot with whom he had conferred. Philip had made everything ready for the Persian war before his death. A number of heretical sects, in revolt against the abuses of the Roman communion, preceded Luther, Calvin, and even Wycliff.

❦ It is commonly believed that Peter the Great woke up one morning with the idea of forming everything in Russia. M. de Voltaire himself asserts that his father Alexis had planned to transport the arts there. There is in everything a maturity that must be waited for. He is a fortunate man who arrives at the same moment that it does.

❡ The National Assembly of 1789 gave the French people a constitution that was above its strength. Now it must hurry to raise the nation to the requisite level by means of a good system of public education. The legislators must act like clever doctors, who, in treating the illness that is subsiding, administer tonics along with their palliatives.

❡ Considering the large number of deputies at the National Assembly of 1789, and the prejudices with which most of them were stuffed, one would have said that they had smashed prejudice only so that they could pick up the pieces, like those who knock down a building in order to make off with the rubble.

❡ One reason why organizations and assemblies never manage to do anything sensible is that in a public debate the most telling thing that could be said for or against the matter or person in question can seldom be said aloud without considerable dangers or great awkwardness.

❡ At the moment when God created the world the movement of chaos must have made chaos more disorderly than when it was lying in peaceful disorder. So in our case, the disturbance of a society that is reorganizing itself must seem like an excess of disorder.

❡ Courtiers and those who lived on the monstrous abuses that were crushing France never stop saying that it would have been possible to reform the abuses without the destruction that has occurred. They would have suggested that one clean out the Augean stables with a feather duster.

❡ In the old regime a philosopher wrote bold truths. One of those whom birth or favorable circumstances had placed in office read them, diluted them, modified them, stole the twentieth part of them, and passed not for a hothead but a man of wit. He tempered his zeal and met with success. The philosopher was put in the Bastille. In the new regime it is the philosopher who is successful. His ideas do not serve merely to get him locked up or to provide quotations and advancement for a fool; they lead to his own advancement. How on earth will the crowd whom he pushes aside be able to accustom themselves to this new order of things?

℃ Is it not laughable that the Marquis de Bièvre (the grandson of the Surgeon-General) imagines that he must flee to England along with M. de Luxembourg and the other great nobles who have been in flight since the catastrophe of the fourteenth of July, 1789?

℃ The theologians, always true to their purpose of keeping men in blindness, and the delegates of governments, always true to theirs of keeping men oppressed, assume, with no grounds for their assumption, that the great majority of men are condemned to the stupidity that is the consequence of purely mechanical and manual labor. They assume that artisans are incapable of rising to the level of knowledge that is necessary in order to make good use of the rights of men and of citizens. One would have to conclude that this knowledge is very intricate indeed. Let us imagine that a quarter of the time that has been spent in brutalizing these classes had been spent in instructing them; let us imagine that instead of putting into their hands an absurd and unintelligible metaphysical catechism, they had been given one containing the first principles of the rights of men and their duties based on those rights; it would be astonishing how far they would have advanced along that road, with the guidance of a good primer. Imagine that instead of preaching the doctrine of patience, suffering, self-abnegation, and self-abasement to them, for the great convenience of usurpers, the sermons had urged them to a knowledge of their rights, and made clear their duty to defend them. One would then have seen that nature, who made men for society, gave them the good sense necessary to form one that was based on reason.

APPENDIX ONE

❧ A MAN WHO HAD set upon a woman before he was ready said to her, "Madame, would you mind keeping your virtue for another quarter of an hour?"

❧ M. de Pl——, when he was in England, tried to dissuade a young English girl from marrying a man who was too far her inferior in every sense. The young person listened to everything that was said to her, and answered very calmly, "Well, when he comes to see me, it's a change of air in my room."

❧ M. D—— I—— told M. D—— of how badly he had been treated in some affair, and said, "What would you do in my place?" The latter, a man who has suffered great injustices and as a result has become indifferent, a man whom his own misanthropy has turned into an egoist, answered coldly, "Sir, in cases of that kind I look after my stomach, keep my tongue rosy, and pay close attention to the color of my urine."

❧ One of the Duchesse d'Olonne's lovers, catching her making eyes at her husband, said, "God strike me, having no morals is one thing, but that's going too far."

❧ In the capitals the old are more corrupted than the young. It's there that corruption succeeds maturity.

❧ Definition of a despotism: an order of things in which the superior is base and the inferior debased.

℃ The ministers brought about the destruction of the royal authority, as the priests brought about the destruction of religion. God and the king were punished for the stupidities of their valets.

℃ A man of wit, finding himself the butt of two malicious wags, said to them, "Sirs, you are mistaken. I am neither a fool nor a dunce, I am between the two."

℃ A man who was known to have shut his eyes to his wife's misdeeds, and who had profited by them more than once, displayed profound grief at her death, and said to me gravely, "I can say what Louis XIV said at the death of Marie-Thérèse: 'This is the first grief she ever caused me.'"

℃ M—— was passionate and thought himself wise. I was quite mad, but suspected as much, and from that point of view I was nearer to wisdom than he was.

℃ A doctor said, "Only heirs pay well."

℃ M. le Dauphin, the father of Louis XVI, passionately loved his first wife, who had red hair and the unpleasant characteristic that goes with it. It was a long time before he could love his second wife, and his explanation was that she did not smell like a woman. He thought that was the odor of the sex.

℃ M. D—— had refused the advances of a pretty married woman. Her husband conceived a detestation for him, as though he had accepted them, and laughed at M. D——, who said, "Good God, if only he knew the joke."

⟪ A pretty woman whose lover was sullen, with a manner no better than if he had been married to her, said to him, "Sir, let me tell you that when you and my husband are both out in the world, it is only right for you to be more agreeable than he is."

⟪ M——, who was asked frequently to read his verses, and was tired of being asked, said that when he started to read, he was always reminded of what the charlatan on the Pont-Neuf said to his monkey when they started their tricks: "Come, my dear Bertrand, we are not here for our own pleasure. We must amuse the honorable company."

⟪ It was said of M—— that his attachment to a certain great lord was stronger for all the base things he had done for him; like ivy, that clings to climb.

⟪ An ugly woman who covers herself in finery when she is to appear among young and pretty women acts, in her way, as people do in arguments when they are afraid of losing them. They try to find some sly way of changing the subject. The question was who was the most beautiful. The ugly one wants them to talk about who is richest.

⟪ "Forgive them for they know not what they do," was the text the preacher took at the marriage of d'Aubigné, aged seventy, to a young lady of seventeen.

⟪ There is a melancholy that goes with greatness of spirit.

⟪ There are philosophers who are like monks, some of whom are what they are in spite of themselves and rage against the fact all their lives. Others learn to be patient. A small number, in the end, are happy, say nothing, and do not try to make converts; whereas those whom their vows have driven to despair undertake the impressing of novices.

℄ M—— said wittily that in Paris every honest man contributes to the livelihood of police informers, as Pope says that poets nourish critics and journalists.

℄ A man said naïvely to a friend, "This morning we condemned three men to death. Two of them richly deserved it."

℄ A very rich man, speaking of the poor, said, "It makes no difference that I give them nothing, the clowns go on asking." There is more than one prince who could say the same of his courtiers.

℄ M. de——, passionately in love after having lived for some years in indifference, said to his friends who laughed at what they called his premature old age, "Your timing's poor. I was very old indeed a few years ago, but I'm very young at the moment."

℄ There is a base kind of gratitude.

℄ When, M. le Duc de Richelieu was received into the Académie Française his speech was warmly praised. One day at a large gathering he was told that its tone was perfect, full of grace and facility; and that whereas men of letters might perhaps write more correctly, their writing did not give as much pleasure. "Thank you, sirs," said the young duke. "I am charmed by what you have said. I should tell you that my speech was written by M. Roy, and I shall compliment him on having a style that is approved of at court."

℄ The Abbé Trublet was asked how long it took him to write a book. He said, "That depends on who I am seeing at the time."

❡ One could write a short chapter entitled, "The Vices Required in Good Company." And append to it one on "Mediocre Qualities."

❡ At the royal mass a man from the provinces plied his neighbor with questions: "Who is that lady?" "The Queen." "And that one?" "Madame."[4] "And that one?" "The Comtesse d'Artois." "And that one?" The man from Versailles, losing patience, answered, "That's the late queen."

APPENDIX TWO

❡ A PRETTY ALLEGORY shows Minerva, goddess of Wisdom, rejecting the flute when she realizes that the instrument is not becoming to her.

❡ A man of wit said of M——, a former friend of his who had returned to him in his prosperity, "He not only wants his friends to be well off, he insists upon it."

❡ Love, says Plutarch, silences the other passions. It is the dictator in whose presence all the others hide their faces.

❡ M——, on hearing a sermon against licit love because of its bad effects on the imagination, said, "For my part, it doesn't worry me. When a woman suits me and makes me happy, I give myself up to the feelings she arouses in me, apart from taking care not to become her dupe if she doesn't suit me. My imagination is the decorator whom I send to furnish my apartment when I see that I can be comfortable there. Otherwise I give him no order at all, and save money."

---

[4] *Madame*: title given to the King's eldest daughter, whatever her age and without reference to whether or not she was married.

℃ M. de L—— told me that the moment he learned of the infidelity of Mme. de B—— he felt, in the midst of his grief, that he would not love again, that love had disappeared forever, as a man hears, in a field, the sound of a partridge rising and flying away.

℃ Clumsy benefactors have been compared to the goat being milked, who stupidly kicked over the jug she had filled with her milk.

℃ Her imagination gives birth to an illusion as soon as it loses one, like those rosebushes that produce roses at all seasons.

℃ M—— said that what he liked above all was peace, quiet, and darkness. "In fact," they said to him, "a sickroom."

℃ A woman, in herself, is nothing. She is what she appears to be to the man who concerns himself with her. That is why she is so furious with those who do not see her as she wishes to appear. She loses her existence. A man is injured less because he remains what he is.

℃ Greatness of soul had led him to take a few steps toward fortune, and greatness of soul had led him to despise them.

℃ M——, an old bachelor, said wittily that marriage is too perfect an estate for imperfect man.

℃ "A man of letters," said Diderot, "may have a mistress who makes books, but he must have a wife who makes shirts."

℃ A man with a great indifference to living said as he died, "How wrong Doctor Bouvard was after all."

℃ Strange, the power of fashion. M. de la Tremouille, separated from his wife whom he neither loved nor respected, learns that she has smallpox. . . . He shuts himself up with her, catches the disease, dies, and leaves her a large fortune and the right to re-marry.

℃ There is a bad kind of modesty, based on ignorance, which sometimes hinders superior characters and keeps them in a sort of mediocrity. This reminds me of the remark of a man of acknowl-edged distinction, at luncheon with certain courtiers: "Ah sirs, how I regret the time I wasted learning that I am your better."

℃ Conquerors will always pass for the first of men, just as the lion will always be called the king of the beasts.

℃ M—— had been traveling in Sicily and was disputing the prevalent notion that the interior of the island is full of thieves. To prove it, he said that wherever he had gone, he had been told, "The brigands are somewhere else." M. de B——, a merry mis-anthrope, said to him, "That, at least, is something that would not have been said to you in Paris."

℃ It is a Turkish proverb, that lovely sentence: "Oh sorrow, I give you thanks, if you are alone."

℃ To justify Providence, St. Augustine said that he leaves the wicked on earth to become good, or to help the good become better.

℃ Men are so perverse that the mere hope, and indeed even the desire to correct them and see them become reasonable and hon-est, is an absurdity, a romantic notion which is excusable only in the simplicity of extreme youth.

℄ M——, a disabused old man, said to me, "The rest of my life looks to me like a half-sucked orange, to be squeezed heaven knows why, for the juice is not worth it."

℄ Our language is said to love clarity. That is, as M—— observes, because one loves what one needs most. For if it is not very adroitly handled, it is always on the point of falling into obscurity.

℄ A man of letters was offered the *Mercure* complete at three pennies a volume. He said he would wait until it was remaindered.

III

CHARACTERS
AND ANECDOTES

❡ M—— SAID TO ME, "I am reduced to finding all my pleasures within myself, in the exercise of my own intelligence. Nature placed in the human brain a little organ called the cerebellum, which acts like a mirror. There one projects a picture, for better or worse, large or small, in outline or in detail, of all the objects in the universe, and even the products of one's own thought. It is a magic lantern, of which man is the owner, and in front of which pass scenes in which he is both actor and spectator. It is, in fact, what man is, properly speaking. It contains the limits of his empire. Everything else is foreign to him.

❡ "Today, the fifteenth of March, 1782," said M. de——, "I have performed a good action of a rather rare kind. I have comforted a man who is honest, has many virtues and 100,000 a year rent, a great name, a great deal of intelligence, and excellent health. And I am poor, unknown, and sick."

❡ Everyone knows of the Bishop of Dol's fanatical speech to the King on the subject of the recall of the Protestants. He spoke in the name of the clergy. The Bishop of St. Pol asked him why he had spoken for his colleagues without consulting them. "I consulted my crucifix," he said. "In that case," the Bishop of St. Pol answered, "you should have repeated exactly what your crucifix told you."

❡ There are witnesses to confirm that Madame, the King's little daughter, playing with one of her maids, looked at her hand and, after counting the fingers, said in amazement, "What? You have five fingers too, just like me?" And she counted again to make sure.

❡ The Maréchal de Richelieu suggested to the King a certain great lady, I forget which, for his mistress, and the King refused, saying that she would be too expensive to dismiss.

❡ The Maréchal de Biron was very gravely ill. He wished to make confession, and began to recount, in front of several of his friends, "What I owe to God, what I owe to the King, what I owe to the State . . ." One of his friends interrupted him. "Hush," he said, "you'll die insolvent."

❡ Duclos was in the habit of using b——'s and f——'s at every turn, in the Academy itself. The Abbé de Renal (whom, they used to call the venomless snake, because of his long body) said to him, "Sir, in the Academy it is not done to use words that are not in the dictionary."

❡ M—— said to me, "I have studied women of every country. The Italian will not believe that her lover loves her unless he will commit a crime for her. For the Englishwoman it must be a folly. For the Frenchwoman, a foolishness."

❡ For thirty years a man went to spend his evenings with Madame de——; he lost his wife; everyone expected him to marry the other, and encouraged him to do so. He refused. "If I did," he said, "I wouldn't know where to spend my evenings."

❡ Madame de Tencin, whose manners were of the sweetest, was a woman of no principles, and capable of anything, precisely.

One day someone was extolling her sweetness. "Yes," said the Abbé Trublet, "if she stood to profit by poisoning you, she would choose the sweetest possible poison."

⟪ Some opinion or other of M——'s about a piece of literature was contested with the statement that the public did not share his opinion. "The public, the public," he said, "how many fools does it take to make a public?"

⟪ M. d'Argenson said to the Comte de Sébourg, who was his wife's lover, "There are two posts for which you would be suitable: director of the Bastille or of the Hospital of the Invalides. If I give you the Bastille, everyone will say that I sent you there, and if I give you the Hospital, everyone will say it was my wife."

⟪ M—— said, after reading the letter in which St. Jerome depicts with great energy the violence of his passions, "I am more envious of his temptations than awed by his penitence."

⟪ M—— said, "The only good thing about women is their best thing."

⟪ A man was so infatuated with the priesthood that he said, "Even if I knew I'd be damned for it, I'd become a priest."

⟪ A man was in heavy mourning: long weepers, black wig, long face. One of his friends asked him, sympathetically, "Heavens! Whom have you lost?" He said, "I haven't lost anyone. I'm a widower."

⟪ Madame de Bassompierre, living at the court of King Stanislas, was the recognized mistress of M. de la Galaisière, the Polish

King's chancellor. One day the King presented himself in her apartments and took certain liberties with her which were not successful. "I shall say no more," said Stanislas. "My chancellor will tell you the rest."

❡ Two weeks before Damien's attempt on the King's life a merchant from Provence, on his way through a little town six leagues from Lyon, and staying at the inn, heard in a bedroom that was separated from his own by nothing but a partition, that a man named Damien was going to assassinate the King. The merchant came to Paris, and went to see M. Berrier[5] but did not find him in. He therefore wrote to him what he had overheard, and then went back again, found M. Berrier in, and told him what he knew. He set off again for his province, and while he was on his way, Damien's assassination attempt occurred. M. Berrier, realizing that the merchant would tell his story, and that the discovery of his own negligence would undo him, sent a detachment of police and guards down the Lyon road, had the man seized, gagged, brought back to Paris, and put in the Bastille, where he was left for eighteen years. M. de Malesherbes,[6] who delivered a number of prisoners in 1775, told this story in the freshness of his own indignation.

❡ M. de Roquemont, whose wife was extremely sportive, slept once a month in her bedroom to avoid awkwardness if she became pregnant, and said as he left, "There, I'm clear now, plant who will."

❡ M. de——, whom bitter griefs kept from regaining his health, said, "Show me the river of oblivion, and I will find the fountain of youth."

---

[5] Berrier, Nicolas: one of the chiefs of police.
[6] Malesherbes; an administrator of the royal household; he defended Louis XVI before the Convention.

℀ A sensitive young man who behaved with honesty in love was laughed at by certain libertines who made mock of his tender feelings. He answered them simply: "Is it my fault if I prefer women I love to women whom I don't?"

℀ They took up a collection at the Académie Française. They were a crown or a *louis d'or* short, and one of the members, known for his avarice, was suspected of not having contributed. He insisted that he had paid his contribution, and the one who had passed the box said, "I didn't see it, but I believe it." M. de Fontenelle ended the discussion by saying, "I, on the other hand, saw it, but I don't believe it."

℀ The Duke of Marlborough was in the trenches with a friend and a nephew when a cannonball knocked out the friend's brains and covered the nephew's face with them, so that he recoiled in horror. Marlborough, unmoved, said to him, "What's this, sir, taken by surprise?" "Yes," said the young man, wiping his face, "I'm surprised that a young man with so much brain should have exposed himself unnecessarily to an unprofitable danger."

℀ Madame la Duchesse du Maine, when her health failed, grumbled to her doctor. She said, "Is it really necessary to impose so many privations on me and force me to live shut in by myself?" "But Your Highness has forty guests at the château at this moment!" "And if I do! Don't you know that forty or fifty guests is privacy for a princess?"

℀ The Duke of Chartres, on learning how his sister, Mme. la Duchesse de Bourbon, had been insulted by M. le Comte d'Artois, said, "How pleasant it is to be neither her father nor her husband."

℃ M— told me, "It is because no one engaged my true feel-ings that I came to behave in love as everyone else does. It was a poor second choice, like that of a man who goes to the theater, and finding no seat at *Iphigénie,* proceeds to the music hall.

℃ "Love," said M—, "is a pleasure that should be reserved for delicate souls. When I see coarse individuals concerning them-selves with it, I am tempted to say, 'Mind your own business. There are gaming, eating, and ambition for the likes of you.' "

℃ Do not extol N—'s character to me. He is hard, unyielding, sustained by a cold philosophy, like a bronze statue on a marble base.

℃ "Do you know," M. de— asked me, "why the young, those under thirty, are more honest in France than those who have passed that age? It is because after that they are disillusioned: in our country one must be either the hammer or the anvil, and they see clearly that the evils under which the nation is groaning are incurable. Up until that age they are like the dog who defends his master's dinner against other dogs. After that they go along like the dog, who ends by taking his share with the others.

℃ Madame de B—, who despite all her influence and prestige was unable to do anything for her lover, M. de D—, a man of a defeating mediocrity, married him. He was not worth showing off as a lover. As a husband, of course, there is no point in hiding him.

℃ M. d'Autrep said of M. de Ximenes, "He is a man who likes rain better than fair weather, and at the sound of the nightingale says, 'Oh the vile beast!' "

℃ When Czar Peter I was at Spithead, he wished to observe the punishment of keel-hauling, which is practiced in the fleet. They could find no one who was guilty. "Take one of my men," said the Czar. "Prince," someone said to him, "your men are in England, and consequently under the protection of laws."

❦ "My ideas and my principles," said M——, "are not suitable for everybody, any more than the Ailhaut powders and several other tonics which have done so much harm to frail constitutions and have been extremely beneficial to those who were already robust." He gave this as a reason for not encouraging the friendship of M. de J——, a young courtier whose acquaintance was being pressed upon him.

❦ M. d'Argenson, at the battle of Raucoux, learned that an army batman had been wounded by a cannonball behind the spot where he and the King were standing, and said, "That clown will not do us the honor of dying."

❦ During the misfortunes of the last years of the reign of Louis XIV, after the defeats at Turin, Oudenarde, Malplaquet, Ramillies, and Hochstet, the good souls at court said, "At least the King has his health, and that's the main thing."

❦ "I have seen in society," said M——, "nothing but dinners without digestions, suppers without pleasure, conversations without trust, associations without friendship, and love-making without love."

❦ I said to M. R——, a witty misanthrope who had introduced a young acquaintance of his, "Your friend knows nothing of how to behave; he knows nothing about anything." "Yes," he said, "and he's already as sad as if he knew everything."

❦ M—— said that a wise and penetrating mind which could see society as it is would find nothing but bitterness everywhere. It is essential to look at everything from its amusing side and form the habit of regarding man as nothing but a jumping jack and society as the board on which he jumps. Thereupon everything changes. The mentalities of the different social states, the vanity peculiar to each of them, individual variations, elaborate dishonesty, etc. all become things to be laughed at, and one keeps one's health.

℘ "It is only with great difficulty," said M——, "that a man of merit can maintain himself in the world without a name, without rank, and without fortune. The man who has these advantages, on the other hand, is maintained there as it were in spite of himself. They are as different as a diver is from a swimmer."

℘ M—— said to me, "I have renounced the friendship of two men: one because he never spoke to me about himself; the other because he never spoke to me about me."

℘ A man of letters was occupied at the same time with a poem and a business matter on which his fortune depended. He was asked how his poem was progressing. "Ask me instead," he said, "how my business is progressing. I am like the gentleman who let his beard grow while he was on trial in a criminal case, because he said he saw no point in being shaved until he knew whether or not his head was going to belong to him. Before I am immortal I want to know whether I can live."

℘ The relics of St. Genevieve were taken out in a procession to pray for dry weather. The procession has scarcely set out when it started to rain. Whereupon the Bishop of Castres said wittily, "The saint has made a mistake. She thought we were asking for rain."

℘ "Considering the general level of literature during these last ten years," M—— said, "literary celebrity, it seems to me, is by now a kind of disgrace which is not quite so damaging as the pillory, but soon will be."

ℭ M. de Malesherbes told M. de Maurepas that the King must be taken to visit the Bastille. "Heaven forbid!" said M. de Maurepas. "He would never want to send anyone there again."

ℭ During a seige a water carrier cried through the town, "Water! Six sous a bucket." A cannonball carried away one of his two buckets. Unperturbed, and without losing a moment, he cried, "Water! Twelve sous a bucket."

ℭ The Abbé de Molière was a poor and simple man, abstracted from everything except his work on the Cartesian system. He had no valet and worked in bed, for lack of firewood, with his trousers on his head over his nightcap, one leg hanging down on one side and one on the other. One morning he heard a knock on the door. "Who's that? Come in." He pulled a rope, and the door opened. Without looking up, the Abbé de Molière asked, "Who are you?" "I want money." "Money?" "Yes, money." "Ah, I see. You're a thief." "Thief or no thief, I want money." "Really. Yes. Well, you must have it. Very well, look in here." He stretched his neck, presenting one side of his trousers. The thief rummaged in the pocket. "No, there's no money in here." "Of course not. But there's my key." "Well, the key . . ." "Take it." "I have it." "Go over to the secretary. Open it." The thief put the key in the wrong drawer. "Let that alone. Don't mess up things in there. Those are my papers. In the other drawer, that's where the money is." "I've found it." "Well, take it. Shut the drawer." The thief fled. "Mister thief! Shut the door! My heavens, he's left the door open! . . . Nasty thief! I have to get up in this cold. Cursed thief!" The Abbé got up, went and shut the door, and went back to work.

ℭ The Comtesse de Boufflers told the Prince de Conti that he was the best of tyrants.

❡ Mme. de Montmorin told her son, "Now that you are going out into society, I have only one word of advice for you. Be in love with all the women."

❡ In M. de Machaut's time the King was presented with a prospectus for a royal audience, as they wished to see it enacted. Everything was agreed upon beforehand by the King, Mme. de Pompadour, and the ministers. The King was prompted as to what he should say, in each instance, to the president. It was all set out in a memorandum, complete with: "Here the King will look stern. Here the King will assume a gentler expression. Here the King will make such-and-such a gesture, etc." The memorandum still exists.

❡ M—— said, "One must either entice men's cupidity or threaten their self-esteem. They are monkeys who never jump except for nuts on the one hand or the whip on the other."

❡ M. de Boulainvilliers, a man of no wit and great vanity, and proud of being able to wear a *cordon bleu* that had been dealt out to him after a payment of fifty thousand crowns, said to someone as he was putting it on, "Wouldn't you like to have an ornament like this?" "No," the other said, "but I would be happy to have what it cost you."

❡ The Marquis de Catelux, who was as much in love as though he were still twenty, saw his wife giving close attention, during dinner, to a handsome young man, and as they left the table, he very humbly reproved her. "Move on, move on, my good man," the Marquis de Genlis said to him, "you've had yours" [a formula used for beggars who return asking for alms a second time].

❡ M——, well known for his knowledge of the world, said to me that what had helped him most had been the ability to sleep, on occasion, with women of forty, and listen to men of eighty.

❡ M—— talked like a great libertine on the subject of love, but in fact he was softhearted and given to the tender passions. As a result someone said of him, "He pretends to be a deceiver lest women should have nothing to do with him."

❡ M. de Richelieu said of the seige of Mahon under the command of M. le Duc de Crillon, "I took Mahon foolishly. M. de Crillon seems to be even better acquainted with that method than I was."

❡ At the battle of Raucoux or of Lawfeld, the young M. de Thyanges had his horse killed under him, and he himself was thrown some distance, but not hurt. The Marechal de Saxe said to him, "Thyanges, my boy, you must have been frightened." "Yes, M. le Marechal," he said, "I was afraid you might be wounded."

❡ Mme. Denis was complimented on her performance as Zaïre. She said, "It requires someone young and beautiful." "Ah, Madame," the flatterer said naïvely, "you are the proof that that is not so."

❡ Madame de Tencin said that intelligent people often erred in their conduct because they could never believe that the world in general is as stupid as it is.

❡ A famous gambler named Sablière was arrested. He was in despair, and said to Beaumarchais, who was trying to keep him from killing himself, "I, arrested for two hundred louis! Abandoned by all my friends! When it's I who made them, who taught them how to cheat! Look at B——, and D——, and N—— (all still alive)—what would they be if it weren't for me? And in the end, sir, look how low I have fallen. I have had to turn police informer in order to make a living."

℣ An English banker named Ser or Sair was accused of conspiring to abduct the king (George III) and carry him off to Philadelphia. Taken before the judges, he said to them, "I know perfectly well what a king can do with a banker. But I am ignorant of what a banker can do with a king."

℣ Someone said to Donne, the English satirist, "Thunder against the sins, but spare the sinners." "What," he said, "damn the cards and pardon the card-sharps?"

℣ M. de Lauzun was asked what he would say to his wife (whom he had not seen for ten years) if she were to write to him, "I have just learned that I am pregnant." He thought for a moment and answered, "I would write, 'I am delighted to learn that Heaven has at last blessed our union. Take good care of yourself. I will come and pay you my court this evening.'"

℣ M——, having known the world, chose to live like a hermit, and gave as his reason that, after examining all the conventions of society that concern the relations between the man of distinction and the man who is mediocre and ordinary, he had concluded that it was a dupes' and fools' market. "I was like a great chess player," he said, "who had grown tired of playing with opponents to whom he must give his queen to start with. One plays divinely, one exhausts oneself, and one ends by winning a pawn."

℣ The Maréchale de Noailles, who is still alive [1780] is a mystic like Madame Guyon, with little to choose between them. Such was her zeal that she was inspired to write to the Virgin. The letter was deposited in the poor box at the church of St. Roch, and the reply was written by a priest of that parish. This circus went on for some time. The priest was discovered and was frightened, but the matter was hushed up.

℃ A young man offended a minister's toady. A friend saw it happen, and said to him, when the offended person had left, "You must learn that it is better to offend the minister himself than his successor on the stool."

℃ L'Écluse, who organized the *Varietés Amusantes*, told how, when he was young and penniless, he arrived at Lunéville and acquired the post of royal dentist to King Stanislas on the very day that the King lost his last tooth.

℃ We are assured that Madame de Montpensier, when she had been obliged several times by the absence of her ladies to have her shoe put on by a page, asked him whether he had not felt a certain temptation. The page answered that he had. The princess, who was too good to profit by this admission, gave him several louis to enable him to go and visit a prostitute, and rid himself of the temptation of which she had been the cause.

℃ Mme. de Prie, the Regent's mistress, under the instigation of her father, a grain dealer by the name, I believe, of Pleneuf, was instrumental in a cornering of the wheat market that drove the populace to despair and in the end caused rioting. A company of musketeers received orders to go and silence the tumult, and their officer, M. d'Avejan, had instructions of his own to fire on the rabble, for thus the French people were designated. This worthy man was loath to fire on his fellow citizens, and this is how he undertook to carry out his commission. He gave the preparatory commands for a salvo of musketry, and before saying "Fire" he walked toward the crowd holding his hat in one hand and his instructions from the court in the other. "Sirs," he said, "my orders are to fire on the rabble. I beseech all honest persons to withdraw before I give the order to fire." Everyone fled and disappeared.

℃ A man of quality married without loving his wife, took a girl from the Opera, and then left her, saying, "She's like my wife";

then he had an honest woman, for the sake of variety, and left her too, saying, "She's like so-and-so." And so on.

℄ Several young persons of the court were supping at the house of M. de Conflans. They started with a song that was somewhat daring but not particularly indecent. M. de Fronsac at once began to sing abominable snatches which startled even that gleeful band. M. de Conflans interrupted the universal silence, saying, "Devil take it, Fronsac, there are ten bottles of champagne between that song and the first one."

℄ L'Abbé Baudeau said of M. Turgot that he was an instrument of an excellent temper, but without a handle.

℄ M. de Barbançon had been extremely handsome; he had a very pretty garden, which Mme. la Duchesse de la Vallière went to see. The owner, who by then was very old and gouty, told her that he had been madly in love with her. Mme. de la Vallière answered, "Good heavens, why didn't you tell me? You could have had me like all the others."

℄ L'Abbé Fraguier lost a suit that had dragged on for twenty years. He was reminded of all the troubles that he had been caused, by a suit which in the end he had lost. "Oh," he said, "I won it every evening for twenty years." A very philosophical remark, which could be applied to anything. It explains how one loves a vain and flirtatious woman. She makes you win your suit for six months, for one day of losing it.

℄ M—— said of Mme. de——, "I thought she wanted me for a madman, and I was ready to be one for her, but she merely wanted me to be silly, and I refused her."

❧ M—— said, referring to the ridiculous stupidities of the ministries, "If it were not for the government, one could not laugh at all, now, in France."

❧ "In France," said M——, "we must get rid of the melancholy humor and the patriotic spirit. These are two quite unnatural ailments in the country that lies between the Rhine and the Pyrenees, and when a Frenchman is afflicted with either one, there is cause to be alarmed on his behalf."

❧ It pleased Madame la Duchesse de Grammont, once, to say that M. de Liancourt had the wit of M. de Lauzun. M. de Créqui encountered the latter and said to him, "You're dining with me today." "My friend, it's not possible." "You must; furthermore, it's in your own interest." "How so?" "Liancourt will be there. He's said to have your wit. But he doesn't use it. He'll give it back to you."

❧ M—— said that the gout was like royal bastards, who are christened as late as possible.

❧ J. J. Rousseau, at a performance of his "The Country Parson," at Fontainebleau, was approached by a courtier who said to him politely, "Sir, will you allow me to pay you a compliment?" "Yes sir," said Rousseau, "if it is a good one." The courtier withdrew. "But," they said to Rousseau, "do you realize what you have just said?" "Indeed I do," said Rousseau. "Do you know anything worse than a bad compliment?"

❧ After supper one evening at Potsdam, M. de Voltaire depicted a good king and then, by contrast, a tyrant. Gradually he warmed to his subject and gave a horrifying description of the miseries heaped upon humanity by a despot, a conqueror, etc. The King of Prussia was moved and let fall a few tears. "Look, look," cried M. de Voltaire, "he weeps, the tiger."

℃ Fontelle had been turned down three times by the Académie and frequently said so. He added, "I've told that to everyone whom I've seen suffering from the Académie's refusal, and it's comforted no one."

℃ Speaking of matters here below and how they go from bad to worse, M—— said, "I read somewhere that in politics nothing was so unfortunate for the people as reigns that lasted too long. I hear that God is eternal. There is nothing more to be said."

℃ M—— remarked with much penetration and justice that however importunate and intolerable the faults of those with whom we live may be, we never fail to adopt some part of them; the fact that we have been the victims of these same faults that are foreign to our natures does not immunize us against them.

℃ Yesterday I was present at a philosophical discussion between M. D—— and M. L—— in which one phrase in particular struck me. M. D—— said, "Few persons and few things interest me, but nothing interests me less than myself." M. L—— answered, "Are not both things true for the same reason? Do they not explain each other?" "What you say is all very clever," M. D—— answered coldly, "but I am merely telling the truth. I have been brought to this point by degrees. Living among men and observing them, the heart must either break or turn to bronze."

℃ Madame Brisard was well known for her love affairs, and at Plombières several ladies of the court did not wish to see her. Among the ladies was the extremely pious Duchesse de Gisors; it was obvious to Madame Brisard's friends that if she were to receive Madame Brisard, the others would present no obstacle. They undertook to arrange the matter and were successful. Madame Brisard was excellent company; la Duchesse de Gisors soon came to like her, and they became intimate friends. One day Madame de Gisors led her friend to understand that, although she could perfectly well imagine how one might succumb to a weakness, she could not understand how a woman could multiply the number of her lovers to such a point. "Alas," Madame Brisard said, "I thought each one would be the last."

❧ The Regent wanted to go to the ball and not be recognized. "I know a way," said the Abbé Dubois, and at the ball he gave him several kicks in the behind. The Regent, who thought they were rougher than necessary, said, "Abbé, you're disguising me too hard."

❧ La Fontaine heard someone express pity on the fate of the damned in hell fire, and said, "I like to think that they get used to it, and in the end are like fish in water."

❧ M. de Soubise was Madame de Nesle's lover. M. de Nesle, who despised his wife, quarreled with her one day in her lover's presence. He said, "Madame, everyone knows that I pay no attention to what you do. Even so, I must tell you that you have certain fancies that I find too degrading to ignore: for instance your predilection for my lackeys' wigmaker, whom I saw you go out with and take to your chamber." After a few threats he went out, leaving her with M. de Soubise, who slapped her face, for all her protestations. The husband then went and recounted the whole exploit, adding that the story of the wigmaker was false, ridiculing M. de Soubise for believing it and his wife for having been slapped.

❧ His courtiers wanted to cure Louis XV, then still a young man, of the habit of tearing their lace. M. de Maurepas undertook to do it. He appeared before the King in the finest lace imaginable. The King came up to him and tore off one side. M. de Maurepas coolly tore off the other, and then said flatly, "I did not enjoy that." The King was taken aback, blushed, and from then on tore no more lace.

❦ Beaumarchais, who had allowed himself to be ill-used by the Duc de Chaulnes without fighting with him, received a challenge from M. de la Blache. He answered, "I've refused better."

❦ M. de R—— had just read, to a small gathering, three or four epigrams against as many persons, none of whom was then living. They turned then to M. de —— as though to ask him whether he did not have a few with which to regale the company. "I?" he said naïvely. "Everyone I know is alive; I can't say a word."

❦ M. de Fontenelle, aged ninety-seven, had just said innumerable pleasant and gallant things to Madame Helvetius, who was young, beautiful, and just married. A moment later on his way to the table he passed in front of her without noticing her. "You see," Madame Helvetius said to him, "how much importance I can attach to your courtly speeches. You pass me without looking at me." "Madame," said the old man, "if I had looked at you, I would not have passed at all."

❦ The Duc de Lauzun said, "I often have heated arguments with M. de Calonne. But as neither of us has any character, the question is which of us will be quicker at giving in, and whichever of us first finds a nicely turned phrase upon which to retreat, is the first to withdraw."

❦ M. de Brissac, drunk with being a gentleman, often referred to God as, "The Gentleman up there."

❦ M. Lorri, a doctor, told how Madame de Sully summoned him when she was not feeling well, and recounted to him an insolence of Bordeu's, who had said to her, " 'Your illness is the consequence of your needs.' What a man!" and at the same time he had presented himself to her in a state that was scarcely decent. Lorri apologized for his colleague and himself plied Madame de Sully with a series of compliments that were courtly but respectful. He added, "I have no idea what happened after that. All I know is that she summoned me once again, and after that went back to having Bordeu."

℺ The Curé of Bray had moved three or four times from the Catholic to the Protestant faith, and his friends expressed surprise at his indifference. "Indifferent?" said the Curé. "Inconstant? Not at all. On the contrary, I don't change at all. I want to be the Curé of Bray."

℺ The familiarity which the King of Prussia allowed certain of those who lived with him is well known. General Quintus-Icilius was the one who took advantage of it most freely. Before the battle of Rosbak the King of Prussia said to him that if he lost it, he would retire to Venice and live as a doctor. Quintus answered, "An assassin to the end."

℺ The Chevalier de Montbarey had been living in I forget which provincial town, and upon his return, his friends commiserated with him about the society with which he had had to content himself. "You're quite mistaken," he said to them. "The good company in that town is like good company everywhere, and the bad is excellent."

℺ A peasant divided all that he owned among his four sons and went to live with each of them in turn. He was asked, on his return from one of these visits to his children, "Well, how did they receive you? How were you treated?" "They treated me," he said, "like their child"—an answer that, in the mouth of such a father, has a certain sublimity.

℺ M. de——, for whom the sources of the degradation of the human species were the Nazarene sect and the feudal system, said that in order to be worth anything, one would have to de-Frenchify and de-Christen oneself, and go back to having a Greek or Roman soul.

❡ M——, paying court to Prince Henry, at Neufchâtel, told him that the inhabitants of the place adored the King of Prussia. "It's very easy," said the Prince, "for subjects to love a master who is three hundred leagues away from them."

❡ M. de la Reynière was to marry Mademoiselle de Jarinte, who was young and charming. He came back from seeing her, enchanted to think of the happiness that was in store for him, and said to M. de Malesherbes, his brother-in-law, "Don't you think my happiness will be perfect?" "That depends on several circumstances." "What do you mean?" "It depends on who her first lover is."

❡ Diderot had among his friends an incorrigible young man who through some recent misdeed or other had just forfeited the friendship of an uncle, a rich canon, who resolved to disinherit him. Diderot went to the uncle, assumed a grave and philosophical air, preached in favor of the nephew, and tried to arouse the uncle's passion with his own pathos. The uncle then told of two or three of the nephew's misdemeanors. "He's done worse than that," Diderot answered. "What?" asked the uncle. "He wanted to murder you one day in the sacristy, as you came from mass, and it was only the arrival of two or three other people that prevented him from doing it." "That's not true!" cried the uncle. "It's a calumny!" "So it is," said Diderot, "but even if it were true, you should still forgive him because of the genuineness of his repentance, his present situation, and the miseries that are in store for him if you leave him penniless."

❡ M. de Voltaire found himself in the company of Mme. la Duchesse de Chaulnes; the latter, among the many compliments that she paid him, praised in particular the harmony of his prose. Suddenly M. de Voltaire flung himself at her feet. "Ah, Madame, I live with a pig who does not have a single sense, not an inkling of harmony, measure, etc." The pig he was referring to was Mme. Duchâtelet, his Emilie.

❦ I asked M—— why none of the pleasures seemed to have any hold on him. He answered, "It's not that I'm insensible to them. But there is not one of them that I think is worth what it costs. Fame lays one open to calumny. Reputation requires continual attention. The pleasures necessitate movement, physical fatigue. Society involves one in numberless difficulties: Everything is seen, examined, judged. The world has offered me nothing which I could not find in a better form by looking into myself. Having tried all these things a hundred times over, though I am neither apathetic nor indifferent by nature, I have become as it were immobile, and my present position always seems the best one to me because its very goodness seems to arise from its immobility and to grow with it. Love is a source of suffering. Sensuality without love is a pleasure that lasts only a few minutes. Marriage is judged even more harshly than other things. The honor of being a father brings with it a train of calamities. To own a house is to set oneself up as an innkeeper. The wretched motives that lead to a man's being sought after or highly regarded are transparent and could deceive no one but a simpleton, nor flatter anyone who was not ridiculously vain. I have come to the conclusion that rest, friendship, and thought are the only pleasures that suit a man who has passed the age of folly."

❦ Lord Bolingbroke gave Louis XIV many proofs of his sympathy during the latter's grave illness. The King was surprised and said to him, "I am especially touched because you English do not care for kings." "Sire," said Bolingbroke, "we are like husbands who do not love their wives but are not thereby prevented from paying court with redoubled ardor to the wives of our neighbors."

❦ In a dispute between the representatives from Geneva and the Chevalier de Bouteville, one of the former grew heated, whereupon the Chevalier said to him, "Do you know that I represent the King my master?" "Do you know," said the one from Geneva, "that I represent my equals?"

❰ A philosopher who had been reproached for his extreme liking for retirement said, "In society everything tends to lower me. In solitude everything tends to raise me up."

❰ I have paid close attention to M—— and find his character extremely interesting. Very charming, with no wish to charm anyone except his friends and those whom he respects. On the other hand a great dread of giving displeasure. This is a just feeling, and harmonizes what one owes to friendship with what one owes to society. It may be that someone will do more good than he; no one will do less evil. Some may be more zealous; none will be less importunate. Some may flatter more; none will shock less.

❰ M. de la Popinière took off his shoes one evening among his hangers-on and warmed his feet; a little dog licked them. Meanwhile the gathering talked of friendship, of friends. "A friend," said M. de la Popinière, pointing to the dog. "There's a friend."

❰ The Archbishop of Toulouse (Brienne) said to M. de Saint-Priest, the grandfather of M. d'Entragues, "There has never been, in France, under any king, a minister who carried his views and his ambition as far as they would go." M. de Saint-Priest said to him, "And the Cardinal de Richelieu?" "Stopped in midcareer," answered the Archbishop. A phrase that depicts a whole character.

❰ M. and Mme. d' Angev—— and M. and Mme. N—— appear to be unique couples, each in their way. It looks as though each belonged exclusively to the other, and as though love could go no further. I have studied them and have come to the conclusion that the heart has little to do with keeping them together, and that when it comes to character, they are yoked to each other for the most part by contrasts.

❡ The Maréchal de Noailles spoke scathingly about a new tragedy. Someone said to him, "But M. d'Aumont, in your own box, says it moved you to tears." "Not at all," said the Maréchal. "But as he was weeping himself from the first scene on, I thought it was only decent to share his sorrow."

❡ M. Th—— said to me one day that usually in society when one has performed a decent and courageous action, out of some motive worthy of it—in other words a thoroughly noble one— the doer must ascribe to the action a shabbier and more vulgar motive, in order to quiet envy.

❡ Louis XV asked the Duke d'Ayen (later Maréchal de Noailles) whether he had sent his household silver to the mint. The Duke admitted that he had not. "I," said the King, "have sent mine." "Oh Sire," said M. d'Ayen, "when J. C. died on Good Friday he knew perfectly well that he would be resurrected that same Sunday."

❡ Mme. de Créqui said to me, of the Baron de Breteuil, "He's not stupid, the Baron, he's just a fool."

❡ A man of wit said to me one day that the French government was an absolute monarchy tempered with songs.

❡ Lord Hervey, traveling in Italy and finding himself near the sea, crossed a lagoon, dipped his finger in it on the way, and said, "Ah! Salt water! It's ours!"

❡ Duclos asked a man who was bored by a sermon at Versailles, "Why did you sit through it to the end?" "I was afraid of disturbing the congregation and shocking them." "My God," said Duclos, "rather than sit through that sermon, I'd have been converted right at the start."

℄ M. d'Aiguillon, while he was Mme. Dubarry's lover, contracted an ailment elsewhere. He feared that he was lost because he thought he had given it to the Countess. Fortunately this was not the case. During the treatment, which seemed to him to go very slowly, and which obliged him to abstain from Mme. Dubarry, he said to the doctor, "This will be my undoing unless you can make it go faster." The doctor was M. Busson, who had cured him, in Brittany, of a mortal illness, when the other doctors had given him up. After M. d'Aiguillon's ruin, the recollection of this bad turn played on Providence had led to the loss of all M. Busson's posts, and of his practice among the nobility. Later, when M. d'Aiguillon became minister, it was some time before he did anything for M. Busson, who said (referring to the way the Duke behaved toward Linguet[7]), "M. d'Aiguillon neglects nothing except those who have saved his honor and his life."

℄ Diderot was asked what sort of man M. d'Epinay[8] was. "He's a man," he said, "who got through two million without saying a witty thing or doing a good one."

℄ M. de Th——, in order to indicate the insipidity of M. de Florian's sheepfolds, said, "I wouldn't mind them if he had put some wolves in."

℄ M. de Lassay, a very gentle man but with a great knowledge of society, said that one must swallow a toad every morning, when one had to go out in the world, so as not to find anything more disgusting during the day.

℄ M. d'Alembert had occasion to see Mme. Denis on the morning after her marriage to M. du Vivier. He asked whether she seemed happy. "Happy?" he said. "You can take my word for it. So happy it would make you sick."

[7] Simon Linguet, a lawyer who defended d'Aiguillon.
[8] A *fermier-général;* his wife was a famous patroness of Rousseau.

❦ M. de Voltaire, seeing religion grow weaker by the day, once said, "It's annoying, just the same. What will we have to ridicule?" M. Sabatier de Cabre said, "Oh, you needn't worry. There will be no more lack of occasions than of means." "Ah sir," M. de Voltaire said sadly, "there is no salvation outside the church."

❦ The Prince de Conti told Beaumarchais, during his last illness, that he had no hope of surviving it because of the exhausted state of his constitution, racked by war, wine, and sensuality. "As for war," said Beaumarchais, "Prince Eugene fought twenty-one campaigns and died at seventy-eight. As for wine, the Marquis de Brancas drank six bottles of champagne a day and died at eighty-four." "Yes," said the prince, "but coitus . . ." "Think of Madame your mother . . ." Beaumarchais answered. (The princesss was seventy-nine when she died.) "Quite so," said the prince. "I may recover after all."

❦ Someone, on reading in the *Journal de Paris* a very foolish letter of M. Blanchard's about the balloon, said, "With a mind like that M. Blanchard must get very bored up in the air."

❦ I was walking with a friend one day when he was greeted by a suspicious-looking man; I asked who it was and was told that it was someone who did for his country what Brutus would not have done for his. I begged my friend to make this great idea comprehensible to me. I learned that the man in question was a police spy.

❦ A philosopher who had retired from the world wrote me a letter full of virtue and reason. It ended thus: "Farewell, my friend. Keep, if you can, the interests that attach you to society, but cultivate the feelings that separate you from it."

❦ At sixty-two, Diderot, still in love with all women, said to a friend, "I keep saying to myself, 'Old fool, old mischief, when will you stop risking the humiliation of a refusal or of ridicule?' ”

ℭ M. de C—— one day was speaking of the English government and its advantages, in a gathering that included several bishops and several abbés, one of whom, the Abbé de Seguerand, said to him, "Sir, from the little I know of that country I have not the slightest wish to live there, and I am sure I would not be happy there." M. de C—— answered, ingenuously, "M. l'Abbé, it is because you would not be happy there that the country has so much to commend it."

ℭ When Mme. Desparbès was in bed with Louis XV, the King said to her, "You have gone to bed with all my subjects." "Oh, Sire!" "You have slept with the Duc de Choiseul." "He is so powerful." "The Maréchal de Richelieu." "He is so witty." "Monville." "He has such a pretty leg." "Heavens! Well, but the Duc d'Aumont—he has none of those attractions." "Oh Sire, but he is so devoted to Your Majesty!"

ℭ Mme. de Maintenon and Mme. de Caylus were walking by the lake at Marly. The water was very clear and the carp could be seen moving slowly, looking sad and thin. Mme. de Caylus pointed them out to Mme. de Maintenon, who answered, "They are like me: they miss their mud."

ℭ The English Ambassador to Naples gave a charming reception but had not spent a great deal of money on it. This was known, and the guests went away to denigrate the festivities, which had been a great success to start with. The ambassador avenged himself in a manner that was at once thoroughly English, and that of a man to whom guineas meant very little. He announced another reception. Everyone thought that he was planning to make up for the other one and that the entertainment would be magnificent. Everyone went. A huge assembly. Nothing for them. Finally an alcohol stove was brought in. The guests expected some miracle. "Sirs," said their host, "it is the expenses and not the pleasure of an entertainment that matter to you. Watch. (He opened his coat and showed the lining.) This is a sacred painting worth five thousand guineas. And that is not all. You see these ten bank notes. They are worth a thousand guineas each, payable on demand at the Bank of Amsterdam." He rolled them up and put them in the lighted alcohol stove. "I have no doubt, sirs, that this entertainment met with your entire approval, and that you will leave with a good opinion of me. Good-night, sirs; the entertainment is over."

ℭ "Posterity," said M. de B——, "is nothing but one public which follows another. Well, you can see what the public is at the moment."

ℭ "Three things," said N——, "annoy me both morally and physically, both figuratively and literally: noise, wind, and smoke."

ℭ "Madame de G.," said M——, "has too much wit and is too shrewd ever to be despised as heartily as many who are far less despicable."

ℭ The late Madame la Duchesse d'Orléans, at the beginning of her marriage, was very much in love with her husband, and there were few recesses of the Palais-Royal that were not witnesses of the fact. One day the young couple went to pay a visit to the dowager duchess, who was sick. During the conversation she fell asleep, and the Duke and Duchess were pleased to enjoy each other on the foot of her bed. She saw it and said to her daughter-in-law, "Madame, it took you to make me blush at marriage."

ℭ When the Maréchal de Duras was annoyed with one of his sons, he said, "Wretch, if you go on I'll make you have supper with the King." The young man had supped twice at Marly and been bored to death.

℄ Duclos, who never stopped vilifying the Abbé d'Olivet, said of him, "He's such a scoundrel that in spite of all the harsh things I say about him, he doesn't hate me any more than he hates everyone else."

℄ Duclos was talking of Paradise, one day, which everyone imagines in his own way. Mme. de Rochefort said to him, "When it comes to you, Duclos, it's clear what yours would consist of: bread, wine, cheese, and the first woman to hand."

℄ When M. de Bissi wanted to leave la Presidente d'Aligre he found on her mantlepiece a letter in which she told a man with whom she was plotting an affair that she hoped to maneuver M. de Bissi into leaving her first. She had, in fact, left the letter there on purpose. But M. de Bissi pretended he had seen nothing, and stayed with her for another six months, maddening her with his attentions.

℄ When M. d'Ormesson was Contrôleur-Général he said, in the presence of twenty people, that he had long tried in vain to understand what use men like Corneille, Boileau, and La Fontaine might have been. The company let it pass. When one is Contrôleur-Général they let anything pass. But M. Pelletier de Mort-Fontaine, his father-in-law, said to him gently, "I know that that is what you think. But for my sake have the prudence to keep it to yourself. I entreat you not to boast of your own incapacities. You occupy a post that was held by a man who was on intimate terms with Racine and Boileau, had them to stay often at his country estate, and said, when he was informed of the arrival of several bishops, 'Have them shown the castle, the gardens, anything, as long as it is not me.' "

℄ The cause of the Cardinal de Fleury's malevolent behavior toward the Queen, the wife of Louis XV, was the fact that she had repulsed his amorous advances. The proof has come to light since the Queen's death, in the form of a letter from King Stanislas, in reply to one from her asking him what she should do in the circumstances. The Cardinal, at the time, was seventy-six, but he had raped two women only a few months before. Mme. la Maréchale de Mouchi and another woman have seen the letter from Stanislas.

℃ For the lying-in of the late Dauphine, the celebrated Levret was summoned to the Court. M. le Dauphin said to him, "I imagine you are pleased, M. Levret, to be in charge of the delivery of Mme. la Dauphine. It will make your reputation." "If my reputation were not made," said Levret calmly, "I would not be here."

℃ Duclos one day told Mme. de Rochefort and Mme. de Mirepoix how prudish courtesans tended to become, how they would not listen to any story that was even a little bit daring. "They are far more prim," he said, "than virtuous women." And with that he launched into a very gay tale, then another that went somewhat further, and finally when his third story began even more lustily, Mme. de Rochefort stopped him and said, "Be careful, Duclos. We may not be as virtuous as you seem to think."

℃ The King of Prussia's coachman overturned his carriage, and the King flew into a terrible rage. "Well," said the coachman, "it's too bad. But look at you, haven't you ever lost a battle?"

℃ Even in his old age the Maréchal de Villars was addicted to wine. When he went to Italy to lead the army in the war of 1734, he went to pay his respects to the King of Sardinia so far gone in wine that he could not stand up, and fell headlong. Even in that condition he kept his head and said to the King, "Here I am, brought quite naturally to Your Majesty's feet."

℃ Some time after the death of Louis XV, the King had a concert stopped before the program was finished, because it bored him. "That's enough music," he said. The performers were told, and one of them said to another, "My friend, what a reign this promises to be."

❡ It was the Comte de Grammont himself who sold, for 1500 pounds, the manuscript of the memoir in which he is so clearly shown to have been a swindler. Fontenelle, who was the book's censor, refused to pass it, out of consideration for the Count. The latter complained to the Chancellor, to whom Fontenelle explained why he had refused his approval. Rather than lose his 1500 pounds, the Comte forced Fontenelle to pass Hamilton's book.

❡ M. de L——, a misanthrope in the manner of Timon, had just had a somewhat melancholy conversation with M. de B——, also a misanthrope, but a less somber one, and even occasionally quite merry. M. de L—— spoke of M. de B—— with interest, and said that he hoped they might become friends. Someone said to him, "Be careful. In spite of his grave manner he is sometimes extremely merry. You must not count on him."

❡ M. d'Invau, when he was Contrôleur-Général, asked the King for permission to get married. The King, when he learned who the young lady was, said, "You are not rich enough." The other mentioned his post, as something which made up for his lack of capital. "Ah," said the King, "posts come and go, but a wife remains."

❡ During the American war a Scot, pointing to some American prisoners, said to a Frenchman, "You fight for your lord and master, and I fight for mine, but who are these people fighting for?" An attitude that deserves a place beside the King of Pegu's, who thought he would die laughing when he heard that the Venetians had no kings.

℄ An old man who thought I was too sensitive about some injustice or other said to me, "My dear child, you must let life teach you how to endure it."

℄ A woman of ninety said to M. de Fontenelle, then ninety-five, "Death has forgotten us." "Shh," said M. de Fontenelle, putting his finger to his lips.

℄ M. de Vendôme said of Mme. de Nemours, who had a long curved nose above red lips, "She looks like a parrot eating a cherry."

℄ M. le Prince de Charolais surprised M. de Brissac with his mistress. "Go," he said. M. de Brissac answered, "My lord, your ancestors would have said, 'Let us go.'"

℄ M. de Voltaire was a guest of Mme. du Châtelet, and in fact was in her bedroom, playing with the little boy who was to become the Abbé Mignot, holding him on his knee. He began to chatter to the child and ply him with instructions. "My friend," he said, "in order to succeed with men, one must have the women on one's side. And to have the women on one's side, one must know them. Now, you should know that all women are false and licentious . . ." Mme. du Châtelet flew into a rage. "What! All women! What are you saying to him, sir?" she said. "Madame," Voltaire answered, "one must not deceive children."

℄ M. de Turenne was asked by M. de Lamoignon, with whom he was dining, whether his courage was never shaken at the beginning of a battle. "Yes," said M. de Turenne, "I am terribly agitated, but in the army there are quite a number of junior officers and a great many soldiers who are not troubled that way at all."

❧ I proposed to M. de L—— a marriage which I thought would be to his advantage. He answered, "Why should I marry? The best I could hope for would be to escape being a cuckold, and I can do that with greater certainty by not marrying at all."

❧ Fontenelle had written an opera containing a chorus of priests which shocked the pious. The Archbishop of Paris wanted to suppress it. "I don't meddle with his priests," Fontenelle said, "I don't see why he should meddle with mine."

❧ King Stanislas of Poland was well disposed toward l'Abbé Porquet and had not yet done anything for him. The Abbé reminded him of the fact. "But my dear Abbé," said the King, "it's largely your own fault. You maintain such revolutionary opinions. It's said that you do not believe in God. You must be a little more moderate. Try to believe. I'll give you a year."

❧ M. Harris, a famous London merchant, was in Paris in 1786 at the time of the signing of the trade treaty, and said to some Frenchman, with regard to that agreement, "I am convinced that France will only lose a million sterling a year for the first twenty-five or thirty years. After that things will even out."

❧ A very poor man who had written a book against the government said, "Good heavens, they haven't put me in the Bastille, and my rent's almost due."

❧ When the Archbishop of Lyon, Montazet, went to assume his charge, an old canoness of ——, the Cardinal de Tencin's sister, complimented him on his success with women, mentioning in particular the child he had had by Mme. de Mazarin. The prelate denied the whole thing and added, "Madame, you know, calumny has not spared you either. The story about me and Mme. de Mazarin has no more truth to it than the one that is told of you and M. le Cardinal." "In that case," said the canoness calmly, "the child is yours."

❦ Madame de C— said to M. B——, "What I love in you . . ." "Ah, Madame," he said fervently, "if you know what it is, I am lost."

❦ I knew a misanthrope who had good-natured moments, when he would say, "I wouldn't be surprised if there were an honest man hidden away somewhere in a corner, whom nobody knows about."

❦ The Maréchal de Broglie was needlessly exposing himself to danger and did not wish to withdraw; all his friends tried in vain to persuade him to do so. Finally one of them, M. de Jaucour, went up to him and said in his ear, "M. le Maréchal, remember that if you are killed, M. de Routhe will be in command." This personage was the stupidest of the staff generals. Stunned at the thought of such a danger to the army, M. de Broglie withdrew.

❦ A man drank excellent wine at table without praising it. Whereupon his host had him served some that was very mediocre. "This is a good wine," said the taciturn drinker. "It's a ten-penny wine," said his host, "whereas the other is a wine fit for the gods." "I know," his guest said, "which was why I did not praise it. This is the one that needs to have someone speak well of it."

❦ "Despite all the witticisms that are leveled against marriage," said M——, "I do not see how a man of sixty can be criticized for marrying a woman of fifty-five."

❦ "I beg you to believe," said M—— to a very rich man, "that I do not need what I do not have."

❦ A man of wit who had read M. d'Alembert's little essays on oratory, poetry, and the ode, was asked what he thought of them. He answered, "Not everyone can be dry."

℄ M—— clings to his ideas. One could say that there was a consistency in his intelligence, if he had any intelligence. Something might come of it if his prejudices could be turned into principles.

℄ A girl whose mother was jealous of her and her thirteen years said to me one day, "I keep feeling I should beg her pardon for having been born."

℄ I asked M. N—— why he no longer went out into society. He answered, "I no longer love women, and I know men."

℄ M—— was both insolent and vain when his first play was moderately successful. One of his friends said to him, "My friend, you are sowing brambles in front of you, and you will find them on your way through, the next time."

℄ "When I see how praise and blame are parceled out," said M. de B——, "I think that the more honest a man is the more he would prefer slander."

℄ M—— was told, "You are very fond of respect." I was much taken with his answer. "No. I respect myself, which sometimes leads others to respect me as well."

℄ M—— said of Mlle. —— (who was not venal, heeded only her heart, and remained true to the object of her choice), "She is a charming creature, and lives as honestly as one can, outside marriage and celibacy."

℄ A husband said to his wife, "Madame, that man has certain claims upon you, and he was disrespectful to you in my presence, a thing which I will not tolerate. He may abuse you when you are alone, but in my presence it is a mark of disrespect to me."

❡ I was at table beside a man who asked me whether the woman across from him was not the wife of the man sitting beside her. I had noticed that the latter had not addressed a word to her, and was able to say to my neighbor, "Sir, either he does not know her, or she is his wife."

❡ M——, when asked to dilate on various public and private abuses, answered coldly, "Every day I add to the list of things which I will no longer discuss. The more of a philosopher one is, the longer one's list."

❡ M. de L——, who was known to be a misanthrope, said to me one day, "One has to be very fond of someone to see him."

❡ A bachelor who was being urged to marry said, "If God will save me from women, I will save myself from marriage."

❡ A man was speaking of the respect that was due to the public. "Yes," said M——, "the respect that is born of prudence. Everyone despises fishwives. But who will risk offending them on his way through the market?"

❡ I asked M. R——, a man of great intelligence and talent, why he had not come forward during the revolution of 1789. He answered, "For thirty years I have found men so malevolent in private and singly that I could not hope for much good from them in public and collectively."

❡ "What they call 'the police' must be a dreadful thing," Mme. de —— said wittily, "if the English would rather have thieves and assassins, and the Turks would rather have the plague."

℃ "What makes the world disagreeable," M. de L—— said to me, "is swindlers in the first place, and honest folk in the second. For things to be endurable one would have to get rid of the former and reform the latter. One would have to destroy Hell and rearrange Heaven."

℃ M. said to me that he had always thought well of the following maxims about women: Always speak of the sex in general; praise the ones that are charming; say nothing about the others; see little of them; never trust them; and never let one's happiness depend on a woman, whoever she is.

℃ A philosopher told me that, having examined the civil and political order of societies, he now studied nothing except the savages in the books of explorers, and children in everyday life.

℃ Mme. de—— said of M. B——, "He is honest and worthy, but mediocre and prickly, like the perch: white, harmless, but tasteless and full of bones."

℃ I asked M—— why he had refused several posts. He said, "I want nothing that puts a role in the place of a man."

℃ It is worthy of note that two authors, both well acquainted with their subject and both of them, one in verse, one in prose, eulogists of immoral and libertine love, Crébillon and Bernard, both died passionately in love with prostitutes. It is even more astonishing to think of Mme. de Voyer possessed to her last moment with romantic love and passionately desiring the Vicomte de Noailles, while on his side M. de Voyer left two boxes full of love letters, in fair copies in his own hand. Which makes one think of cowards who sing in order to disguise their fear.

⟨ "For a man of intelligence," M. de—— said, laughing, "to have doubts about his mistress, that's reasonable; but about his wife, that's plain stupid."

⟨ M—— said, "In society you have three kinds of friends: your friends who are fond of you, your friends who don't care either way, and your friends who detest you."

⟨ M—— said, "I don't know why Mme. de L—— is so insistent on my going there, because when I haven't been there for some time I despise her less." One could say that of the world in general.

⟨ D——, a witty misanthrope, said to me, referring to the evil of men, "It's only the uselessness of the first flood that keeps God from sending a second."

⟨ M—— said that the disadvantage of being inferior to princes is richly made up for by the advantage of being far away from them.

⟨ M—— said, when a marriage was suggested to him, "I have loved two things to distraction: women and my single condition. I have lost the one passion; I must cling to the other."

⟨ The rarity of an honest feeling makes one stop sometimes on the street to watch a dog gnawing a bone. "It's on my way back from Versailles, Marly, Fontainebleau," said M. de——, "that this spectacle attracts me most."

⟨ M. Thomas said to me one day, "I have no need of my contemporaries. All I need is posterity." He cared passionately for fame. "A fine result of philosophy," I said, "to allow you to dispense with the living and make you depend on the unborn."

❡ N—— said to M. Barthe, "I have known you for ten years, and I always thought it would be impossible to be your friend. But I was wrong; there is a way." "What is that?" "Absolute self-abnegation, and a perpetual adoration of your egotism."

❡ At one time M. de R—— was less hard and denigrating than he is today, but he has used up his indulgence, and what little is left, he keeps for himself.

❡ M—— was accused of being a misanthrope. "No," he said, "I'm not, but I thought I was becoming one, and took the best way of avoiding it." "What did you do?" "Kept to myself."

❡ "It is time," said M——, "that philosophy had her own index, like the Inquisitions of Rome and Madrid. She should draw up a list of books that she forbids; her proscription would be more extensive than that of her rival. Even in the books that she approved in the main, how many individual ideas would she not condemn as being contrary to morality and indeed to good sense?"

❡ "That day I was very affable, not in the least brutal," M. S—— said to me, when in fact he had been both.

❡ M—— said one day, speaking of women and their faults, "One must choose between loving women and understanding them; there is no middle course."

❡ M——, who had published a book which had had a great success, was urged to publish a second, which his friends spoke of with enthusiasm. "No," he said, "one must give envy time to wipe off the froth."

❡ M——, a young man, asked me why Mme. de B—— had rejected his suit and had pursued M. de L——, who did not seem to welcome her advances. I told him, "My dear friend, Genoa, rich and powerful, offered its sovereignty to several kings who refused it, whereas wars were fought over Corsica which produces nothing but chestnuts, but which is proud and independent."

❡ M. de—— asked the Bishop of —— for a country house where the latter never went. The Bishop answered, "Don't you know that one must always have some place where one does not go, but where one thinks one would be happy if one did?" M. de ——, after a moment's silence, answered, "That's true. It's what has made heaven's fortune."

❡ I urged M. de L—— to forget the ill turns that he had been done by the M. de B—— who had formerly done him several kindnesses. He said, "God said we were to forgive the evils that were done to us. He said nothing about the favors."

❡ M—— was asked why nature had made love independent of our reason. He said, "It is because nature considers only the perpetuation of the species, and to achieve this she has to resort to our foolishness. If I am drunk and address myself to a barmaid or a prostitute, the goal of nature is fulfilled as satisfactorily as it would have been if I had won Clarissa after a two year suit, whereas my reason, left to itself, would have kept me from the barmaid, the prostitute, and perhaps from Clarissa herself. If he heeded only his reason, what man would choose to be a father and lay up for himself so many cares, so far in advance? What woman, for the sake of a few minutes' epilepsy, would make herself sick for a whole year? Nature, in separating us from our reason, insures her own rule, which is why, in this matter, she has put Zenobia and her goose-girl on the same footing, and Marcus Aurelius and his groom."

℄ "What can princes, and those in power, do for me?" said M——. "Can they give me back my youth, or can they take away my mind, the use of which consoles me for everything?"

℄ M. de B—— saw Mme. de L—— every day, and a rumor arose that he was going to marry her. When he heard it, he said to one of his friends, "There are few men whom she would not marry more willingly than she would me, and I feel the same way about her. It would be odd if, in fifteen years of friendship, we had not come to realize how antipathetic we are to each other."

℄ A gathering was debating whether it was more pleasant to give or to receive. Some said giving; others that, if friendship was perfect, the pleasure of receiving might be as delicate, and more keen. A man of wit, when his opinion was asked, said, "I would not like to consider which was the livelier pleasure. I would prefer giving. It seems to me, at least, that it is the more durable of the two, and I have always noticed that it was the one that was remembered longer."

℄ M——'s friends wanted to bend his character to suit their whims, and finding him always the same, said he was incorrigible. "If I were not incorrigible," he answered, "I would have been corrupted long ago."

℄ M—— said, "I have rejected M. de B——'s overtures because I have little respect for the qualities that make him want to know me, and because if he knew the qualities that I do respect in myself, he would not receive me."

℄ A man who had refused the advances of Mme. de S—— said, "What good is intelligence if it does not allow one to escape from Mme. de S——?"

℄ The Duke of —— was formerly a man of wit, and sought out the conversation of company that one could respect. At fifty he turned into an ordinary courtier. That calling, and the life at Versailles, suited his decaying intelligence, as cards do old women.

℄ A young man of the court was accused of being too passionately addicted to whores. There were a number of respectable and influential women present whose favor might have been lost to him through such an accusation, and one of his friends answered, "It's an exaggeration! It's a slander! He has other women too."

℄ M. de L—— said that marriage should be subjected to the same conditions as the renting of houses, which one leased for three, six, or nine years, with an option to buy if the place suited one.

℄ "The difference between you and me," said M——, "is that you have said to all the masks 'I know you,' while I have let them imagine that they were deceiving me. That is why the world is kinder to me than to you. It is a ball at which you have spoiled the others' game and your own amusement."

℄ "Man," said M——, "is a foolish animal, judging by myself."

℄ "I have seen," said M——, "few prides that satisfied me. The one that I admire most is that of Satan in *Paradise Lost*."

℄ "Happiness," said M——, "is not easily come by. It is very hard to find within ourselves, and impossible to find anywhere else."

℃ M—— was blamed for his taste for solitude. He answered, "I am more accustomed to my own faults than to those of others."

APPENDIX ONE

℃ IN PERU ONLY the nobles were allowed to study. Here they think differently.

℃ The Montgolfier brothers, after their triumphant demonstration of the balloons, applied, in Paris, for a tobacconist's shop for their parents. Their request was beset with numberless difficulties, the work of several persons, among them M. de Calonia, upon whom its success or failure depended. The Comte d'Antraigues, a friend of the Montgolfiers, said to M. de Calonia, "Sir, unless they are given what they have asked for, I shall publish how they fared in England, and then how, thanks to you, they are now faring in France." "And what happened in England?" "M. Étienne Montgolfier went to England last year. He was presented to the King, who welcomed him and invited M. Montgolfier to ask a favor of him. M. Montgolfier told Lord Sidney that as he was a foreigner, he did not know what he could ask for. The peer pressed him to make a request of some kind. Then M. Montgolfier thought of a brother of his, a poor priest in Quebec. He said it would give him great pleasure if his brother were to receive a little award of fifty guineas. The peer answered that such a request was worthy neither of the Montgolfiers, the King, nor his minister. Some time later the bishopric of Quebec fell vacant. Lord Sidney asked it of the King, who gave it to him, at the same time telling the Duke of Gloucester to abandon his suit for it in the name of someone else. It was with some difficulty that the Messieurs Montgolfier were able to prevent the royal bounty from going to such lengths. . . . It is a long way from that to the tobacconist's shop they are refused in France."

℃ "I can tell you the moment when I gave up love," said M——. "It was when women started to say, 'M——? I love him very much, I love him with all my heart,' etc. Once," he added, "when I was young, they said, 'M——? I have the deepest respect for him; he is a most excellent young man.'"

⊄ Before Mademoiselle Clairon brought in costume at the *Théâtre Française*, all tragedies were performed in the same garment, called a Roman gown, which was worn whether the characters were Greeks, Americans, Spaniards, or something else. Lekain was the first to consent to wear a real costume; he had a Greek gown made to play Oreste in *Andromaque*. Dauberval came into Lekain's dressing-room just as the wardrobe manager of the *Comédie* was bringing in the gown for Prestes. The novelty of it made a great impression on Dauberval, and he asked what it was. "It's called a Greek gown," said Lekain. "Ah! It's beautiful!" Dauberval said. "The next time I need a Roman gown, I'll have them make me a Greek one."

⊄ After deliberate crime and evil, one must list the ill effects of good intentions, the good actions that are injurious to the public weal, such as kindnesses done to scoundrels, stupidities of the good-natured, the distressing consequences of misapplied philosophy, clumsiness in trying to help one's friends, the false applications of useful or true maxims, etc.

⊄ Nature, in loading us with misery as she has done, while at the same time endowing us with an invincible attachment to life, appears to have behaved toward man like an incendiary who sets fire to our house after first posting sentinels at the door. The danger has to be very great indeed before we will jump out of the window.

⊄ Ministers in power sometimes (when they chance to have any wit) speak of the day when they will be in power no longer. One is often deceived by this, and imagines that they believe what they are saying. It is nothing but a flight of fancy, on their part. They are like sick persons who often speak of their death, but do not believe in it, as one can tell from other things they let fall.

℟ Someone said to the mesmerist doctor Delon, "Well! M. de B—— died in spite of your promise to cure him." He answered, "You were not there. You did not follow the progress of the cure. He died cured."

℟ A gazeteer published this: "Some say that Cardinal Mazarin is dead; others say he is alive; I do not believe either of them."

℟ They asked Madame de Rochefort whether she wanted to know the future. "No," she said, "it's too much like the past."

℟ L'Abbé Vatri was urged to ask for a post that had fallen vacant at the Collège Royal. "We'll see," he said, and did nothing about it. The post was given to someone else. One of the Abbé's friends ran to his lodging. "Now then! See how you are! You didn't ask for the post, and now the appointment has been made." "It's been made, has it?" he replied. "Well, then, I'll go and ask for it." "Are you mad?" "Indeed I'm not. I had a hundred competitors before, and now there's only one." He asked for the post, and got it.

℟ L'Abbé de Fleury had been in love with Madame la Maréchale de Noailles, who scorned his suit. He became prime minister; she had need of him, and he reminded her of her severity. "Ah, Monseigneur," she said ingenuously, "who could have foreseen it?"

℟ "You're yawning," said a wife to her husband. "My dear," he said, "husband and wife are one flesh, and when I'm alone, I'm bored."

℃ Maupertuis, sprawled in his armchair and yawning, said one day, "At this moment I'd enjoy solving some splendid problem if it weren't too difficult." A sentence which portrays the whole man.

℃ Mademoiselle d'Entragues, annoyed at Bassompierre's refusal to marry her, said to him, "You're the most foolish man at court." "You can see for yourself that that's not so," he said.

℃ A woman shed no tears at a performance of *Mérope*. They were surprised. She said, "I'd like to weep, but I'm dining in town."

℃ L'Abbé de Canaye said that Louis XIV should have given Gahusac a pension. "And why?" "Gahusac kept him from being the most despised man in his kingdom."

℃ Henri IV used a singular method to show the Spanish ambassador the different characters of his three ministers, Villeroi, Jeannin, and Sully. He summoned Villeroi. "Do you see that beam that looks as though it's about to give way?" "Very well," said Villeroi, without looking up. "It will have to be fixed. I'll give orders for it." Next he called in Jeannin, who said, "I'll have it examined." Then Sully was sent for, looked at the beam, and said, "Oh Sire, do you think so? That beam will outlast both of us."

℃ Marivaux said that style has its sex, and that one could recognize a woman from one sentence.

℃ La Gabrielli, a famous singer, asked five thousand ducats of the Empress, to sing for two months in St. Petersburg. The Empress said, "I pay none of my field marshals on that scale." "In that case," said La Gabrielli, "'Your Majesty should of course

have her field marshals sing." The Empress paid the five thousand
ducats.

℃ "Atheists are a better influence on me than believers," said M.
D——. "At the sight of an atheist all the half-proofs of the existence of God come to my mind, and at the sight of a believer all
the half-proofs that he does not exist leap to mind."

℃ M—— said, 'I heard something to the discredit of M. de ——;
I would have believed it six months ago, but we have been rec-
onciled."

℃ One day, when several of the representatives were talking
rather too loudly at the assembly, M. de Harlay, who was presid-
ing, said, "If the gentlemen who are talking would make no more
noise than the gentlemen who are sleeping, it would enormously
convenience the gentlemen who are listening."

℃ "I know how to be sufficient unto myself," said M——, "and
if the need arose, I could even do without myself," meaning that
he would die without thinking it a calamity.

℃ Mlle. du Thé had lost one of her lovers; it became known; a
man paid a call on her and found her playing the harp. He was
surprised, and said to her, "Heavens! I expected to find you in a
state of desolation." "Oh," she said, her voice full of pathos, "you
should have called yesterday."

℃ The Marquise de Saint-Pierre was at a gathering where it was
said that M. de Richelieu had had a great many women without
having ever loved one. "Without having loved one! That's easy
enough to say," she said, "but I happen to know a woman whom
he traveled three hundred leagues to get back to." She went on to
recount the story in the third person, but the telling of it got the

better of her: "He flung her on the bed with an incredible violence, and we were there for three days."

❡ A thorny question was put to M——, who answered, "That is
one of those things which are wonderfully clear to me as long as
no one mentions them, and which I forget as soon as anyone asks
me about them."

❡ A man who professed a deep respect for women was asked
whether he had had many. He said, "Not as many as if I had
respected them less."

❡ In an argument about the cruel disgrace that blights the
families of those who are found guilty, M—— said, "It's bad
enough to see honors and rewards where there is no virtue, without having to see punishment where there has been no crime."

❡ Lord Tirauley said that if you stripped a Spaniard of everything good about him, you were left with a Portuguese. He said
this while he was ambassador to Portugal.

❡ M. de L——, in an attempt to dissuade Mme. de B—— from
marrying again when she had been widowed for some time, said,
"You know, it's a very fine thing to bear the name of a man who
will never again do anything foolish."

❡ The Vicomte de S—— one day came up to M. de Vaines and
said to him, "Is it true, sir, that in a house where they had the
goodness to say that I had wit, you said I had none?" M. de
Vaines answered, "Sir, there is not a word of truth in it. I was
never in a house where anyone said you had wit, and I never said
you had none."

℄ Man comes to each age of his life a novice.

℄ A man of slender means undertook to help an unfortunate who had been commended in vain to the benevolence of a great lord, and to that of a man of immense wealth and influence. I told him of these two circumstances, with all the details that rendered these two personages still more blameworthy. He answered calmly, "How could the world go on if the poor ever stopped doing the good that the rich cannot be bothered to do, and patching up the harm that they do?"

℄ A young man was told to ask a woman of about forty, with whom he had been very much in love, to return his letters. "I don't suppose she still has them," he said. "Oh yes, she does," they said. "Women start keeping love letters somewhere around thirty."

℄ Madame de Talmont noticed that M. de Richelieu, instead of paying attention to her, was laying suit to Madame de Brionne, who was very beautiful but was not known for her wit. She said to him, "Monsieur le Maréchal, you are not blind, but I think you are a little deaf."

℄ There is an Italian farce in which Harlequin says, of the troubles of the sexes, that we would all be perfect if we were not men or women.

℄ M— said of Mme. la Princesse de—, "She's a woman whom one must deceive because she is not the sort one can leave."

℄ M. de—, a man of violent temper, when reproached for certain wrongs he had done, flew into a rage and said he would go and live like a hermit. One of his friends answered calmly, "I see you would rather keep your faults than your friends."

❡ When he heard the account of the battle of Ramillies, after the defeat, Louis XIV said, "God seems to have forgotten all that I have done for him." (The story was told to Voltaire by the old Duc de Brancas.)

❡ A man said to Voltaire that he worked too hard and drank too much coffee, and was killing himself. "I was born killed," he said.

❡ A wife had just lost her husband. Her confessor (in an honorary capacity) came to see her the next day and found her playing cards with a very well-dressed young man. "Sir," she said, "you look surprised; if you'd come a half hour ago, you would have found me bathed in tears. But I staked my sorrows on a card with this gentleman, and I lost."

❡ M—— said of the way in which people live in the world, "Society would be delightful if people were interested in each other."

❡ The Baron de la Houze had performed a number of favors for Pope Ganganelli, and the latter asked him whether there was not something he could give him that would please him. The Baron de la Houze, who was a sly fellow, asked for the body of a saint. The Pope was surprised at a Frenchman's asking for such a thing, but he arranged to have it given to him. The Baron had a little estate in the Pyrenees which brought in next to nothing and had no market for its products; he had the saint taken there and accredited. The customers flocked in, the miracles started, a village sprang up, the prices of local products went up, and the Baron's revenues tripled.

❡ Lord Hamilton, a most eccentric personage, killed a serving boy while he was drunk in a tavern in England, and retired without realizing what he had done. The innkeeper went to his room in great agitation and said, "My lord, do you know you killed that boy?" The lord stammered out, "Put him on the bill."

℃ They say of an extremely unfortunate man: "He falls on his back and breaks his nose."

℃ M—— said, on his return from Germany, "I know of nothing that I would be less suited to be than a German."

℃ King Stanislas of Poland dined a little earlier every day. M. de la Galaisière said to him, "Sire, if you go on this way, you will end by dining the night before."

℃ A Catholic of Breslau stole from a church of his own faith some little gold hearts and other offerings. Taken before the court, he said the Virgin had given them to him. He was condemned. The sentence went to the King of Prussia for his signature, as is customary. The King summoned a number of theologians to inquire whether it was absolutely impossible for the Virgin to make little presents to a devout Catholic. The theologians of that faith, deeply embarrassed by the question, decided that it was not absolutely impossible. Thereupon the King wrote on the bottom of the sentence, "I pardon the aforenamed N——, but I forbid him, on pain of his life, to accept any more presents of any kind from the Virgin or the saints."

℃ M. the Bishop of L—— was having lunch when the Abbé de —— arrived. The Bishop asked him to lunch; the Abbé refused. The prelate insisted. "Monseigneur," said the Abbé, "I have already lunched twice, and besides today is a fast day."

APPENDIX TWO

℄ A WOMAN OF WIT, at a performance of *Rinaldo and Armida*, in which the one was hideous and the other deformed, said, "Those lovers don't look like people who chose each other; they look like the two who were left when everyone else had chosen."

℄ Mme. Cramer, returning to Paris after several years in Geneva, was asked, "What is Mme. Tronchin (a very ugly woman) doing?" "Frightening?" she answered.

℄ The King of Prussia had built a barrack which shut out the daylight from a Catholic church. A complaint was sent to him. He returned it with these words written at the bottom: "Blessed are they who have not seen but believe."

℄ "When I have a temptation," said M——, "do you know what I do?" "No." "I keep it."

APPENDIX THREE

℄ AN ENGLISHMAN CONDEMNED to be hanged was pardoned by the King. "The law is on my side," he said. "Hang me."

℄ Julius Caesar, after listening to a bad orator, said, "If you meant to be speaking, you were singing. If you meant to be singing, you were singing very badly."

℄ A gambler wanted to sublet the remainder of his lease. He was asked whether the light was good in his apartment. He said, "Alas, I don't know. I go out so early and come in so late."

❡ Speech of a man hastily condemned to be hanged, by the Court of Exchange (Paris, 1775 or 1776): "Sirs, I am grateful to you. In your haste to have me hanged in order to exercise your jurisdiction, you put me everlastingly in your debt. I have committed twenty thefts and four murders. My legal deserts are far worse than my sentence. I am innocent of the present crime. Thank you."

❡ The Maréchal de Luxembourg was imprisoned in the Bastille for two years on an accusation of practicing magic. He was let out to command the armies. "They still need magic," he said with wit.

❡ M. de——, a well-known liar, had just told some improbable tale. "Sir," someone said to him, "I believe you. But you will agree that it is very wrong of Truth not to deign to be a bit more likely."

❡ An Indian chief under the orders of M. de Montcalm had a conversation with him in which the General became angry. The Indian said to him impassively, "You command, and you get angry?"

❡ Mme. la Duchesse du Maine one day had need of the Abbé de Vaubrun and sent one of her valets to find him wherever he might be. The man went, and to his great surprise, found the Abbé de Vaubrun saying mass in some church or other. He caught the Abbé as the latter was coming down from the altar and gave him the message, after expressing his surprise at finding him saying mass. The Abbé, who was a great libertine, said, "I beg you not to tell the Princess of the state in which you found me."

❡ They were telling tall tales one day in front of Louis XV. The Duc d'Ayen told of a certain Franciscan Prior who shot a

Franciscan every day as they came from matins, always waiting for his man at the same doorway. The rumor spread. The provincial of the order paid a visit to the monastery, counted the Franciscans, and found, fortunately, that not a single one was missing.

℀ A little boy asked his mother for jam. "Give me too much," he said.

SHORT PHILOSOPHICAL DIALOGUES

DIALOGUE IX

A: He was trying to humiliate you.
B: He who can be honored only by himself can be humiliated by no one.

DIALOGUE XVI

A: I would gladly do him a bad turn.
B: He never did you one.
A: Someone has to start.

DIALOGUE XXIV

A: One must live with the living.
B: Not true. One must live with the dead.

DIALOGUE XXXVIII

MME. DE ——: Who's that coming toward us?
MME. DE C——: It's Mme. de Ber——
MME. DE ——: Do you know her?
MME. DE C.——: What? Don't you remember all the dreadful things we said about her yesterday?

DIALOGUE XLIX
(Between the Nuncio Pamphili and his secretary)

THE NUNCIO: What do they say of me out in the world?
THE SECRETARY: They accuse you of having poisoned so-and-so, a relative of yours, to get the inheritance.
THE NUNCIO: I had him poisoned for quite a different reason. And then?

THE SECRETARY: And of having murdered Signora——for being unfaithful to you.

THE NUNCIO: Not at all. It was because I feared for a secret that I had told her. And what else?

THE SECRETARY: Of having given one of our pages the——

THE NUNCIO: Quite the contrary. It's he who gave it to me. Is that all?

THE SECRETARY: They accuse you of having pretensions to wit, and of not being the author of your last sonnet.

THE NUNCIO: Blockhead! Scoundrel! Out of here at once!

DIALOGUE LV
(Between a Master and his Valet)

THE MASTER: You rogue! Ever since your wife died you get drunk every day. You used to get drunk only two or three times a week. I want you to get married again tomorrow.

THE VALET: Oh sir! Allow me a few more days' grief.

DIALOGUE LVI

A: I suppose, sir, that you owe me ten thousand crowns. . . .

B: I beg you, sir, to start with a different hypothesis.

DIALOGUE LXXI

CHLOÉ: Madame, were you never young?

ARTÉMISE: Never as young as you, Madame.

DIALOGUE LXXIII

DAMON: (at the ball, to Eglé, in her mask) Are you pretty?

EGLÉ: I hope so.

THE TAKING

OF THE

BASTILLE[1]

JULY 14, 1789

---

[1] It should be remembered that this essay, like the others in the series *Scenes of the Revolution,* was written to be published as a text accompanying illustrations of the events.

In a huge enclosure, surrounded by a wide, deep ditch, rose eight round towers, with walls six feet thick, joined together by sections of even thicker masonry. Such was the appearance of the castle that was the Bastille, defended besides by bastions within the walls, guardhouses, ditches crossed by drawbridges between different courtyards, the first of which presented three pieces of artillery loaded with grapeshot and facing the entrance. Fifteen cannons ringed the ramparts and twenty thousand-weights of powder, brought in two days before, at the moment when the Parisians became soldiers, were there to fire the artillery. Eighty Swiss or *invalides* made up the garrison. Mounds of stones were piled up on the ramparts and bastions to protect them from assault. It was from this place that the governor, detested by the people, thought that he could defy them. But all eyes were turned toward this fortress. From the morning onwards, the words "To the Bastille! To the Bastille!" were repeated throughout the whole of Paris, and starting the evening before, several citizens had sketched plans for attacking it. The fury of the populace served as a plan. One could see the cannons trained on the city. A single citizen, in the name of his district, went to request the governor to spare the people this sight. He boldly gave his advice, which sounded like warnings. At his voice the cannons turned away, and the people applauded the brave citizen, who made an appearance at the top of the towers. Soon a new multitude came demanding arms and ammunition. They were received in the outermost courtyard, but they had scarcely entered when, either through some misunderstanding on the part of the soldiers inside, or perfidy on the part of the governor himself, a large number of these unfortunates perished under a rolling salvo of musket fire. The cries of the dying echoed outside, together with shouts of "Murder!" and "Treachery!" Fury, desperation, rage, seized all hearts.

Two intrepid men, climbing onto a guardhouse, hurl themselves across the drawbridge and break the irons and bolts with hatchet blows, under the enemy fire. The crowd surges across. It floods that courtyard, is repulsed for a moment by the musket fire. Meanwhile a first, and soon a second deputation, preceded by a drum and a white flag, arrive and are exposed to the same dangers. A new fury seizes the populace. The representatives try to restrain them, to prevent them from rushing to a useless death. "Useless!" cries the multitude, with howls of rage. "No, no, our dead will fill the ditches." The attack begins again; the blood runs in the gutters. Accidents, mistakes, haste, multiply the dangers and disasters. Finally a detachment of grenadiers and a troop of townsmen commanded by a military man whom they had elected to be their leader advance on the fortress, followed by cannons, which they set up at strategic points. They take up positions, deploy themselves like men of experience. Wagons loaded with straw and set alight at the foot of the ramparts send up a cloud of smoke, which hides the actions of the besiegers from the besieged, while from the top of the neighboring houses the fusiliers stationed along the rampart are driven back with rifle fire. Soldiers, citizens, artisans—maneuvers, armed, unarmed, are of the same quality; their fury is the same. Fathers see their sons killed, grandchildren their grandfathers; children of seven collect musket balls, still burning hot, to take to the grenadiers. A young girl in military uniform is to be seen everywhere at her lover's side. A wounded man cries out, "I am dying, but hold firm, my friends; you will take it."

During this attack some of the populace forced the arsenal and the central powder store, and brought their defenders munitions of every kind. In every courtyard, at every doorway, a new combat, marked by acts of heroic courage. Elie, Hulin, Tournai, Arné, Réole, Cholat, your names, dear to your country, and rendered immortal by that day, will survive those of so many other warriors, however famous, who shed their blood only for their masters, and served, in futile combats, nothing but the ambition of ministers or the vain quarrels of kings.

This last attack, so impetuous and so terrible, renders them masters of a bridge, and the besiegers, encouraged, and more enraged than ever, bring up three pieces of artillery and place them before the second bridge. Already their success seems certain. Launay [the governor of the Bastille; translator's note] trembles, and some of his soldiers talk of surrendering. At that word he loses control; he seizes a lighted taper and runs to the powder magazine to fire it. He is forced back by his own men. He begs, as a favor, for a barrel of powder with which to blow himself up. The garrison shows the white flag and asks to be allowed to surrender. "No," is the answer from the crowd. A paper emerges from a battlement, on the outside of the fortress. An intrepid citizen moves out along a rocking plank to seize it; he falls into the ditch. Another replaces him; he is luckier, takes the writing, returns it, hands it to the brave Elie. The writing said, "We have twenty thousand-weights of powder; we will blow up the garrison and the whole neighborhood if you do not accept our surrender." "We accept it, on my word as an officer," says Elie. "Drop your drawbridges." The bridges come down. The crowd rushes in. What does it see? The *invalides* on the left, the Swiss on the right, putting down their arms and shouting their acclaim of the victors. Launay is seized and taken off to the Hôtel de Ville, where he was not destined to arrive.

Meanwhile the multitude rushes on and covers the entire enclosure of the fortress. They climb into the rooms above, along the platforms, where they are still under the fire of those who had been too far away to hear of the surrender. The assailants, without realizing it, kill their friends and defenders. The courageous Arné, braving almost certain death, advances along the parapet, his grenadier's hat on top of his pike, and stops this disaster. The joy is redoubled, the crowd grows larger, rushing in from the neighboring streets. The prisons are forced, the cells; they are entered; all the cellars are broken into; the prisoners are freed; they had imagined that this tumult heralded their death, and are astonished at being embraced. Their chains are broken. They are led toward the light, which some of them, grown old in their cells, had forgotten, and which their eyes could not bear. Astonishment is expressed at the weight of their chains, which are broken, are torn up, and presently are carried around them, around the litters on which these unfortunates are borne into the public squares, into the gardens. These instruments of duress are spread out before the astonished multitude, iron corselets and other instruments of torture, refinements of an inventive barbarity. The odds and ends that were taken from beneath these dark vaults, bolts, irons, everything that a first effort can tear loose, become trophies in the hands of whoever seizes them. The keys to the cells, borne to the Hôtel de Ville as a proof of this happy victory, pass from hand to hand, through the hands of an elector who is known to have inhabited that execrable keep. These memories, these contrasts, redouble the public's delight, which is soon further increased by the arrival of the conquerors with the flags of the *invalides* and the Swiss, rescued from the first fury of the populace, and now protected against it by those who have conquered them.

What pen, what brush, could even suggest the shifting and varied scenes that then met the eyes, in the vast rooms of the Hôtel de Ville, on the staircases, on the Place de Grève, the bloody weapons, the fluttering streamers, the national colors, the strange and impressive trophies of an unexpected victory, the triumphal and civic crowns awarded by the universal enthusiasm, the movement from fierce passions to generous passions, from terrible deeds to the gentlest tenderness, whose unheard-of-mixture, whose sublime expression, bore the soul and the imagination back to heroic ages?

History has already consecrated acts of virtue, magnanimity and grandeur that soften the painful memory of the people's revenges. They shed blood, it is true; but their own has just been shed. The Bastille is still standing. The dead, the dying, surround it. Parents, friends, carry the wounded into nearby houses, into hospitals which piety has consecrated to humanity. One of them, dying, asks, "Is it taken?" "Yes," someone tells him. He raises joyful eyes and breathes his last. A mother looks for her son among the disfigured corpses. Surprise is shown at a curiosity that appears barbarous. "Can I look for him," she asks, "in a more glorious place?" Did liberty speak a fairer language in the lands that she honored longest with her presence?

PASSAGES
FROM
ESSAYS

I

FROM "ON THE *MEMOIRES DE RICHELIEU*"
(*written around 1791 for the* Mercure de France)

. . . The editor of Richelieu's *Memoirs* consecrates several chapters to a portrayal of the interior of the court during the last fifteen or twenty years of his (Louis XIV's) reign. Saint-Simon's memoirs, which have been published recently, or at least extracts from them, had already made us familiar with this scene. Richelieu's add several details to the picture. They are, in fact, no more than anecdotes, but they are often linked to great events or interests, or to famous or imposing names. It is vain for philosophy to scorn details of this anecdotal kind, as she seems to do, or to inveigh against the pleasure which she herself takes in lingering over them. An involuntary interest detains us in spite of ourselves before these contrasts between the greatness of events and the pettiness of their protagonists, the apparent happiness and the real misery. So many means of glory reduced to court vanity, so many sources of real pleasures producing nothing but pointless amusements and sometimes painful bitterness: these, whatever may be said, are considerations that are far more likely than hackneyed human ill will to lead our eyes to the weaknesses of the courts. The philosopher and the man of the people can almost equally find matter for thought, or at least for feeling, in the spectacle of a dauphin of France, forty years old, honored by several military successes, the pupil of Bossuet and Montauzier, born with a happy disposition but a weak character, led by degrees and then kept in a sort of annihilation at court; a son of the King of France, father of a King of Spain, not daring to lay claim to the slightest favor for himself or for anyone else; and so discouraged by the King's severe despotism that he spent whole days propped on his elbows, blocking his ears, with his eyes fixed on the bare table, or sitting in a chair tapping his feet with the end of his cane for the whole of an evening; at last dying at Meudon, almost forgotten at court, abandoned by his officers, buried without even the ceremony appropriate to his rank, his coffin covered with the ordinary pall that was used for peasant funerals in the village.

In reading this edition of the *Mémoires de Richelieu*, one is not reading Tacitus, but one's attention is frequently caught by personages and objects that remind one of his pen: an old despot, long cloaked in a mendacious glory, now eclipsed, that had been bought with the tears and blood of his people; gloomy, languishing between his favorite and his confessor who applaud him for expiating the errors of his youth by torturing the conscience of his subjects; surrounded by his illegitimate children who make him the pawn of their intrigues and the tool of their ambition; virtually detesting, in his legitimate son, his needful heir; with too little love for his grandson, in whom he sees nothing but the pupil of Fenelon, a prince who thinks that kings are made for their people and not the people for their kings, which at the time was a kind of blasphemy; loathing his capital, which pretends not to know about a serious illness in its king, while it regards that of the dauphin as a public calamity; crushed with boredom in a court in which his pride is humored with absurd suppositions, by the reception of a make-believe ambassador from Persia, a Portuguese adventurer paid by the Jesuits to perform his comedy and rehearsed by them in his part; the honors due only to public emissaries accorded to two generals of Franciscan orders, come from Rome on the pretext of visiting their establishments but actually there on the instigation of the favorite, to keep the King occupied; finally the death of the despot, given up, for three days, to the care of a few inferior domestics, abandoned by his confessor, who had come to Paris to start intrigues for the regency; by his wife, who had fled to Saint-Cyr and returned only upon his command; the capital celebrating its joy with festivities, fanfares, and dancing, all the way from Paris to the tomb, to which the procession made its way across fields and by little-known lanes in order to escape the indignation of a people that in the midst of its loud rejoicings calls him a bad king. What a thing to be called by a people that has been famous until then for its love of its monarchs, "so anxious to love them," to use a phrase quoted from Richelieu himself! Let no one be surprised that Louis XIV did not continue to be called "the great" in the common tongue, as his flatterers had referred to him, and as the whole of Europe had seemed almost prepared to do, in its momentary seduction. . . .

One is forced to admire the fatality that presides over the destinies of nations when one sees the composition of circumstances, prior and contemporary, that prepared and served the despotism of this prince; the conjuncture of his capabilities and his faults, his tastes, his habits, and his preferences, selected as though by design, and brought into agreement, to conduct him to this fated end; the length of his reign, during which all the political prejudices that are injurious to a society took root and grew strong; in which all the institutions, all the establishments bore the mark of a more or less ornate, more or less decorated servitude; in which public slavery, dazzled by the sovereign and developed from that dazzled state, seemed to take pride in growing daily into a religious cult, and foretold the apotheosis of the monarch; finally the result of this enfeebled but not abolished illusion, which toward the end left Louis XIV with his pride and his griefs, France with her misfortunes, her misery, and her degradation, given over to the pleasant arts or to futile tastes, without knowledge of the principles of society or of government, or the means of ridding herself of her troubles or preventing their recurrence; in a word, abandoned to all the hazards of an uncertain future, and the whims that she had deified for sixty years in the person of the prince who had longest and most constantly abused her. . . .

II

FROM "ON *LA VIE PRIVÉE DU MARÉCHAL DE RICHELIEU*"

. . . One might say that Richelieu set out, at fourteen, to begin his amorous career with a princess, an heir presumptive to the throne. It is believed that he was distinguished by the Duchess of Burgundy. This is what is believed, and that opinion, in the eyes of Richelieu, was almost equivalent to reality. He acquired a precocious celebrity as a result of this adventure, which was somewhat precocious in itself; and he was rewarded with marriage and imprisonment in the Bastille. The very scandal of the punishment lent credit to that rumor that was so favorable to the young man's self-esteem. He admits that he was at pains to confirm this suspicion. His chief excuse, apart from vanity, was that it could do the princess no harm, since she was dead; and it is true that the dead allow one to slander them as much as one likes. Richelieu suddenly found himself the object of the kindness of several ladies of the court. . . .

But as long as the King was alive, his gallantries were decent—that is, unknown. No one knew, for example, of an adventure with a certain Mme. Michelin, an adventure in which Richelieu displayed a cold atrocity, monstrous at his age. It is this fundamental barbarity that Richardson says is at the heart of the true libertine, and which he has expressed so clearly in the character of Lovelace. Richelieu himself has preserved for us all the details of this horrible anecdote . . . Mme. Michelin was a mere bourgeoise . . . a young woman of a rare beauty, of a most modest and touching demeanor, respectable, demure, religious, and up until that time thoroughly devoted to her duties. Unfortunately these duties were not all equally agreeable: her husband was old, a worthy man occupied with his business. He was a dealer in mirrors and furniture in the Faubourg Saint Antoine. The Duc de Fronsac (his name at the time) saw her, became enamored, disguised himself, visited the merchant as a prospective buyer of furniture, tried to render himself attractive to the wife, failed to obtain a hearing, saw nevertheless that she was attracted, and that the only obstacles to his passion were in the respectability of its object. He decided to resort to crime and violence; but he was short of money: his father was alive. What does he do? The young duke visits a lady of the court, of whom he is enamored and who returns his passion, and he borrows from her the money he needs in order to be unfaithful to her. He had already had an apartment furnished by the worthy Michelin, who was not surprised that a young man should have a haven to offer his mistresses. But it was a question of leading the worthy man's wife into this haven. It was not possible that she would come of her own free will; how was she to be brought? He indicates that a certain duchess wishes to give M. Michelin her custom and place an order for furnishings. But with that in view she wishes to speak with Mme. Michelin. The duchess was in the country. A carriage would come for the furnisher's wife, come for her in fact, on a day when the husband had been carefully induced to be elsewhere. The conveyance took the wife to an unknown house. She entered an apartment where she found the Duc de Fronsac. Surprise, fright of the unfortunate woman. She defends herself against his advances, but the duke had had all the doors locked. The victim succumbs. The guilty one was beloved; he obtained her favor, and a second rendezvous besides, not in that house but in Mme. Michelin's own. There, continuing to warm the heart and senses of a woman who was weak, but decent and worthy of consideration even in her error, banishing remorse with love, he succeeded, one night agreed upon in advance, in sharing the nuptial bed.

What was his goal? He had noticed a friend of Mme. Michelin's who lived in the same house and was as young and beautiful as her neighbor, but it was a different kind of beauty. He chided himself for not having paid enough attention to her, for having been unjust with regard to her. The harm was easily repaired. She, having nothing in her favor but her face, was a vain and silly bourgeoise, flattered at having attracted the attentions of a duke; she gave the impression of being a woman who was born for vice, as Mme. Michelin was for virtue. The negotiation did not take long, but the Duc de Fronsac needed something to compensate for this facility and give the adventure more relish. It was his fancy to choose for his rendezvous with Mme. Renaud (the name of this woman) the same night, won with such pains, which should have been Mme. Michelin's; a night whose anticipation had been bought with terrible remorse, redoubled by the idea—horrifying to a pious bourgeoise—of drugging a servant with opium. Imagine her surprise when, before two in the morning, the Duc de Fronsac, deceiving his mistress with some tale, some romantic story, quitted her apartment and apparently left the house. He went up to Mme. Renaud's and stayed with her until nine in the morning.

But if he had a taste for scenes with a certain spice, he had every reason to be satisfied. Here is Mme. Michelin, who, probably in search of distraction from her sorrow, or in order to escape for a moment from her remorse, has come to pay her friend a visit. There before her eyes is the Duc de Fronsac. She does not recover from her surprise; neither woman is in the other's confidence. Mme. Renaud had gone in awe of her pious friend, whom she had thought unapproachable. Her pious friend can scarcely believe that she had been deceived, and is far from imagining that she had been betrayed. And indeed she has not been betrayed, yet: M. de Fronsac had said nothing to Mme. Renaud. But he was not a man to deprive himself of the additional delight that the revelation of the mystery flung into this scene. He informed Mme. Renaud, in her extreme humiliation, that her friend had reasons for being indulgent, that a night shared between two respectable rivals provided no grounds for misunderstanding between them, nor with their lover. . . . And yet this scene required still further inducements to gaiety, and with this in mind he urged the two rivals to live amicably together, to form among three hearts a truly gentle and charming society, and by the way of precedent he cited numerous examples drawn from history, both sacred and profane. His proposal, which did not seem to fill Mme. Renaud with infinite horror, stunned and overwhelmed Mme. Michelin; but at last he managed to calm her, to console her, and left alone with her, he even obtained her pardon.

That is not all: still seduced, still enticed, she consents to lunch at the Duc de Fronsac's. This time at least she expects to be alone, with no rival to fear. But Fronsac held to his plan and meant to see it in operation. Mme. Renaud appears: a new portrayal of the delights involved in a sentiment shared by three beautiful souls; and continuing to add to the confusion of their ideas by his tone, his vivacity, his manners, he obliges the two ladies to draw lots to see who should pass first from his salon into his private chamber. Each in turn having had this audience, they returned, the one rather satisfied, the other with death in her heart. It is easy to guess that the latter was poor Mme. Michelin. A decent bourgeoise, not born for such behavior, and finding only a source of suffering in the error that had seduced her, confused, rent with remorse, degraded in her own eyes, she became mournful, she languished, she fell ill. He found her merely boring . . . He was finished with Mme. Michelin. She wished to see him, and spoke to him like Clarissa to Lovelace, as a tender and devout soul who renounces the life but contemplates with horror the future and salvation of the object of her love. One can imagine her welcome. He went to tell this exquisite adventure to the duchess, who had lent him the money for the furniture bought from the dealer, and to savor the effect of this lovely tale on a woman whom he had loved, and whom he liked to torment from time to time.

Meanwhile his victim went into a decline, and finally died, as he learned upon meeting her husband in mourning, and inviting him into his carriage. He admits, or pretends, that he was touched by the account of her death: "But I had learned already," he said, "that it is not prudent to concentrate on one's sorrow, and I went to call on the Duchesse de ——, where the talk was all of the travels of the Princesse de —— (one of his new mistresses), and the pleasure of hearing her talked of soon restored my good humor."

This is what Richelieu was like at sixteen, and the portrait is by his own hand. But what renders this adventure still more odious is that one perceives that this cowardly and cruel atrocity has its source not in the giddiness and frivolity of his age but in a fierce scorn of everyone who did not belong to his class, a feeling that he expresses again and again. . . .

. . . what can one say of the following passage? It is at the moment when he wishes to leave the unfortunate woman whom he has seduced, and whom he describes, himself, as the most estimable woman he had known: "And like Mercury," he continues, "who had been disguised as Sosia, and afterwards went to cleanse himself in Olympus with ambrosia, I promised to rid myself of the dirt of these two plebeian affairs at the side of the celestial Princesse de ——."

. . . The disorders into which the Duke of Richelieu plunged his youth were shared with all the young nobility of France, but he surpassed all his rivals in the art, then so celebrated, of embellishing vice, of clothing it in the charm of manners, and in all the graces of wit, of lending seduction an amusing spriteliness which turns the injury it does into a pastime, and takes pleasure in the scandal it causes. These were talents that were highly regarded by the descendants of the ancient knighthood, and it was by their exercise that Richelieu had become the object of general emulation. He could flatter himself with being the best student of the famous Comte de Grammont, or rather of Hamilton, his biographer. This book, as we know, has long been the breviary of the young nobility. More than any other it has contributed to founding in France a school of immorality that is said to be agreeable, and of a perversity reputed to be charming. To succeed with women, to begin with, was the first distinction; to deceive them was the second; and as all the arts tend to perfect themselves, delivering them up to disgrace and public derision became the most delicious pleasure of all. . . .

III

FROM "ON *LA VIE PRIVÉE DU MARÉCHAL DE RICHELIEU*"
(*written for the* Mercure de France)

. . . Such was the destiny of this singular man; such was his character, if one can give that name to a bizarre mixture of disparate qualities. No one would have been happier if the pleasures of the senses were the sole requisite for human happiness. No one knew better how to preserve himself in a way of living that might have been calculated to shorten his days. Furthermore it has been thought that most of the excesses to which he seemed to abandon himself were, as a general rule, only apparent. It is said that in his debaucheries, more indecent than frequent, and his sensualities, of which everyone has heard so much, he knew how to maintain a prudent and studied husbandry of his powers. In a word, he was merely a prodigal miser, here as elsewhere.

Fortune favored him in almost everything; but it must be admitted that he elicited her favors with intelligence, dispatch, and energy. Above all, he was clever at turning to his own profit the vices of his age, of which he could say *Et quorum pars magna fui.* He had brilliant gifts and not one virtue. He broke off the hunt after being so unfortunate as to kill a man who was there with him, but at the same time he allowed a number of innocent persons to languish and die in prison, whom he had sent there for having hampered his tastes or impeded his fancies. And the few decent actions that managed to emanate from him in the course of a long life seem to have been mere caprices, whims that surprise more than they please; just as in certain works of the mind one may see a few details that are striking in themselves, but out of place, and thereby rendered void. . . .

BIBLIOGRAPHY

❦ ❧

PRINCIPAL EDITIONS OF CHAMFORT:

Oeuvres de Chamfort, Paris, Directeur de l'Imprimerie des Sciences & des Arts. 3rd Year of the Republic (1795). 4 vols. Edited by Guingené, and prefaced by his memoir of Chamfort; the first collected edition.

Oeuvres Complètes de Chamfort, Paris, Chaumerot jeune, 1824-1825. 5 vol. Edited by P. R. Auguis. The most complete edition of the whole of Chamfort's writing.

Oeuvres Choisies de M. Chamfort, Paris, Librairie des Bibliophies, 1879. 2 vols. Edited by M. de Lescure. The last volume edited from the original manuscripts, which later disappeared; it contains over a hundred maxims and anecdotes which had not previously been published.

Chamfort: Produits de la civilisation perfectionée, Collection Nationale des Classiques Français, 1953. Preface by M. René Groos. Biographical introduction, Bibliography, Glossary, notes and textual criticism by M. Pierre Grosclaude. The first serious critical edition.

Chamfort: oeuvres principales. Éditions Jean-Jacques Pauvert, 1960. Edited and with bibliographical foreword by M. F. Duloup. Excellent representation based on the Grosclaude edition; *Products of the Perfected Civilization* and the Guingené memoir complete; selected letters and five essays.

PRINCIPAL BIOGRAPHICAL STUDIES:

Chamfort, by Maurice Pellisson, 1895. The first attempt, after Guingené's, a hundred years before, at a full-length biography. Incorporates more recent material.

Chamfort et son temps, by Emile Dousset, Fasquelle, Paris, 1943. Work of little critical originality, but the most complete survey of the known facts, when written.

Chamfort: sa vie, son oeuvre, sa pensée, by Julien Teppe, Paris, Pierre Clairac, 1950. With a preface by Jean Rostand. Teppe is an impassioned partisan; the work incorporates a few new details and an excellent survey of the history of Chamfort's reputation.